ALSO BY ROSS A. LAIRD

Grain of Truth: The Ancient Lessons of Craft

A STONE'S
THROW

A STONE'S THROW

THE ENDURING NATURE OF MYTH

ROSS A. LAIRD

National Library of Canada Cataloguing in Publication

Laird, Ross A., 1964-
    A stone's throw : the enduring nature of myth / Ross A. Laird.

Includes bibliographical references.
ISBN 1-55199-091-1

    1. Mythology.   2. Laird, Ross A., 1964-.   I. Title.

BL727.L28 2003   291.1'3   C2003-901961-6

Design by Terri Nimmo
Maps by VisuTronx
Photos by Elizabeth Laird

We acknowledge the financial support of the Government of Canada through the Book Publishing Industry Development Program and that of the Government of Ontario through the Ontario Media Development Corporation's Ontario Book Initiative. We further acknowledge the support of the Canada Council for the Arts and the Ontario Arts Council for our publishing program.

Typeset in Sabon by M & S, Toronto
Printed and bound in Canada

McClelland & Stewart Ltd.
The Canadian Publishers
481 University Avenue
Toronto, Ontario
M5G 2E9
www.mcclelland.com

1 2 3 4 5   07 06 05 04 03

DEDICATION

To Elizabeth, for her courage, patience, and remarkable wisdom;
and to Rowan and Avery, for the great gift of their presence.

CONTENTS

ACKNOWLEDGMENTS

I'm grateful to my father, Allan Laird, for his companionship on the mountain journeys which were this book's genesis. Once the stone was found, the geologist Bill Stephen helped me identify it and the stone sculptor Lorenzo Di Francesco provided artistic guidance. Don Lowe generously assisted with genealogical research, and Jennifer Richardson's translation of French sources helped illuminate early ancestral records. Bernice Bell, my aunt, kindly shared and clarified several family stories. Jacquelyn Dwoskin, Gladys Foxe, Craig Mosher, and Sherry Reiter offered insight into mythological, political, and philosophical themes in the narrative. Gary Ross, my editor, and Barbara Czarnecki, copy editor, provided further assistance and support.

Thanks must also go to Tony and Mary Ann Milobar, whose recollections of their childhood in Nordegg are a fine gift of memory for my own children.

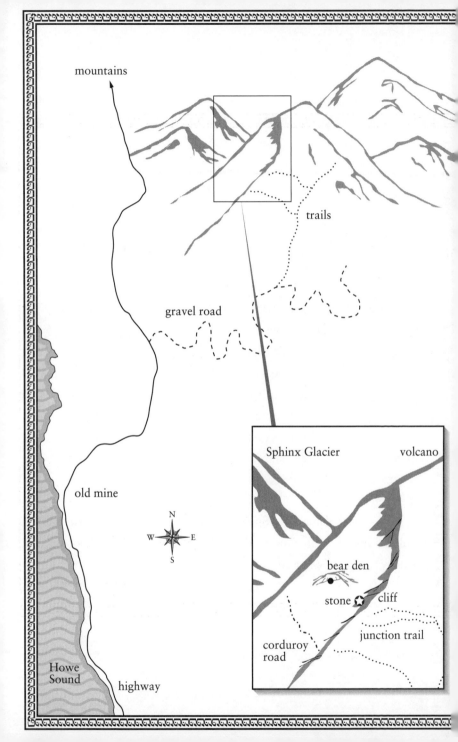

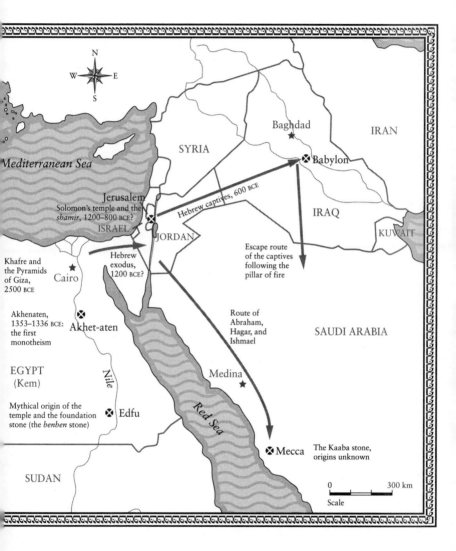

N

W   E

S

Mediterranean Sea

SYRIA

Baghdad

IRAN

Babylon

Jerusalem
Solomon's temple and the
shamir, 1200–800 BCE?

ISRAEL

JORDAN

Hebrew captives, 600 BCE

IRAQ

KUWAIT

Khafre and
the Pyramids
of Giza,
2500 BCE

Cairo

Hebrew
exodus,
1200 BCE?

Escape route
of the captives
following the
pillar of fire

Akhenaten,
1353–1336 BCE:
the first
monotheism

Akhet-aten

Route of
Abraham,
Hagar, and
Ishmael

SAUDI ARABIA

EGYPT
(Kem)

Nile

Medina

Mythical origin of the
temple and the foundation
stone (the *benben* stone)

Edfu

Red Sea

Mecca

The Kaaba stone,
origins unknown

SUDAN

0   300 km

Scale

PREFACE

If history were the past, history wouldn't matter. History
is the present, the present. You and I are history.
                                                    – James Baldwin

At the beach near our house, on a warm day in early autumn when the tide is low and gulls coast on the blustery breeze, my son scours the shore for a skipping stone. He finds one, thin and smooth and black, that precisely fits his small hand. He ambles toward the water, heedless of tangles of seaweed and shallow pools sculpted by the tide's egress. His rubber boots make rough imprints in the ridges of the sand. He passes the trails of white foam made by the strongest wavelets and keeps going, past the threshold of the beach and into the water. He stands with his feet covered, his arm poised, his gaze alternating between the passage of incoming water and the languid surface of the outgoing sea. It stretches across the bay, out past the peninsula of dark trees, and meets the sky at a horizon flecked with the shreds of clouds.

He throws the stone. It tumbles in the air, startling three gulls from their perch atop the breakwater, and descends in a shallow arc toward the water. It grazes the surface, makes a small splash, skips once through the veil of the splash, then falls again, vanishing. The water closes over it, restores itself like a dreamer waking from sleep. But deep inside the sheltering water, the black stone will continue to turn and spin. Far down, it will sing its forgotten songs in the dark.

This is a book about stones and memory, about what we preserve and what we discard, about the claim of the past on the present. Stones are often the carriers of that past, and their influence is not limited to archaic mythologies. The foundation stone of the Temple Mount in Jerusalem, the Washington Monument, and the sacred Kaaba stone in Mecca are examples of ancient symbols pressing their way into modern life. They lie at the heart of the world's most troubling conflicts. Their gravity reaches across the ages we've tried to forget, peels back the facade of the present, and reveals the past still working out its unfinished dreams.

Stones inspire myths, which in turn create the histories of the human spirit. But myths are necessarily complex and contentious; their narratives interweave with the details of archaeology, anthropology, literature, religion, and many other fields of inquiry. Myths, which are impossible to untangle from the clamor of voices that would lay claim to truth, are never true to fact, as facts are never the whole truth. We craft persuasive tales from fragments of the past, from silhouettes, from footprints in the sand muddied by countless crossing tracks. We make interpretations, we reconstruct the old voices. And when we speak in those voices, which are also our own, the dialect of our discourse is mythological.

The scission between the mythic impulses of the heart and the intellectual imperatives of the mind lies at the crossroads of human history. The tension between them is the source of art, science, and politics. The structure of these pages is intended to mirror this tension: contextual and historical themes, artifacts of the intellectual quest – about a quarter of the book – appear in endnotes (marked in the main text by the symbol *). The notes are a view from the shore, from the secure footing of the modern self seeking to understand the roots and conflicts of family and culture. The myth narratives, by contrast, follow the path of a stone thrown by a child: into the ocean, down to where hidden things sing and dream and wait.

PART I

EMERGENCE

PROYET

O N E

It is quiet on the dock. A speckle of frost on the handrail melts into the wood as I touch it. Trees on the far shore appear black against the slate sky, though a fringe of November light has begun to spread across Point Grey to the south. The eastern horizon is crimson. The water of the bay is now still. An ebbing tide sweeps the rocky beach without a sound.

I walk across fir planks to the corner of the dock, where my view of the channel widens. A row of moored sailboats blocks the open water and the tiny island with its cluster of residences; but I look in that direction, and listen.

Presently, I see a ripple curving along the white hull of the farthest sailboat: the day's first stirring. And I hear the sound of oars in the water: quiet creak, soft splash, silence, then the patter of droplets. The day unfolds into the rhythm of these sounds.

A yellow dinghy comes into view from behind the moored boats. A set of spruce oars moves through the black water. I can see from the shape of the hull – steep rake of the bow, wide thwart – that it's a Davidson dinghy. Upon the thwart seat, his back to me, his face looking along the channel to the open water, wearing a red windbreaker and a blue hat, my father rows.

I wait at the dock's edge. As the dinghy approaches, my father slows, lifts the left oar from the water, and pulls with the right. The boat swings to starboard and comes alongside the dock. He ships the oars as I reach down to the gunwale. I find the cold painter, loop it through the dock ring, and tie it with a bowline. My father hands me a bag of gear and climbs out. The hull rocks gently, and small ripples skitter out into the bay. We say our good mornings. I remark on the cold. He mentions that a Thermos of coffee is in the bag, along with bananas for breakfast.

We drive north along the coast, past the islands of Howe Sound, into the mountains. Before the fjord closes in and we lose sight of the wide ocean to the southwest, we see – around the back side of a large island, fifteen miles to the west, hazy in the oncoming light – the shore where both he and I spent our childhood summers. We can't see the cabin, or the trail that leads up the hillside to a plateau overlooking what seemed, to an eight-year-old, all of creation. But we can see the hill, round and slight at this distance, a bump in a far landscape. The cabin is still in our family, bought by my cousins when my grandmother died, but neither I nor my father has visited there for many years. Sometimes he passes that shore, during trips north on his sailboat. He doesn't stop, though he'd be welcome. He keeps going, into the oncoming breeze that wraps the headland and through the channel to the sea.

Steep treed slopes border the road. Far ahead, white peaks are beginning to catch the gathering day. We stop at the diner adjoining the old mine; I'm surprised to find it open this early on a Saturday morning. A logger's pickup sits out front, its owner the only other customer inside. As we select our snacks, the power browns out, the lights flicker, and the waitress pauses, looking both annoyed and hopeful.

This stretch of the old road has always felt derelict to me. The mine, once the largest copper producer in the British Empire, is long closed. Almost every window in its terraced superstructure is smashed; its tunnels are now a museum not visited much by travelers driving through the mountains. Southward, the city is spreading in this direction; within a generation, this quiet town will be another burgeoning suburb.

Before the mine, in the days when this landscape was not yet populated by ghosts, my great-uncle walked this territory. Just after the First World War, through the days of a long summer, lodging with trappers and homesteaders and sleeping in the rough; hundreds of miles across a land of impenetrable silence. He walked off the ache of his wounds here, along this shore where the sound widens and the glaciers first come into view.

We climb back into the car and head north. The road is wider than it once was and bypasses the old cemetery beside the nesting ground of the eagles. Highway crews have straightened out the tight corner we used to call the death curve, and they've blasted away the cliff face upon which someone once painted a false tunnel opening. We once hit a moose near that cliff face, late at night, the road slick with rain. The front quarter of the car was smashed in, but the moose kept going. We could hear it trundling off into the bush, hurt or unhurt we never knew.

By the time we turn off the highway and crunch onto the gravel track heading eastward, the sky is bright. Ahead, the forest ramparts – green and dark and thick with shadow – stretch across a series of ascending ridges. The distant peaks are cloud-hidden. The road meanders toward them, climbing three thousand feet over the next half hour, switchbacking through stands of fir and cedar along the shoulder of the mountain. The track has been worn into two ruts, now filled with water streaming from the alpine above. The ridged center of the road rises close to the undercarriage of the car. Halfway up a long switchback, my father reminds me that a few years back, along this stretch, the oil pan was ripped loose from the bottom of a car he was traveling in.

We come around a tight bend and the road widens. We must be close now to the trail, so we pull over to check our location on the map. The slope of the road, followed by a tight bend, looks similar to a tiny hooked line that I can see between two altitude markers. The line extends a fraction beyond where we are. Near its end, a small track wanders off into the bush.

We drive another two hundred yards, then park where the road is overhung by a scrim of silvered branches. The temperature hovers around freezing; snow covers the most shadowed slopes. We put on hats and gloves, and I shoulder my pack. Ahead, mottled leaves of birch and alder form a sunburst canopy above an opening in the woods: the trail. Underfoot, the dark ground is broken by skeins of aggregated volcanic rock. Fragments of arkose, a sandstone dyed with red feldspar, lie like tumbled bricks among the scree. Above us, hidden by the forest, up in the alpine where marmots and bears traverse a territory seldom disturbed by human activity, the crater lies dormant. About ten thousand years ago, more than a cubic mile of this mountain exploded with a ferocity similar to the 1980 eruption of Mount Saint Helens. A vast fountain of fire ejected molten rock into the sky. Volcanic gas, pumice, and ash swept down the slopes, feckless, debris thick enough to cover the tallest fir trees, more than three hundred feet high. Nearby forests were either blown down by the searing ash cloud or left standing dead as black spume spread to the horizon.

A whiskey jack flitters among the trees. Beneath this fresh and pristine forest, the old fire lies hidden like a seed.

The trail is narrow at first, and we walk one in front of the other. But it soon widens, and we pull alongside. As we go, we talk about navigating the trail and what the weather might bring. Then the conversation shifts, becomes more imaginal: what it would have been like to be here when the volcano erupted; what my great-uncle Dave saw, when he came here after the war, to see the crater; what we're doing here in late autumn, a questionable and perhaps dangerous season. Taking what seems like an opportune moment, my father asks me, as he did when I first invited him on this hike, to tell him about the dreams.

There was first a story, I tell him, a tale of origin – perhaps the oldest tale of origin. I came across it in the summer, at the lake with Elizabeth and the kids, in one of the books I had brought with me. I read it, ruminated upon it, was absorbed by its simplicity. It spoke of water, of a mountain, of a stone rising from the depths. As we sailed our dinghy and the kids swam near the lakeshore, I began to see ways in which the archaic myth renewed itself in every moment. Though it was crafted in a vanished age, the myth seemed to come alive again in my own imaginings: in the way stones on the beach glistened beneath the surface, in the whoops and shouts of my kids after they dunked their heads in the water. As I rebuilt the cabin's break-water – its stones brought from the Rocky Mountains in the back of a station wagon over the course of many long trips and laid down by my father-in-law and his kids – I discovered why old, discarded things cannot be forgotten.

In the oldest Egyptian myth – thousands of years older than the Book of Genesis – white wings against a dark sky do not yet trace the morning twilight. Bones do not yet speak of the weather, or of what lies over that ridge, itself not yet formed by the broken earth. No scents come from there – of cinnamon or smoke or the salt of a green sea. A dinghy has not yet rounded the point on a November morning.

There are no paths upon which to follow yearnings, no rustlings of trepidation. Rain is not yet falling on the shake roof. A world is not yet formed by the call of a child. No touch, no night, no time. Only a well of black water, not yet formed but waiting.

The sea of beginnings possesses neither surface, nor shore, nor bottom.* Its depths are still. Nothing rises there. Ghost forms and long stories lie wrapped tight, cocooned. The under-world, dreams, all that is lost or on its way back to knowing. Secreted inside the waters is the mountain trail I will follow with my father – ramparts of hemlock and black spruce – as well as those paths we have not yet walked, perhaps will never walk, where goldenrod and loosestrife mark the trail's edge. All the journeys lie here, dark and untrodden, those I must follow and those I will, of necessity, pass by.

From within this singular sea, a black stone of fire – relic of a vanished age – draws up from the formless. It separates the waters into above and below, fracturing the infinite. The stone is an embodiment of nameless ancestors, those who created themselves in the primeval age. Within the stone, emblem of beginnings, are concealed all the words of the sacred language.

The emergence of the foundation stone (it shines, though there is no light to shine upon it) is the first act of the universe remembering itself. The water, bereft of its unity, retreats from an emerging shore. Above, a firmament stretches out, presses back the thick darkness of the waters. They recede but remain forever a boundary beyond which the unknowable extends, far past the reach of gods.

The stone inscribes circles that widen and grow solid in its wake. These revolutions are like a mouth opening, voicing the first vowels – a herald, a lament, an ululation for what has been and what will come to be. Slowly, beneath the stone's passage, land rises. An island awakens into a world of darkness.

In the oldest histories, this emergent atoll is named the Island of the Egg.* It is an enclosure crafted by a stone of stones: a *benben* stone. Its genesis – like every genesis – is a recapitulation of forgotten but never derelict paths.

The trail rises, then flattens out and runs alongside the mountain slope. As we walk, I tell my father that my discovery of the old origin myth prompted in me dreams of stones and fire and water.* I dreamed of herons gathering at a shore, of tall reeds shining with dew, of a roving flame. A falcon wheeled in an empty sky. I dreamed of a breeze ruffling the water and of boats heading out. Beneath a broken limestone wall, the shadows of an old temple dwindled. I walked on red earth beneath a black cliff. The scents of the desert came to me like a distant memory, a lost tale. Sometimes I heard a voice calling: *Come to the river.* When we returned from our summer holidays, I tell him, I started looking for the river.

I unshoulder my pack and retrieve the map. I trace my finger eastward from the highway, up the gravel road, and from there northward, to where the map shows the threadlike trail. A tiny line snakes across a ridge and then stops. I've extended the trail, with a small pencil line, until it intersects with a river flowing down from the crater. This is our destination: a volcanic deposit in the middle of nowhere, marked only on geological surveys. I found the deposits on a government map in early September, while looking with the eye of intuition for where I might find a stone of origin. I've marked the spot with an X.

In the Egyptian tale, the island that rises from the sea of beginnings is signified by a glyph meaning sacred place: an X within a circle. X marks the spot.

We continue on until the path diverges. One track leads up the slope, the other down toward the valley. We pause to consult the map again, but we've passed the end of the trail indicated upon it. There's a considerable stretch of terrain between the terminus of the marked trail and our goal. The paths ahead are phantom trails, and we have only the indications of the forest to follow. On the principle that it's easier to backtrack going downhill than up, we take the upper trail. It winds across the contour of a ridge and heads toward the open alpine above.

My father leads off. I pause to replace the map in my pack. He is well down the path by the time I'm ready to get going. I look ahead to where he is – blue hat and red jacket, that distinctive, purposeful walk, the curve of the trail beyond which he will disappear from sight – and I realize, in a moment of mingled sadness and love, that this is how it will be. When it comes, in ten or twenty or perhaps thirty years, when he departs on that definitive journey, this is how it will be: my father going ahead, into a world of soft autumn light, his back turned, his face hidden but shining, I'm sure of it, with a radiance I can't see.

"Rise up, Father," says the Egyptian Book of Illumination. "Reclaim your place in the broad and welcoming sky. You will stand among the radiant ancestors as a companion to the sun. And I, your son, will with words of praise cradle your abandoned bones. I will preserve for you a place by the river, even as I look upward, searching the sky for a trace of your shadow, vanishing."*

The trail takes us into the shadow of the mountain. The ground cover thickens, and the going is slow in spots. The sound of flowing water comes to us distantly, audible for a moment and then gone again as we pass into a tangled grove.

We come upon a bare blueberry patch beneath which the trail disappears. We forge through, pushing the branches aside, and emerge at the stump of a massive cedar, six or seven feet across, cut cleanly through by loggers perhaps eighty years ago.

I clamber onto the flat top of the trunk, high above the undergrowth, and search the forest ahead. The sound of water is continuous now, and I can make out the cleft of a gorge – a patch of white, a granite boulder.

We follow the trail, now faint underfoot, toward the gorge. It leads through a stand of devil's club: the seer's plant, the healer. Devil's club is actually a kind of ginseng; in addition to its reputed sacred powers – the ability to offer heightened perception of the spirit world, among others – it can be used to help heal broken bones and to balance the body's energy. Bears eat its fruit, though its spines, filled with organically produced silica, are sharp as glass. As I pass through, I brush up against a branch and feel a prickle. I remove my glove to find a row of small red welts already rising on my skin. My hands are warm. I remove the other glove, put the pair in my coat pocket, and continue on.

The trail ends at the edge of a high cliff above the river gorge. White water tumbles through below, rumbles against black stones on the riverbed. Near-vertical banks of smooth rock guide the water around a roaring corner downstream. A tall fir has toppled over from the cliff top and now lies almost upside down, its branches lost among a jumble of boulders pressed into the far bank.

According to my reckoning (which is usually poor), we should be almost on top of our destination. But aside from the riverbed, I don't see an outcropping of stone anywhere. And there's no way to explore further, to cross the white water, without climbing equipment.

We sit down on a fallen log above the river, listen to the

sounds of the waters, watch the rushing eddies slide up along the bank. My father remarks on how beautiful it is. He offers me a banana from his bag, and we rest a moment. I wonder aloud, not for the first time, about my great-uncle Dave's experience in this territory; limping from the wound in his leg, searching for respite from the echoing sounds of the guns. Perhaps he sang as he walked, or was quiet with his own echoes. It was so long ago; no one remembers, there are no children to whom he would have told the tale. My father, too, wandered here, when he was a boy: sailing up the sound, hiking the cliffs, skiing the glacier south of where we are now. A few valleys east of us, in the years when the Trans-Canada Highway was a gravel track, he ran alongside his parents' car because he was too carsick to ride. They drove slowly. Besides, the canyon road was barely safe at ten miles an hour. He jogged and loped and puffed his way, stopping frequently. He was five years old. Sometimes, when the track widened and lay level for a stretch, he'd climb into the car and they'd speed up, kicking the dust behind them into clouds that trailed off into the forest. Every time I drive that road, going north with my wife and kids to visit our family, I think of my father, galloping toward the next bend and a drink of mountain water.

These old roads – the one below us, and its companion eastward, over the mountain – were first trails, crossed by travelers in unremembered ages. Then, in the generation of my parents and grandparents, the trails were widened into gravel roads. In my own life, the flanking forests have been thinned and the asphalt widened. The roads have changed as I've grown older; my own history is wrapped up with them, and with their woods.

I drive the road below several times a year, though I haven't walked upon this mountain since I was a teenager. I return here now, bidden by dreams, by memories, by a feeling awakened in me by an archaic tale. Who else has come this way: forgotten ancestors, refugees, ghosts?

A black bird, high up, turns and turns. Perhaps he's eyeing my banana. The old Egyptian myth spoke of such a bird – dark wings against a gray sky. What struck me about the myth, I tell my father, was not only its age, but its persistence. Its authors were gone; yet it remained, undaunted, inscribed upon the walls of a Nile temple built more than two thousand years ago, during the reign of a queen who had virtually the same name as my grandmother, Bernice. I do not think of myself as having ancient Egyptian ancestors, though I am – along with every person alive today – directly descended from them.* My attraction to the myth did not arise from my own cultural roots or from an academic impulse. No, my motivation was entirely personal. This artifact, which described the world's beginning as an ancestral gift, spoke of the presence of the past. As I make my own family, as I shape the lives of my children, together we choose what to reclaim – and discard – from our familial stories. Every day, we entertain an important question: What must we preserve?

I look upstream to where a layer of new snow covers a patch of open ground, and I wonder about the day. Perhaps I won't find the stone after all. But I have the feeling I'm near the hidden place. I'm sure it's just a little farther, across the water. Or perhaps beneath the water. But where?

I want to think it through, revisit the dreams and indications and hunches that have grown into this journey. I want to enter into the labyrinth of my questioning. But I refrain. Instead I wait, watching the water, looking with the eye of intuition, until the doubt fades and I see, with growing clarity, that we must go back to the junction and take the other trail. That's all. We took the wrong turn. This certainty comes without fanfare, not a revelation but a neutral, almost indifferent knowing.

The path along which we have come, with its speckled wood and high promontory and pristine water, is the guide to another journey. We will take it again, another day.

We head back, past the devil's club and cedar, through the barren blueberries, along the overgrown trail to the junction. It's eleven o'clock by the time we reach it. Today is November 11, Remembrance Day. Right now, in many parts of the world, people are observing silence. I mention the time to my father. He proposes that we stop for a couple of minutes, share in the ritual. We stand on the trail, quiet, listening to water dripping from leaves. I think of my great-uncle, the war veteran, and of the long line of forebears that stretches behind me, bolstering the foundation of my own life.

The ancestral thread has no beginning. It is a loop, tied off and punctuated with infinite, tiny knots. But where the two ends meet and interwoven strands twist the cord into a seamless unity, origin myths reside. In one of these, a stone rises from the waters to make an island: the first land of a renewed age. The island spreads. The shore widens, fringed with black stone. At the island's center, within the enclosure of the foundation stone's smallest revolution, a well stretches down into the surrounding sea. Within this contained column, the spirits of the aged ones ascend, undulating through the water, redeeming the magnificent catastrophe that is the world. They move, lissome, summoning forms. Their whispering voices gather the shapes of creation – fallen, scattered, waiting – and sing them light, soft songs of return. At the edge of the well, the black stone glows. The ancestors rise through the waters, languid.

Slumber departs from the shapes of things. Slowly, threading radiance through the old darkness, the Island of the Egg comes again to life (for origin is only a reawakening). The well, hiding all the emergent forms within its waters, lies at the center of creation like the pupil of an eye: searching, remembering, far-seeing. The island encircles it like a dark corona. The ancestors rest here, dreaming the world, gazing back and forth along the avenue of time. They dream of a sun, fierce and orange, on the crest of a new day. They dream a winter bird, on the topmost branch of an evergreen – a swish of wings, the branch trembling as the bird launches into sky. Stirring and turning, their faces the only forms yet manifest, the old ones dream deep into the well. They glimpse a man in a yellow dinghy, rowing. Ripples spread from the bow into the dark water, as though the boat is an island rising from the sea. Everything that will ever be dreamed is first dreamed here: every form, every light, terror and wonder, memory, love, the moon, a far shore glimpsed from the car as you round the bend. All the threads of time, together, weaving.

The island is illuminated by dreaming, glows within a cocoon of light. We are wrapped, even now, inside that radiance, inside the bright eye of becoming with its dark pupil.

When their dreaming is complete, the ancestors depart. The

next tasks, spinning the world out from the well of vision, are not theirs. The aged ones fashion the light but do not carry it forward. They awaken the world into its dream and then vanish, leaving a legacy of desire. They depart into the surrounding sea, return to dark waters, wait for the wheel of time to make its circle.

High up, turning and turning, silent, a falcon glides. It is a spirit of long traveling, wanderer of untrodden paths, companion to the vanished shapes of longing. From far off it has come, drawn by a myth, a dream, by the promise of time. Its origin is hidden. The god is genderless, ageless, freed of form. It is the earth maker, the divine heart. It is called Pn, meaning the Unnameable.

The black stone is a perch upon which the Unnameable descends. Warm, risen from surrounding waters, the stone is the first seat of creation. Latent forms begin to stir – a dream flower opens, pebbles tumble down the bank of an imagined river, a woman, not yet born, pauses at the edge of a field of barley, looks back across the golden stalks. Every age of the uncreated world unfurls from darkness, waits for the pupil of the well to dilate.

The first sound rises into the first sky. The call of the Unnameable spreads across the waters, radiates from the perch of awakening, coalesces into air, then into dust, then into ground. From the circular shore of the island, new land rises: sand and tumbled boulders and clay. Pebbles, small and shiny as papaya seeds, are washed by the retreating waters.

"Where there was neither heaven nor earth," says another archaic tale, in the Mayan Book of Spirits, "sounded the first word of God, unloosed from the stone, declaring divinity. The vastness of eternity shuddered. The word was a measure of grace, which broke and pierced the backbone of the mountain. Who was born there? Who? Father, you know."*

My father looks up at the sky, overcast with scuttling clouds. The day is drawing on. A crow calls through the trees, and we get moving. The trail leads slightly downward at first, but then turns east, climbing along the ridge. I hear the river again, quieter now than at the gorge. The sound is more subdued, softer, hinting at a wider course. The air grows cold, the forest more dense. We pass slowly beneath a canopy woven by white pines and large, dark cedars.

We emerge at the bank of the river, not a steep cliff here but an easy slope. I can just make out, far up the hillside, the river bend we could see from the cliff top. Careful footing on a fallen log and a hop across wet stones take us to the far side. The path drives straight north from here, bolstered by cordwood laid down by loggers generations ago. This would have been a thoroughfare at one time – steam donkeys hauling themselves along on massive sledges, cabled to trees ahead, winding themselves up the mountain. This abandoned road, hidden past the threshold of a river at the end of a forgotten trail, has likely not seen a traveler in many years. It lies near none of the regular hiking trails, does not appear on the maps, wanders now purposeless toward the Sphinx Glacier far ahead. Yet it is not overgrown.

I want to follow this old path, but it leads off in the wrong direction. We need to travel east from here, up the mountainside. I traverse the fringe of the logging road, sweeping wide along the brush, looking for the opening of a trail. But the ground cover is solid. The road follows the ridge, winds along the slopes of the mountain's lower reaches; it's unlikely that it will curve upward and swing back toward the alpine. We'll have to strike out into the bush, keeping course by the sound of the river.

I check with my father to see how he's doing. We've been moving for more than three hours, in and out of dense brush, along jumbled trails, and I'm becoming worried about him. He's almost seventy, and this is not the kind of environment where help is near at hand if things go wrong. British Columbia possesses the world's densest forests – far more overgrown than the Amazon. If we had an accident, if either of us turned an ankle or fell and broke a leg, we'd be in serious trouble. One of us would have to leave the other and go for help – three hours out, a couple hours driving, three hours back in. It would be dark before help came, if the spot could be found.

I was five years old when I was lost in these mountains, alone, in winter. It happened during the year that my brother and I took ski lessons at the mountain south of here. Early Saturday mornings, our parents dropped us at the charter bus stop near our home; we stowed our skis and poles and lunches, then walked onto the bus with the clunky gait forced upon us by our boots. My brother was a year older, and when we got to the mountain he went off to another class. My group was for the smallest kids. Mostly, we practiced the snowplow. But I'd get cold as the day wore on, especially my feet, and my instructor would send me off to warm up in the ski patrol hut. It was a tiny structure: a bench, a table, and an electric kettle with which someone once made me hot chocolate from a little packet of powder. The ski patrollers would come and go, and I'd sit in the hut until I warmed up. Then I'd try to find my group again, or my brother, or I'd wait until the end of the day. But on one occasion, I left the hut and began wandering. I walked along a trail packed with snow, threaded my way into the woods, and was lost.

My brother didn't know what to do when I failed to show up at the end of the day. In his six-year-old mind, the best course of action was to consult with my parents, so he got back on the bus and went home to them. Consequently, it was dark before anyone else knew I was missing. And by the time a search party was organized, five or six hours of the night had passed.

They didn't find me. The mountain is an enormous territory; even now, dozens of skiers and hikers lose their way every year. A surprising number never make their way out. But I did. By virtue of luck or providence or simple determination, I found my way back to the chalet at the top of the gondola. A bright light in a dark night.

Standing on the old road, scanning the brush for signs of a trail, I mention to my father my fragmentary memory of that night. How different times were, he tells me. He never doubted that his kids would be safe, a five-year-old and his six-year-old brother, gone for the entire day to a mountain, in charge of each other.

I don't see a trail, just solid undergrowth fringing the road. As I look for a point of entry, it occurs to me that I've been trying to find my way in these woods for a long while.

I check with my father again, to make sure he's all right. He's game, as always, to go on. I give him my penetrating stare, the one that's supposed to be appraising, critically honest, forceful. I don't usually have much success with that look, and it doesn't help me now. I can't tell whether he's doing fine or bluffing, not wanting to spoil the day, conscious of my enthusiasm and willing to push himself – perhaps a little too hard – in service of another of my odd quests.

He offers me his reassuring look, the one that's casual, jocular in the midst of adversity. There's no hint of exhaustion, or anxiety, or even any fatigue. He looks fine, but he could be on the point of collapse. He possesses the stoic reserve so typical of men of his generation – men who went to work the way their fathers went to war, dedicated to the careful siege of feeling. For many of them, the ramparts of an enclosed heart grew tight with pressure, and one day erupted like a volcano. My father has managed the trick of avoiding that fate. He was saved from it by my mother, whose presence evoked the strongest feelings in everyone she knew. She was a fountain of fire.

We leave the old road and head uphill, into the bush. Immediately our progress slows as the forest thickens and presses us inward. The sky is blocked by branches, and the ground underfoot is tangled. We stumble through more devil's club, salal, vine maple, and patches of stinging nettles. It is not possible to follow a straight course. Moss growing on over-hanging hemlock branches blocks our view of the sky. Every few steps, an impenetrable screen of branches forces us aside. We plod around, searching for a way through the gloom. We clamber along the silvered trunks of fallen cedars, slippery with frost but clear for ten or twenty feet. The visibility is so poor, sometimes only to the next tree, that it might as well be twilight already. It's hard going. In half an hour we progress less than a hundred yards.

This terrain – partially regrown after logging, dead gray snags littering the ground in the wake of an old forest fire – is ideal for underbrush. The returning trees have not yet grown large enough to block the sun entirely, and there's enough ground light for plants to thrive. Mountain hemlock, with its starlike needle clusters, will eventually form a screen thick enough to curtail the ground cover, leaving thickets of rhododendron and blueberry; but now, in this intermediate condition, the landscape is a diverse and winding labyrinth.

Higher up, several hundred feet from where we are, the alpine begins. Clear stretches of rocky ground lead to meadows carpeted with flowers in summer, where solitary whitebark pines, old as history, breathe the rarefied air. Here and there, algae in the glacial snow lie poised between ice and fire. Their peculiar biochemistry catches the sunlight and stains the spores the precise color of watermelon. As the continental temperature slowly rises, the islands of alpine tundra above the timberline will be squeezed ever smaller; on the lower peaks, many of them will soon disappear.

As we trundle through the undergrowth, we see purple lupines, named for the wolf but small and delicate, that lie like paw prints on the shadowed ground. The petaled flowers are bright splashes of color against a background of wet moss and dark branches. We're higher now. Tendrils of the alpine are starting to reach down and draw us onward. Niches in the hillside are filled with new snow.

We climb quietly, careful to avoid slips, wary of the sudden shifting of a branch as we grab hold. We move side by side, staying close, calling out discovered passages and dead ends. I try not to worry about my father as he breathes hard, hefts himself over a fallen trunk.

The terrain opens as we come to the crest of a slope. We slow, easing into the wider space. And there, as we pass on either side of a tangled cedar stump covered with fungus and creeping branches, a black bear rises up from the undergrowth.

In countless myths of origin – from Egypt, Greece, Russia, the Americas – a bear guards the gate between the temporal and celestial worlds; between the eternity of the gods and the constantly transforming realm of earthly experience. The Inuit believe that polar bears can see the future. My four-year-old son trusts his teddy bear to guard the night and dreams. Bears are mythic sentinels who never leave their posts. Ursa Major, the constellation of the Great Bear, is so named for this very reason: in the northern hemisphere, it never sets.

In the Egyptian tale of sea and stone, the first speech of the Unnameable is directed north, toward the stars that never set. The sound rises heavenward, invoking nameless powers. And they respond. The nomads come, the Shebtiw who are both magicians and immortal sages.[*] They come from a single family, and there are two of them: one each for all the shades of duality. Male and female, young and old, above and below. Their names are Aa and Wa.[*]

The Shebtiw are the creators of substance and the speakers of words. Upon the stone perch of the island, they name "all substances, all food, all that is liked and loathed, life to the peaceful, every craft, the life and movements of every body." They enter "into these bodies made of every wood, every stone, and every clay thing."* They immerse themselves in the world, merging with all its forms, calling out with the light of voice. They speak the true names of things, names which will be forgotten in the flowering of new language.

But these names still reverberate: in the sounds of water, in the voice of my wife and the calls of my children, in the rhythmic footsteps of a boy running on gravel. My own voice, that of my father, that of each of our remote and forgotten kin – in every one of us, the remnants of the Shebtiw's speech prevail. As for the sages themselves: when the tasks of naming were completed, they sailed away, across the dark sea over which a ceaseless wind now blows.

And yet, because all myths are one myth, the departing Shebtiw found their way across the ocean, to the land of the Maya. There another chapter of the tale of the twins Aa and Wa was told in the Popol Vuh, the Mayan sacred book. They became Hunapu and Ixbalanqué, warriors of the first age. Their stories – of origin, of emergence, of manifesting a world reckless with diversity – unfurled, gathering the weight of time.

"They do not lose their substance when they go," says Hun-Hunapu, the father of the sacred twins, "but they bequeath it to others. The image of the lord, of the sage, of the orator does not vanish but he leaves it to the sons and daughters whom he procreates."*

The twins of the origin tales are the first earthly ancestors, the first parents. To find them, to catch up with them in their long wandering, seems to me a both daunting and imperative task. They hold the promise of the thread's unraveling, so that I might teach myself, and my children, about their own beginnings. But the Shebtiw did not leave open the gate to the ancestors. There's a bear guarding it, and this presents no small difficulty.

I should know by now that the guardian never sleeps. He emerges from the ground, almost silent, fur swishing against the fallen wood. He's no more than an arm's reach away. I can see the individual hairs of his coat, jet black and glistening. He heaves his body out of the den and swivels his snout toward me, searching for the source of this irksome intrusion. He does not yet see my father standing on the other side of the stump. My father does not yet see the bear.

A moment of startling exhilaration – if this mythological creature has come to challenge our passage, our destination must be close – is followed by alarm of such immediacy that I don't have time to panic. I become acutely conscious of my vulnerability. Running seems like a poor idea, just the thing to activate the bear's natural instincts. Besides, the terrain is so overgrown with obstacles that I wouldn't move very fast, and the bear, whose habitat this is, would easily catch me.

The bear orients himself to my conveniently bright blue jacket. I couldn't be more exposed. In the absence of a viable escape strategy, I just stand there, waiting.

The bear looks at me. It's hard to tell if he's appraising, or alarmed, or indifferent. He has probably not seen humans before. The air is cold, and I'm suddenly aware of its clarity, the rarefied quality with which it renders the colors of the forest.

It's as though I'm looking through stained glass, bright and rippled with liquid texture. The green branches of a nearby hemlock sweep across the sky.

The bear's black eye swivels within a ring of smoke. He turns his head and looks south along the slope, to where my father plods through the underbrush. They see each other at the same time, both in motion, gliding on momentum. My father looks up, draws back, frightened, and then roars. An inarticulate cry, replete with every vowel, rises through the air.

I laugh, which surprises me. And in the ensuing moment of silence – my father red-faced, the bear beginning to react – it occurs to me that if the bear is a guardian, what he needs from us is a password, and that cry, with its vowel keys to the sacred language of myth, should do the trick. The Egyptians, from whom all Western notions of magic ultimately derive, never wrote down the vowels of their sacred texts. Knowledge of the magical uses of vowels was the mark of power. "When a god or man was declared to be *maa-kheru* – true of voice, or true of word," says E.A. Wallis Budge in his *Legends of the Egyptian Gods*, "his power became illimitable. It gave him rule and authority, and every command uttered by him was immediately followed by the effect required."[*]

A tremor of fast movement works its way through the bear's body. His paws churn the undergrowth. He lunges forward, twisting for a moment toward my father – at this, I experience a flare of anxiety mixed with aggression – and then away, slanting uphill toward the alpine and the river. He makes hardly a sound. His black form dissolves into the trees, and I am amazed that such a lumbering beast, four or five hundred pounds of fur, teeth, and claws, can move this way; lithe and sinuous, a phantom.

I retrieve the map from my pack, find our location, and mark on it "bear." The notation is slightly north of the X. I suggest we follow the bear, up and toward the river. I don't wish to run into him again, but his appearance is an unequivocal gesture: the guardian challenges, then guides.

We get moving again, following the sounds of the river, calling out to the bear that we are in the vicinity. The recent excitement has reinvigorated us, and thrashing through the undergrowth is now less of a chore. Our movements are freshened with a sense of imminence.

We approach the river again, first smelling its cold air and then catching glimpses of it through the brush. We emerge at the bank, find it eroded and overhung with trees balanced over the gorge. Water cascades along turbulent paths, boulders shift with a rumbling sound. Directly in front of us, rising over two hundred feet in a vertical slash against the November sky, is a cliff of cooled lava.

High up, where the cliff meets the forest above, we can see our perch from earlier in the morning. I think of the first seat of the Unnameable, from where the Shebtiw spoke the names of things. We've come out below the first trail, the one we back-tracked along because it ended above the river. We had been sitting on top of the cliff. Its face was shielded by our position above it, its crown covered by the forest undergrowth. We had reached our destination after all. Yet, even if we had known it, there would have been no way to climb down. We would likely have given up, assuming that special equipment was needed to get at the deposits. We would not have been led here by the bear.

The cliff extends roughly three hundred feet along the bank of the river. It's exposed here because of erosion: more than ten thousand years of water traveling in this cleft, deepening it, etching the surface into relief while the surrounding forest concealed traces of the old volcano. The river lays bare the old flame, cools it, dreams with it – slow, rhythmic dreams of clear water, lucent fire.

The face of the cliff is aggregated, filled with black rocks embedded in solidified ash and pumice. Upstream, where water rushes fast and white, a jumble of huge volcanic boulders has fallen from the cliff face. Five or six of them lean against and on top of one another. Each is as big as a truck. Beneath this edifice, surrounded by water and outlined by the gray mass of rock, is a shadowed space that looks like a cave.

We clamber down the bank to the water's edge. The rocks are slippery, treacherous. Everything is coated with a quarter inch of clear ice. The riverbed is only rock – nothing like a sandbar here – and the gloss of ice renders the colors bright: slate, black like the bear's fur, caramel. White stones lie here and there like scrimshaw.

Arms out for balance, we walk carefully across the river, treading upon the largest stones, trying to stay out of the water, slipping and grabbing with every step. I would have thought nothing could be slower going than the rain forest, but the crawl of our progress here is absurd. Two or three hunched steps a minute, struggling for purchase, arms wheeling. I fall in twice, first up to my knees in the water and then on my side, soaking the right half of my pants.

Eventually we reach the shadowed place. It's a grotto, formed by the fallen boulders and natural contours of the river. A small waterfall cascades down onto the stones. The grotto lies beneath the waterfall; the water rushes above and around it, while the boulders preserve its dolmen shape.

The old Egyptian myth relates that the stone of origin will be found along the winding waterway, "at the boundary of the sky, in darkness, surrounded by fire."*

We approach the cavern. Water sluices through from above. The interior is small, perhaps a dozen feet across. Ice hangs from the dark ceiling, coats the volcanic walls, and covers the faceted stones of the floor. I step gingerly ahead, out of daylight and into shadow, the sounds of the river now muted. I hear water trickling down from the icicles. A frozen pool lies at the center of the cavern floor, its surface glistening with clear ice, its fringe marked by granite stones and flakes of obsidian. Behind and above the pool, at the rear of the cavern, the river flows down through a gap in the boulders.

Light is carried on the white water as it spills over the threshold of the pool. I bend down, cup my hands, take a sip. It tastes of green branches, the alpine, minerals, all tumbled into it as it cascades down the mountain. The water feels light in my hand. Its surface refracts the skin of my palm, webbed with soft lines. Errant drops make small splashes on the rocks.

My father comes into the mouth of the cavern. We stand beside each other, gazing into the shadows and then up, past the overhanging boulders of the cavern roof to the cliff above. The lava flow covers the sky. Around us, the water sound is like many voices speaking together.

My father sits down on a boulder at the water's edge. I wander around, becoming curious about the entry of the river at the back of the cavern. I climb around the side, skirt the small waterfall, climb over a fallen cedar, and scramble across the frozen rocks. Behind and above the cavern, I discover another pool. Its surface is white with snow and frost. I can't see into the pool – there are no glossy stones visible here – but a dark rock, black and flecked with snow, protrudes from the surface.

Come to the river, said the dreams. This is what I've come for. A black stone beneath a cliff of fire.

I retrieve my rock hammer from my pack and strike the carapace of ice on the stone. Shards break loose, glancing against my face and falling aside. I inspect the stone, see that I'm not yet through the ice, and continue hammering. The percussion from the blows causes the ice on the surface of the pool to crack. A single, wide fissure works its way five or six feet upstream from the stone. There's a brittle, cracking sound. Water seeps through from the pool beneath, soaks the snow and clears my view into the pool. At the end of the crack, lying in about a foot of clear water, I see a second black stone. It is a rough and flattened cube. The ice-encrusted stone I had been hammering on is the marker, as the bear was a marker. It points the way; I follow its unequivocal gesture.

I step into the pool, reach into the frigid water, and touch the black stone. There's warmth to it, or so it seems. I lift it from the pool. It's heavy, perhaps a hundred pounds; a hard, igneous rock. The word *igneous* means, literally, "of fire." The six faces of the stone are cleaved sharply, yielding corners that are almost square. Water skitters off the dark surface, revealing shades of color. The rock is not quite black: a dark-hued blue sweeps across it, and speckles of white lie on the textured surface like scattered snowflakes. There is such beauty in it that I am stilled.

I stand on the shoulder of an exploded mountain, up to my knees in frigid, fast-running water, beneath a cliff from which boulders – weighing hundred of tons – and tree trunks have fallen. I am overshadowed by a forest of virtually impenetrable bastions. It is Remembrance Day. And I hold, dripping in my hands, a stone of beginnings. A seed stone, black, hinting at color, hiding the secret, as the myths relate, of the world's creation.

I heft the stone onto my shoulder and step out of the pool. Carefully, I remove my fleece jacket from my pack, wrap it around the stone, and place the bundle back inside. I hoist the pack onto my back, reel under the weight, correct my posture, and move out toward the river's edge. I walk down slowly, skirting the waterfall, adjusting my footfalls to the weight of the stone. At first, my steps are shuddery. My feet come down too hard on the riverbed, and my gait is unstable. Walking downhill is more stressful on the legs than walking uphill; the large muscles in the upper legs can be shredded by the exertion of continually halting the body's momentum. And I have more than the weight of my body to contend with; I'm carrying an extra hundred pounds of stone. I take it slow, reminding myself how unpleasant it would be to fall headlong into the river.

My father waits below, at the entrance to the grotto. I sit on a nearby log, unshoulder my pack, and prepare to show him the black stone. He begins to climb over to where I am, loses his footing on the ice, and slides sideways, flailing for a moment and then falling, with a cry of frustration, into the water. He lands on his side. The water is so cold that he thrashes up, struggling among the jumbled boulders of the shore. I rush forward, reaching, but he's too far out. I step into the water, and by the time I reach him he's up, chagrined, the bloom of exertion spreading across his face.

He plods to shore and sits down on the log. I ask if he's all right. Once again he nods, tells me he's fine, laughs a little at this inconvenient turn of events. The right side of his body is soaked, as are his arms. It's one thing to have wet feet – if you keep moving, they usually warm up – but to be wet along the trunk of the body, in weather like this, is not good. It's time to get moving. We'll look at the stone later.

We backtrack along the riverbed, down the slope of the mountain, past the cliff with its glittering obsidian and dark ash. We move with urgency now, traveling fast, but not rushing. We head back into the underbrush and struggle across the shadowed ground. We stay closer to the river this time, knowing the trail crosses it downstream, no longer searching for an unknown destination but navigating directly.

Ten minutes into our return journey, my father's hands grow numb. The ends of the truncated fingers of his right hand are white. Several years ago, while he was oiling the cable on the funicular that leads from the dock to his house, a flayed tendril of the cable seized his hand and carried it into the flywheel of the motor. He's lucky to have lost only the tips of his fingers. Since then, both his hands have been much more susceptible to the cold.

His gloves are wet and of little use; frostbite is not far off.

Suddenly the situation seems serious. And then I remember that I took my gloves off, back at the first patch of devil's club. If I had kept them on, grasping wet branches and scrambling across the riverbed, they would now be useless. But they're in my coat pocket, warm and dry. I take them from my pocket and give them to my father. So often when I was a boy, my gloves wet and cold from falls in the snow, my father gave me his pair, large and cozy and warm.

We move on, seeking a clear path through the tangle. I take the lead, turning to the left and emerging accidentally at the water's edge. I pivot back toward the forest, but my father notices a clearing in the bush, across the river. It's the old logging track we had come across, but farther south along its line. There must have been a jog in the road where it crossed the river: perhaps the crossing here was precipitous at one time, and further down, where it joined the trail, the bed was wider, more accommodating to logging sledges and pack ponies. The road runs straight south, between the upper and lower trails, and we decide that following it is a fair gamble, especially when stacked up against two tired hikers – one with oncoming frost-bite, the other carrying a pack heavier than both his kids com-bined – heading back into thick winter underbrush.

We cross the river. The bed is flat, and not too deep. Beneath the moving water, stones of every color shine through a liquid veil. Mud on the bottom is packed tight. Fragments of sand tumble silently toward the valley.

We climb the opposite bank to the remains of the road above. Like the segment farther north, the track is derelict but not overgrown. Thin shoots crisscross the path, but the going is easy compared to the underbrush. Twenty minutes later, we emerge at the upper trail. It's difficult to see how we could have missed this junction; but there are tall grasses here, and the trunks of young alders obscure the view of the old and narrow track. What a windfall: we've avoided a couple of hours of hard slogging through the rain forest. My concern for my father's hands eases, and my mood shifts – confident now of our safety, rolling over to the wonder of the stone's discovery.

The old road leads us to where the two trails join, the intersection of memory and prophecy I encountered earlier in the morning. Bark on the surrounding trees is dark, and shadows migrate across leaves turned down toward the earth. My father is ahead, and he passes the juncture without comment; it is not, for him, a point of opening. I pause, look back at these two paths – one sloping down toward the valley, hiding the river ahead and an old road of forgotten days; the other, an ascending passage, overhung by a yellow wood, rising into a grand gallery of bright sky.

We will come here again, where the path diverges. My father will go ahead, his back dwindling as he walks with gentle footfalls toward the bright air, the rushing water. But today, with daylight still strong and a path of tumbled rock underfoot, we turn and head down the mountain.

T W O

The stone lies on my workbench, the water of the river gone from it, its surfaces lighter. Just rough, dull stone. But something drew me to it, drew me far up the slope of a mountain, across a guarded threshold, and into the dark, chill river.

I call my father to see how he's doing. Yesterday, after we made our way down the mountain and I dropped him off at the harbor, he seemed tired but also invigorated. I want to make sure he's not too sore today; my own joints and leg muscles are tight and sluggish. He answers the phone, upbeat and sprightly, and tells me he's been passing along the story of the bear to anyone who will listen. It's the kind of story we'll be talking about for a long while.

He asks me about the stone, and my plans for it. I'm not sure, I tell him. I need to acquaint myself with it, to understand more deeply the impulse behind my search for it. The dreams, which cracked open and tumbled into the brilliant day, are forging paths inside me, crisscrossing, weaving toward a horizon

I can't quite see. I need to follow them, follow the myth that was their inspiration. I need to sit with the stone until my direction becomes clear.

The November day is dark. Sheets of rain wash the evergreens behind our house; bright drops hang, then fall, from branches. I turn from the window and head back to the shop. The room was designed as a garage, but no car has been in here for years. Except for a clear space in the center, the shop is filled with tool cabinets, stacks of wood, assembly tables, power tool stations. A block of marble from the quarry used by Michelangelo holds up one end of a pile of seasoned beech. An oarlock from an old dinghy lies on the windowsill, its bronze green with age. On my kids' workbench, scattered with offcuts of cedar and pine, a small hammer rests alongside a row of nails hammered into a board. I can see from its rounded edge and scratched surface that it's one of the boards from the old ski rack my father and my brothers and I built for our cabin when I was eleven years old. Along the top, between two holes that once held pegs for securing the skis, one of the kids has used a rasp to abrade a shallow valley in the wood. Fresh fibers of Douglas fir – pale, with a hint of orange – contrast with the old surface, deepened by thirty years of mountain light.

This place is steeped in layers of time. In my own work, in that of my kids, we intersect with other moments: the forest tree, growing for hundreds of years before any of us was born; artifacts old and discarded, made by unknown craftsmen, by my father, by my own hands; tools, new and ancient, whose histories will remain forever obscure. And now a stone, millennia old, lies on the bench beside a bloodstain from a mishap last summer when the power planer took off the tip of my finger. At the time, my father laughed, saying that truncated fingers seemed to be a family tradition. Another story to tell, like that of the bear.

These stories – remembered, adapted, embellished – form the core of our family identity. And of our personal identities as well. Stories are how we make sense of who we are; they are the thread of our connection to the unfathomable.

As I wipe the stone with a cloth, clearing its surface of sand and algae from the river, I wonder about the intersection of the stone's tale with my own. I'm reaching toward something, a way of bringing the dreams out from the shadow of my inner life. A way of holding them to the wind, so that they might lift off and be borne toward the territory of myth. After all, a dream is only a wandering myth, exiled from the source but always on its way back home.

The dreams and myths to which I have been drawn – sea of beginnings, well of fire, black stone spinning – originated with people who called themselves the Kem. Their culture is now long gone, though their country remains: wide desert, red cliffs, black earth. They were already vanishing more than two thousand years ago, and they were gone by the time Christianity began. A few hundred years before Christ, the Greeks, whose civilization borrowed substantially from the Kem, called the land of their cultural forebears Khemia. That name journeyed through ages of forgetting, of secret flame, and was delivered, intact with its essence of mystery, as the modern word *alchemy*.* The land of the Kem is one place, the beginning place of burnished sky and deep river: Egypt.

From a craftsman's point of view, ancient Egypt is the most compelling place on earth. In stonework, in monumental architecture, in artistic finesse, the Kem achieved a level of astounding refinement. In temples, statuary, and sculpture, they were capable of matching – and in some cases, exceeding – what we can accomplish today. Their endeavors, which now lie strewn across the desert, buried and fallen into ruin, served the aims of an enigmatic spirituality about which we know many facts but few truths.

The consciousness of those vanished people is so fantastically distant from our own that we can hardly grasp it. It has been lost on the road of the world's unfolding, somewhere between the present and the crossroads of beginning. The impulse that drew me into a dream and up the mountain involves walking back along that road, reading the signposts in the way that I know – through the work of my hands – trying to discover the traces of a lost age. That odyssey begins with stone.

The black stone lies undisturbed at the edge of the bench. While I wait for the impulse to shape it, I carve a canoe bowl in the tradition of the aboriginal artists of the Northwest Coast, a birthday present for my friend Grant. I glue up two layers of cypress with a slice of purpleheart between. As I work, removing layers of the light, almost yellow cypress, I find myself diverging from the intended shape of the piece. I carve deeper, hollowing out the central section and shaping the edges by instinct. I bore through to the layer of purpleheart deep in the wood. It emerges as an indigo oval at the bottom of the bowl's swept-out interior. A tendril of dark grain threads its way along the wood at the intersection of the contrasting layers. I pause, inspecting the work. The top of the bowl is not narrow and uniform like a canoe but instead flares wide at the center; it's almost a circle that flows into short handles at the ends. Working in imaginative leaps, I inlay shimmering copper along the contour of the handles and polish the cypress to a clear, amber sheen. When it's done, the bowl is an eye – a pupil in a deep well, surrounded by a bright iris.

I finish the bowl with walnut oil, a non-toxic finish, in case Grant decides to use it for serving food. I apply six coats over the course of a week, holding the bowl above my workbench, sliding around its interior with a cotton cloth. After the third coat, the wood begins to shine. I sit in the shop and watch the light play upon the surface. As I wait for the oil to dry enough that I can move the bowl inside, where it's warmer and the finish will dry more quickly, I pick up the stone and hold it in my lap.

It's darker than slate, not quite jet black. The corners are sharp and distinct, as though cleaved level by a colossal hand. The two largest and opposing faces, what I think of as the top and bottom, are parallel. The side planes taper slightly, forming shallow wedges at the corners. The surface, mottled with mineral streaks from water erosion and marked by a ragged crack that runs between two corners, feels smooth. It's not smooth – small fissures and fractured veins crisscross the stone everywhere – but nothing on the surface is remotely loose, and there are no grains that shift under my fingers. My eyes see rough patches – crevasses and ridges roughly sheared off – but when my hand touches the stone, allows itself to glide over the surface, the rock feels smooth as polished bone.

There is blue in it, the color of the northern sea beneath a November sky. Dark, impenetrable blue. And white, like flotsam, or a flock of gulls gliding across the night sky. Flecks of white, in every part of the stone, spreading out like ancestral lights tumbling across the mouth of the well.

The constituent minerals of the stone give rise to these colors. The black-blue background is composed of hornblende and pyroxenes; they are many times harder than tool steel. Microscopically, the hornblende displays precise, six-sided crystals, each one a tessera of the black stone's mosaic. Pyroxenes are a group of minerals: augite, hypersthene, bronzite, and the like. All much harder than iron, all crystalline. Using a magnifying glass, I can also see labradorite, with its distinctive glow, blue and metallic. It resembles lapis lazuli, one of the stones sacred to the Kem.

The white flakes in the rock are of the feldspar mineral group; microcline, probably. There is some olivine, as well, judging by its namesake color, and a host of iron-rich minerals and metals, magnetite and hematite among them. All of it twined together, thrust up from the mountain's core, cooled by hidden waters.

The combination of minerals in the stone denotes it as basalt, a name of Kem origin. Pliny, the Roman savant and author of the celebrated *Natural History*, a work of authoritative scholarship until the Middle Ages, wrote, "The Ægyptians also found in Æthyopia another kind of Marble which they call Basaltes, resembling yron as well in colour as hardnes."[*] Bands of basalt form the crust of the earth beneath the oceans. In this sense, basalt is the foundation stone, a pillar upholding the manifest world.

Basalt forms far down beneath the earth's crust, miles down where the temperature exceeds a thousand degrees Celsius. There its constituent minerals melt together as magma, as molten stone. Volcanic and tectonic activity thrust the magma up to the surface, either directly through the summit of a volcano or along dikes and sills leading to the mountainside. As the magma approaches the surface – quickly or slowly, depending on geologic action – the minerals begin to crystallize. If ascent toward the surface is slow (millions of years), and the surrounding temperature drops gradually, large crystals can form in the aggregate. If the movement upward is rapid (a few seconds, say, with a further few days of cooling), crystals have only a short time in which to develop, and the resulting texture is more uniform. The small flecks of microcline in the stone I found, along with the absence of any other large crystals in the matrix, indicate that it cooled swiftly on the surface.

Along one edge of the stone, its dark color and smooth texture are interrupted by a lighter mass of grainy material, almost like sandstone. This intrusion, called a xenolith, is a mass of compressed ash from the volcano. When still molten, cooling on the surface beneath a sky blackened with pumice, the developing stone flowed around this anomaly. The dense ash is there still, a gray lump the size of a golf ball.

For ten thousand years this stone has lain on the mountain, on an old riverbed, in the shadow of a volcano. A long series of eruptions delivered it from the earth's hidden core, as in the Kem myth of origin. It floated up through the fiery sea, rested upon the summit of an emergent mountain, took its rough and simple shape. As I place the stone back on the bench top, ruminating on its origins, I wonder about the similarity between geological and mythological tales. According to the current scientific view – itself a fluid construction, always changing to accommodate new ideas – the earth was indeed fashioned as the Kem myth describes: out of a maelstrom of solar dust, hot gases, and gravity. The planet coalesced, a great sea formed (no one knows how), and under the protection of its waters the first stones were made. Those stones, some of which have been discovered by geologists, are more than four billion years old. My mountain stone, by comparison, is young indeed. The ratio of its span to that of the most aged stones is as one day to a thousand years. This is about the same ratio as the age of my kids to the age of humanity.

I visit Bill to discuss the age and composition of my black stone. Bill is a geologist, and he's much more interested in the chemical composition of basalt than in its mythological associations. As we're talking, in Bill's den overlooking the forest, he retrieves a stone from the edge of his fireplace hearth. It's about the size and shape of a small Bible. Bill hands me this stone and tells me it's one of the oldest objects in the world. It has been sawn into two parallel planes, banded with black and white striations, edged by rough sides where the rock shows deep weathering. The white bands are quartz and feldspar; the darker ones are mostly biotite. The stone is called a gneiss.* Though it's not large, it's heavy in my hand. There are no loose grains; only a hard, crystalline matrix spread across a background of contrasting hues.

Bill received the gneiss as a gift when he worked as a geologist for the Canadian government, and he counts it among his most prized possessions. I can see why: at almost four billion years of age, such an artifact is astonishing – older, by far, than the dinosaurs, older even than the earliest fossils. It invites questions and ruminations. It encourages within me a sense of my own insignificance. But also, like an anchor offered to the drifting mind, it provides a concrete means of joining with the past. Four billion years is a difficult span to imagine. Measures and metaphors can capture the breadth of that time, but not its depth. Here, though, cradled in my palm, is four billion years.

Looking closely, I glimpse the detail in each of the black bands: whorls, curves, marks like tiny swirls of ink. Dark tendrils extend above and below each striation. Here and there the white breaks through, truncating a long skein of black. As I study the surface, it begins to resemble a text – black on white, linear, structured with letters and punctuation. The similarity is unmistakable. "In the beginning," says the Hebrew legend, the Torah was "written with black fire on white fire, lying in the lap of God."*

Bill shows me, on a map, where the stone was found: at the center of a small island, rising from the waters of an unnamed lake, in the Acasta region of northern Canada.* Islands and nameless waters. I mention the similarity between Kem mythology and the geography in which his gneiss was found. As I look at the map, tracing my eye over a northern territory almost devoid of human habitation, I notice something else: the unnamed lake drains into a river system that adjoins Great Bear Lake. The guardian again, protecting the ancestral land with its stone of origin.

Bill's stone is a fragment of the original continent – what geologists call the protocontinent – that survived asteroid impacts and the turbulence of a formative earth.* From a core veined in black and white, on an island surrounded by fresh and aged waters, the beginning text of the world was written.

As I drive home, past the cedar mill and the bog that reaches to the river, I wonder about time, about what is remembered and forgotten. I drive south, along the new highway that borders the bog's eastern edge. How old is the bog? The highway is fifteen years old; trees on the bog's fringe are standing dead because the blacktop disrupted the drainage of their soil. Old gives way to new. I suspect, however, that the bog will be here long after the highway has vanished. The road stretches into the future; the bog retreats and waits.

This landscape is a metaphor for modern consciousness: the past diminishes as we depart from it, and the future is a road dwindling ahead to a bright horizon. This conception of time – linear and unidirectional – continually shapes our experience. We are governed by its regular sequence; its precise direction leads us toward an irrevocable, unknown destination. The road of time moving forward is a structure upon which we bind our living.

But for the ancients, it was not this way. Their descriptions of time are not straight paths but circles. For them, every step forward led back toward the origin, toward the welcoming light of ancestral fires.*

By the time of Plato, in the fifth century BCE, the old view of time was entirely reversed. Plato maintained that time spreads out behind the present moment, as though we stand on the deck of a boat gazing forward, and the sea of the future assaults us from ahead. Our present is the cleaving prow, our past a turbulent wake drawn across a wide expanse of ocean.

This shift in the perspective of time is the basis of Western culture. We no longer face backward. For us, such a direction is a regression, a betrayal of what we have come to think of as progress. Our immersion in time as a path moving forward makes it difficult for us to understand an alternative perception. We are preoccupied with the idea of evolution. The ancients, conversely, were occupied with notions of return.

They would have understood more easily – in the bones, in the breath – the span of time embodied by the past. Our straight road of time never turns back; we leave our flotsam at the side of the road and move on, forgetting. But if the path of time curves round again, leads us down remembered tracks, rolls toward beginnings, we begin to know the way.

Stones, which unlike people are not circumscribed by time, may live for millions or billions of years. Every pebble underfoot is a relic of numberless days. We dismiss, or are indifferent to, the fact of our fleeting residence on the earth. But stones remember. In the dance of remembering, they constantly move, playing out a rhythm too slow for us to perceive, alive with the thrumming of mountains and the music of the sky. The minerals in basalt, each a crystalline structure tuned to a note of nature, are the individual strings of a volcanic instrument. A song – old, soft – plays as we pass, its music unnoticed as we press forward along the straight road of time.

I pass my hand over the black stone, feeling again its smooth texture, the weight of its age. And I begin to sense, in these opening moments of the work, the well of origin. I move toward it, as though gliding on dark waters. Inside the stone, beneath its implacable surface lambent with the colors of a hidden age, water and fire together begin – are always beginning – to stir.

Winter, the season called *proyet* by the Kem, deepens. *Proyet* means emergence. It is the season of remembering, of reflection, of quiet. In modern times, Remembrance Day marks – inadvertently, though perhaps not accidentally – its beginning. While branches in the yard are ruffled by cold wind and weighted with snow, the stone spins its awakenings within me. It lies on the bench, still and dark, while I work on other projects. It appears in my reading of myths from many cultures. My kids inspect it every time they're in the shop with me, slapping its surface with resounding thwacks, as though testing its resiliency. Something is begun in these moments of engagement and observation. I'm not sure what, exactly, but I can feel a delicate momentum building.

During Christmas week, we make our annual trek to my father's island home. We gather up our gear – gifts, food, life jackets – and head down to the dock. The yellow dinghy waits. There's wind on the water; rigging from the moored sailboats whistles and clangs. On the way across, my kids ask about their cousins, whether they've arrived yet. They don't see their cousins much; about as frequently as I saw mine when I was a boy. I haven't seen any of my cousins since my mother's funeral, and before that, my paternal grandmother's funeral. Almost ten years. The next time will be the funeral of my father, or one of my aunts.

I am troubled by the distance in my family, a gulf that has been growing since the death of my grandmother. Bereft of its center, the family began to scatter – even before my kids or my older brother's kids were born. My mother died soon after my grandmother, and it was as though the wind went out of our sails. We had been held together by a fierce old gentlewoman, and by a mother of desperate intensity; once they were gone, we began drifting. We moved forward through time, but in different directions.

We dock the boat on the far shore, climb the ramp at the head of the dock, and take the funicular up to the house. My brother's kids are here already; when they see Avery and Rowan, the playing begins in earnest. They run together into the forest out back, climb along the rocky hill where springwater bubbles up into a pool, shout and chase and catch one another with reckless vigor. Later, when we've finished opening presents, they make a pile of shredded wrapping paper, dive into it, wrestle until it spreads across the living room in tendrils of bright color.

The winter sun, low in the southern sky, filters light through the trees behind my father's house and illuminates the nest of a heron, ragged bundles of sticks gathered across a high tree's crown in a wide arc. In many myths, herons are immortal birds, beyond time. In Kem tales, the ibis – cousin of the heron – is given this role. The ibis is the animal form of Thoth, god of wisdom, voice of the world's creation.

At the end of our visit, we walk down the winding path that leads from the cliff-top house to the shore. My younger brother goes ahead to ready the boat for crossing. As we descend on the switchbacking trail, Avery holds aloft a red helium balloon that had been attached to one of the presents. His four-year-old fingers wrap tight around the ribbon; the balloon bobs up and down as he walks.

We reach the ramp that leads down to the dock. It's late in the afternoon, Avery is tired, and he asks if I can carry him. I lift him from the ground, cradle him against my shoulder, settle into this simple affection which will carry me through my whole life. But as he reaches his arm around my neck, he lets go of the balloon. Too late, I see the ribbon drifting up, and I snatch for it with my free hand. Realizing, suddenly, that his hand is empty, Avery looks up and with a shout of frustration watches the balloon ascend. Together we watch it meander in the breeze and dwindle slowly upward into the sky. It climbs into the cobalt expanse, a drop of red in a blue ocean. It drifts higher, almost out of sight. When Avery loses track of it, I point with my index finger, holding it still until he finds the balloon again. Eventually it becomes tiny. How high: hundreds, thousands of feet? Distance and perspective are rendered void by infinite blue and infinitesimal red. I could be looking at a galaxy, or a single mote in my son's eye.

One moment the balloon is there, clear but distant, and then it's gone. I search for it, and see it again. Then it disappears once more. I spot it one last time, rising into the far distance, somehow buoyed with the promise of deliverance, of endurance. The balloon fills my vision with a kindled hope – for myself, for my children – that we might be carried aloft on our fragile dreams. It wheels in the empty sky and is gone.

Early in the new year, I visit Lorenzo. His studio, which looks out to the inlet and a series of bridges spanning the water, is fronted by a wide grassy yard populated by slabs of stone. Square columns of white marble, shot through with skeins of apricot and charcoal, lie sidelong on the ground. A dark block the size of a fridge rests beside stacked shards of pale granite. Many of the stone surfaces are smooth, cut with clean lines by a band saw using a steel blade and a slurry of corundum powder. Rough faces appear here and there, their angles and contours shaped by the grain of the stone and a hand chisel. I see remnants of drill holes where some of the blocks were split with wedges.

Lorenzo shows me blocks from Italy, from northern Canada, from diverse places where these treasures have been thrust up from deep in the earth. I wonder about their age, and about the many turns in their spiraling paths that have brought them here. I carry my own dark stone cradled in the crook of my arm.

Inside the studio, a film of stone dust covers every surface. Shelves are stuffed with abrasive wheels and diamond blades and chisels. In many ways, the space is much like my own shop: scattered with cords and tools and worktables, disheveled enough to be interesting as well as hazardous. Lorenzo says precisely the same thing to me that I say to everyone who enters my shop: "I need to clean up a bit more." This is a craftsman's mantra, repeated because it never gets done. A certain amount of chaos seems, for many of us, to be necessary. Clean shops produce clean work – measured and refined. But for most of the craftsmen I know, clean work can be an exercise in the mundane. A bit of mess helps to make things interesting, to loosen up the formality and rigidity of materials that, in themselves, are rigid enough. Besides, why clean up when the work is there, waiting, inviting?

Lorenzo leads me into a corner of the studio and shows me two matched sculptures of amorphous human forms climbing a pillar of marble. Each is about six feet high; hands and backs and legs twist around the stone, merging and separating as they reach upward. These sculptures remind me of the ancestors in the Kem origin tales, climbing up the well, drawn by the radiant stone. When I mention this to Lorenzo, he tells me that his intent is to show the rhythm of time, the cycles of becoming and dissolution. We talk about memory, about the unity of myth and experience, and then he shows me the fire sculpture – twinned human forms, clothed in flame, emerging from a foundation of red marble shaped like a pyramid. I think of the Shebtiw, the twins of Kem mythology.

I place my fire stone on Lorenzo's workbench. We talk about my half-formed plans for it, the kinds of tools I might use, the approach I might take. We make small cuts in the stone, testing its hardness and grain. The smell of dust spreads out in the damp air. As I watch the blade neatly incise the stone's surface, a pressing need grows in me; to get going, to take the images and words of the old tales and coax their shapes from the stone itself. My hands, after a period of waiting and research and simple openness, are ready to work.

Late that evening, I sit out in the yard and watch the northern sky. A rampart of tall evergreens, blackened by the night, is silhouetted against a vault of indigo. I see the Great Bear, turning around the hub of the world. As I gaze up, suddenly, from the blue darkness of the sky, emerging all at once as though swimming up from deep waters, a flock of white birds appear. Their wings, reflecting light from a source I cannot see, are brighter than the surrounding stars. They move like ripples on a sea of obsidian. Then they glide past the trees and vanish.

At the temple of the falcon god Horus, in Edfu – in the south of modern Egypt, along the Nile – limestone inscriptions relate how primeval ancestors reanimated the universe. The black stone is their embodiment. The name of each member of this company of first beings contains the element *hr*, meaning face or countenance. And it is here, reading these myths while the stone perches quietly beside me, that I find a formative impulse: to uncover, and animate, the ancestral face.

I visualize the long backward steps of my family and the many faces of my forebears. I follow the thread of names back as far as I can. I remember some things, and I imagine I remember others. I read the old stories in our family chronicle, and I watch them take shape inside me. I work to refine my vision. And I dream: of a luminous wave splashing through the crack at the bottom of a closed door. The water washes up the wall, erases the room with its brilliance. Outside, a sliver of new moon drifts through an indigo sky. On the far side of the door, there is a sound like the rushing of waters, and a shadowed foot moves across the light. I do not get up. I do not open the door. I lie in bed, waiting, fearful. The figure takes another sidelong step, as though pacing. His foot is bare, and dark, the rhythm of muscles lithe as his heel pivots on the cold floor. As the moment stretches itself out, and a skein of bright tendrils weaves across the wall, I remember black earth under my feet and the cry of a bird, high up. I know, without seeing, that beyond the door's threshold a deep well is encircled by desert. The surface of the water is a glistening disk. The true names of things call out in clear voices. A momentary dislocation jostles me – a flutter, a ripple in the air – and I find myself in the hall, my body a cool and liquid fire. A feeling of urgency draws me down the narrowing corridor. The sound of water comes rushing back. Light and water. I take a step forward, tentative, expectant. The water sound fills the air, and I awake.

It's early; the kids and Elizabeth are still asleep. Conscious but not yet alert, drifting on the fringe of the dream, I wander down to the shop and sit with the stone. It has been sitting, in one place or another, for thousands of years. I inspect, again, its marks and crevices, looking for something to guide me. Despite my itch to get going with the actual work of sculpting, I'm hesitant to push, to rush. I want to allow the stone to speak slowly, the way a pebble makes its measured way down a creek bed.

I ruminate on the Kem myth of the coming of light and the world brought into being by the power of words. This old and fractured story is the first resonant trace of the later sacred myths of Judaism, Christianity, and Islam. The biblical account is a descendant, thousands of years later, of the early origin tales fashioned by the Kem and their neighbors the Sumerians. Beyond the threshold of their storytelling, before writing was invented, the tales stretch back even further. No one knows how far – perhaps as much as seventy or a hundred thousand years, when language and symbolic thinking seem first to have entered human consciousness.*

Stone and word, always together in the old tales: the Unnameable, speaking from the perch of stone; Moses and the tablets of creation; Thoth, writing in a book of stone and throwing it, trailing fire, to the earth. Black fire written upon white fire. I wonder again: How far back does it all go?

I hear the sound of running feet: across the hall upstairs, down the stairs, along the tiles behind the kitchen. The shop door opens, and Avery is there: sleep fading from his face, blue eyes soft and inquisitive, ragged teddy bear in one hand. He asks for breakfast.

Later, after Elizabeth has readied Rowan for her grade two spelling test and I've walked Avery to preschool, I return home and begin the preliminary work. I place a diamond blade over the arbor of my grinder, tighten the bolt counterclockwise, and replace the safety guard. Tiny industrial diamonds, set into the body of the steel blade, lie just proud of the metal – an essential design feature, as basalt is much harder than steel. I lift the grinder from the bench, press the black start button with my thumb, and immediately feel rushing air spin off the accelerating blade. Unlike most power tools, in which the blade is either fixed to a heavy assembly or mounted at the center of the mechanism, grinders are gyroscopes. Because the circular blade lies near the end of the motor housing, its motion is not balanced along the length of the tool. Maneuvering a grinder with the power on feels the same as steadying a spinning bicycle wheel in the air while holding its mounting bolts. Above a certain threshold, the revolutions of the wheel take on their own life: shifting, edging sideways, always trying to rotate away from your grasp. By virtue of this same peculiar physics, grinders possess a unique dynamism.

I steady the blade and move it toward the surface of the stone. I choose a spot near the edge – a location I'm sure will be removed in the later work – and ease the blade down. I hear a rushing, grating sound: pitched high, consistent, but with a rough undercurrent, like gravel tumbling through a tunnel of ice. As the blade spins, a flat spot emerges from the backdrop of the stone's surface. First I see white flecks, more evident now as the darker matrix is smoothed into a uniform texture. Then I begin to see into the stone, layer upon layer of aggregated minerals.

I lift the blade from the stone and release the power switch. The wind settles. I run my finger across the clean patch. It feels polished, though there's no gloss. As I explore the area with the tip of my index finger, I trace the boundary between the stone's cut surface and the surrounding eroded texture. I skate across to the other side, follow the threshold around again, notice that the shape of the worked patch, smooth amid rough, is like the scar that encircles the tip of my finger – an old mishap from cutting firewood in the rain.

The past sneaks into the present, and my mind turns to a developing question: What is my obligation to the histories of the Kem, to the ancestry of my own family, to these ramshackle tales of sacred stones and departed gods? I have been taught, by virtue of the age in which I was born, to separate myself – my values and convictions and aims – from those who have gone before me. We move on. But for the Kem, there was no moving on. They believed in the immediacy of ancestry, the immanence of origin. Each generation was responsible for the past. As I rub the exposed corner free of grit with my finger, I wonder about the unfinished tales I am responsible for, the unremembered heraldry that I and my children have inherited.

Our collective legacy from the Kem – symbols, tales, a persistent iconography – is due entirely to the simple fact of their devotion to stone. They prized the hardest, most enduring stones for their work: basalt, granite, diorite. Many of the oldest artifacts, dating from 2500 BCE and earlier, are made from these materials. One of the statues from that period, of a monarch whose name has come down to us as Khafre, is the sole surviving artifact from a series of twenty-three identical diorite sculptures. It was unearthed in 1869, upside down at the bottom of a pit beneath a temple adjoining the Sphinx. Khafre's lone black statue – battered, portions of the left side sheared off – is magnificent. The monarch is seated on a wide slab of stone that extends beneath and behind him, up to the crest of his shoulder. Both hands are in his lap. The left lies palm down, fingers relaxed and forward, on the crest of his left leg. The right hand, curled firmly into a fist, rests atop his right leg. The face is shaped with a similar polarity: the left side expresses affection and openness; the right is formal, authoritative.

The character of the statue depends on the perspective from which it is viewed. The right side, less damaged than the left, shows Khafre as regal, forceful, yet also conveys a sense of enigma – a commanding presence gazing out from a remote age. From the left side, Khafre looks young; a faint trace of a smile, balancing rebellion and authority, plays upon his lips. His head appears to tilt back from this angle, in humor or repose. The impression is not of a monarch, an icon of power, but of a man, fleeting and vulnerable, embodied by lasting stone but with the face of one who has stopped only for a moment, to rest here on the rock while following the circular road of time.

The ceremonial beard has been broken off below Khafre's chin, but his headdress is still intact. It wraps the back half of his head, flares wide just below his ear and descends, decorated with horizontal stripes, to his upper chest. A thin covering extends from the headdress across the top of this head. A seam of fabric, etched into the stone, follows the contour of the fontanel line from the crown of Khafre's head to between and above his eyes. From there, a narrow band diverges on each side, back along his skull to where the two sides meet the rear of the headdress above his ears. The overall effect of the front portion of the headdress is to emphasize the intersection of the fontanel line and the two bands, low and central on Khafre's forehead. They make a crossroads, a deliberate marker of utmost importance. "On the brow," says the Book of Illumination, "your vision of the veiled god opens. Awaken the eye in calmness, wander the temple halls wrapped in the peace of your own becoming."*

Seated behind Khafre, at the top of the black stone slab, is a falcon. Its wings are extended forward on either side, enfolding Khafre's headdress. Its head is raised, as though sighting movement far off. The falcon is the ancestor, raised up from the sea of beginnings, witnessing and whispering.

The statue, which now lies in the Egyptian Museum in Cairo, is slightly larger than life-size. Streaked with veins of green and gray, the black diorite captures precisely the texture of Khafre's skin and underlying sinuous structure. The portrayal is realistic enough to be eerie: a dark figure, striations of color moving across him, a bird of prey nestled on his shoulder.

Why was the statue at the bottom of a pit? Where did its companions go? What catastrophe overtook this monumental work – and the culture that crafted it, forty-five centuries ago? In modern times, archaeologists working on the Giza plateau have unearthed smashed fragments from other statues in the series. The cause of their destruction is unknown, hidden by the simple erasure of time. It's likely that the damage was done about 2250 BCE, during an anarchic period of two hundred years following the time of Khafre. The chaos and social upheaval of that era, only the first of several waves of mayhem, forged a gap we have not been able to cross.*

I skate the grinder across the stone's surface, getting used to the feel of the work. I smooth more of the top, and wonder about Khafre. I first saw his statue when I went to Egypt as a tourist. His precise and personalized features animated the ruins for me. Of Khufu, Khafre's father and the builder of the Great Pyramid, only the monument remains; but Khafre, builder of the middle pyramid, has persisted through the statue's individuality. It's this persistence that I'm interested in: old things that do not surrender to oblivion. Khafre's likeness in stone is one of the most ancient personal representations that still exist. He has become, for me, a mythopoeic ancestor of sorts, a cultural precursor, perhaps humanity's first individual.*

My kids ask a great deal about where things come from: cars, the moon, ice skates. They want to know about origins, ancestors, the means by which the earth was crafted from nothing. This questioning began, for each of them, when they could no longer recall the incidents of their own early development and birth. Until the age of three or four, their recollections of the womb, of their definitive entry into the world, were clear and simple. Avery used to comment on the feeling of warm enclosure; Rowan remembered sounds drifting into the womb from outside. They had not yet begun to forget.

Now neither of them can recall anything about their personal origin. This, I surmise, is due to the widening of their sphere of awareness. Older memories tend to vivify with age, not diminish; I don't think they've forgotten the womb because time has passed. They have forgotten because the womb of their existence is now the wider world; it insists upon their devotion. They now identify their personal beginnings with universal creation. The answers to the basic questions – Who am I? Where did I come from? – have changed, but the impulse for questioning remains. And it seems to me, as I wipe stone dust from the workbench, that the assistance I provide my kids in their questioning of origins is one of the central privileges of my parenting.

The Kem offer considerable guidance in this regard. They created, for the first time in human history, a means by which tales of origin could be symbolized and preserved. Their means of accomplishing this involved the shaping of hard stones into representations of myth. The falcon perched on Khafre's shoulder, the orientation of his hands, the dais upon which he is seated: folded within each of these is an iconography layered with many meanings.*

The statue is, in fact, a book of stone. It relates the tale of creation, of the world's unfolding, of Khafre's place within the knotted threads of time. For the Kem, who practiced this kind of esoteric craftsmanship in every artifact, book and stone were one.

I decide that the stone from the mountain will be a book in the Kem tradition – not a book of words, but a symbolic narrative, one that we will remember, river and bear and numb fingers, and make part of our larger story. Books, after all, have been the keys to my own origin. I inherited roughly a hundred from my great-aunt Eileen: bound with leather or thick black stock, pages gossamer thin, bindings cracked and crumbling. Books of poetry, fable, science, philosophy. Chaucer and Shakespeare and Milton; illustrated versions of Byron and Homer. Most were published in the eighteenth century and are by far the oldest artifacts in our family. Inside an old black Bible – small, about the size of my outstretched hand, the binding reglued but still fragile – the page edges, once red and gilt, are the color of pale red roses. Secreted between facing pages in the Book of Joshua, a flower was long ago pressed. Fragments, cinnamon-hued, delicate as the wings of dragonflies, are all that remain. The underlying text describes the raising of stones as memorials: "This may be a sign among you, that when your children ask their fathers in time to come, saying What mean ye by these stones? Then ye shall answer them . . . These stones shall be for a memorial unto the children."*

Before paper, before papyrus, stone was the means by which the enduring was crafted from the fleeting. The Kem have preserved, in stone, the entire corpus of their learning for five thousand years. Today much of their stone library shows little sign of wear. But they are long gone.

The devotional importance of stone and the craftsmanship surrounding that devotion have not been surpassed since the reign of Khafre. In scarcely more than a century, the Kem devised the monuments of the Giza necropolis (the centerpiece of that necropolis, the Great Pyramid, was the tallest building in the world until the Washington Monument was completed in 1885); they shaped the Sphinx, and the Valley Temple with its limestone blocks weighing as much as two hundred tons. Using simple copper tools, they sculpted hard stone – as much as fifty times harder than copper – into shapes both massive and delicate.* Then, like their forebears, they were rolled under by the wheel of time.

Kem tales tell of living statues, of stone imbued with sentience. Inside them, nestled within the dark stone matrix, the essence of a god, or of a person, passed into a world of long dreaming.* For the Kem, animating statues was not simply a metaphoric or ritualistic process. The stone, in their conception, was literally alive. Statues spoke and walked. A living statue was said to have healed a young girl sick with grief. When the girl's father tried to keep the statue in his home as insurance against further ills, its spirit was seen to fly out, departing into the sky as a golden hawk.

The black diorite statues of Khafre were intended to make a home for his double, the spirit self that walked his own untrodden paths. During his time, there were many such statues. All but one have disappeared, smashed by the tumult of history. Yet I can't help hoping that some of them walked off into the desert. I imagine that if I knew their true names, if I could gaze past the translations and find the authentic voice of those original words, I could call them into waking.

"What unsuspected marvels we should find," says the alchemist Fulcanelli, "if we knew how to dissect words, to strip them of their barks and liberate the spirit, the divine light, which is within."*

Matzeivot is the Hebrew word for standing stones scattered throughout the Middle East. Every religious tradition of the area claims them as their own. They are found on ridges and along open stretches of ground, singly and in groups, thousands of them. They have been adopted by every age – as talismans, as altars, as signposts – but their origin is obscure. They are part of the mythic landscape from which new tales are dreamed.

I read, in my great-aunt's Bible, about Jacob's vision of a ladder ascending to heaven. After awakening, he makes a pillar from the stone he has used as a pillow, saying it "shall be God's house."* In the Arabic tradition, the term for a standing stone means "house of God." In an old Assyrian chronicle, a campaigning king "camped by the stones in which the gods are dwelling."*

According to the local mythology at Tula, in Mexico, four massive basalt statues of female warriors, called the Atlanteans, become animated at night. Fifteen feet high and three feet across, they walk the grounds of the temple, thundering across the flat-topped pyramid with their stone feet, still enacting the guardianship of a mute and derelict sanctuary. They are sentinels, crafted by the Maya, but unable finally to preserve their lands against history's conflagration.

Tales of moving and speaking stones and statues are commonplace. The bleeding figures of Christ, seen in churches throughout the world, are perhaps the best-known examples. In the same vein, statues of the Virgin Mary sometimes move, or cry, or sing. Along the volcanic slopes of Mauna Loa in Hawaii, tourists gather stones as souvenirs, only to return them (by mail, usually) months or weeks later, having gone home and found themselves subject to ill luck as a result of defying the injunction of Pele, goddess of fire, not to remove her property. The National Park Service in Hawaii receives thousands of pounds of returned stone every year.

To follow the Kem, to discover the consciousness of their surpassing craftsmanship, I must take their assertions at face value. I must enter that world in which statues speak and awareness is a nomadic light taking up residence in the stone. Yet, living as I do in an age so remote from the Kem, immersion in their reality is not a seamless endeavor. It beckons double selves from me. An ancestral and imaginal self, capable of knowing the forgotten ways, offers me dreams of awakening, of light and doors and water, meandering. *Come to the river.* I follow old memories, drawn up from the well of my deepest knowing. I am watched by another self, one who follows the raveled threads of a different kind of awareness. This Other, whose eye is a searchlight dispelling shadow, eases open the mysteries through patient and pressing inquiry. He watches the patterns of leaves growing and falling. He reaches for the tangle of perception, draws together its diversities, and finds for each shining thing a place of understanding. Drawn onward by his gentleness, my awareness blossoms across an unknown territory.

These interwoven selves are not simply the instinctive and rational faculties. They are, to borrow from the Kem, complementary aspects of the unified God. One eye moves forward, the other gazes back.

Wan winter light from the street drifts in through the single window in my shop. I've installed a number of overhead fluorescent lights over the years, but they never seem to provide enough illumination. When spring and summer come, I'll open the garage door while I'm working. It faces east, and laboring on summer mornings can be a surpassing joy. Now, with chill air and an overcast sky, both heaters and five fluorescent fixtures are on. I'm wearing a fleece jacket flecked with yellow cedar sawdust; I can smell its fragrance, like sandstone warmed in the sun. Motes of dark dust from my experimental foray into the stone's surface drift around the shop.

I inspect the stone where the eroded contours and grinder marks meet. Now I've begun, with dreams and myths and memories all wrapped up together, interwoven. There's a growing momentum. I must try to follow. I will fail, as always, to follow it entirely; my devotion, my skill, will be insufficient to the task of manifesting the vision. But my effort will be enough, is always enough, to carry me forward into wonder.

THREE

I mix up a batch of quick-setting modeling compound in a large stainless steel bowl. It's the color and consistency of pancake batter. In a separate bowl, I mix the light blue catalyst. I pour the catalyst into the larger bowl and furiously mix the two solutions together for half a minute. The compound begins to set – I can feel the resistance increasing against my mixing spoon. I toss the spoon aside, take a deep breath, quell my panic, and place my entire face into the mixture.

For forty-five seconds I wait, trying to bring my heart rate down, struggling in my mind, again and again, with an image of my face stuck permanently in the hardening material, my hands desperately trying to pull it away. I'm fairly sure that's not going to happen, but the rising tide of anxiety is pressing and claustrophobic. My air begins to run out long before it should. I hang on as long as I can, my lungs on fire, my hands twitching. Then, with the last of my breath, I blow out. The seal between my skin and the modeling compound releases, and I remove my face from the bowl. I open my eyes, look down, and see a perfect, inverted replica of my face: a negative. At the corners of my negative-eyes, small pockets remain where air bubbles were caught in the mold. The finished form looks and feels like a plastic gel; tiny ripples shiver across its surface as I move the bowl to the back of the bench.

In twenty minutes this mold will harden to the point that it cracks, so I move quickly. I dump a box of plaster of paris into another bowl, add a couple of cups of cold water, and start mixing. I follow the feel of the mixture and not the measuring directions. The plaster should be thin enough to pour, thick enough to dry without too much shrinkage from water evaporation – about the consistency of melted ice cream.

I mix for five minutes, then run the spoon one last time along the bottom of the bowl, looking for material not yet dissolved. Then I retrieve the mold from the back of the bench and pour the plaster into it. The mixture fills the form completely, leaving a flat expanse on its top. I dip my finger into it, feeling for warmth. Nothing yet. I sit down, wipe my hands absentmindedly on a cloth, and listen to the thump of my slowing heart.

Ten minutes later the plaster is hot, and hardening fast. It has begun to darken a little – it's a faint, ashen color – and a thin film of moisture now lies upon its surface. I leave it to dry for another hour, and walk to the school to pick up Rowan. She's excited when I tell her what I've been working on, and runs ahead of me, shouting that we should get going to see how the face has turned out. The day is unseasonably warm. My own face feels as though it has been cleansed by immersion in the compound.

Back home, I grasp the bottom of the bowl, place my hand securely on the top surface of the plaster, and invert the whole works. Then I put it down again on the bench and remove my hand from between the plaster and the bench top. I push the top of the bowl down with one hand and lift along its circular edge with the other. Moving in increments, stretching the form, I ease the hard plaster loose. I feel it release with a *snick* and come to rest on the bench top as the bowl comes free in my hand. There, hardened and delicate and incongruous on my workbench, is an exact replica of my face.

The first thing that occurs to me is that it doesn't look like me at all. The face is too narrow, the nose pinched, the chin snubbish. My features seem flattened and elongated. My mouth is noticeably lopsided: full and fleshy on the left, narrow and descending, as though unsupported, on the right. I didn't know the paralysis there was so evident. I'm used to looking at my reflection in a mirror, but a mirror doesn't show a faithful image; it swaps left for right. I have never seen my face this way, as it actually appears in three dimensions. As a stranger sees it on the street. It looks unattractive, a bit eerie. But the topographic features are all there, providing me with a template for shaping the stone.

An archaic face, swimming in the waters of my family history, lies somewhere behind my own. Layered and interwoven with my countenance, gazing back toward a horizon limned by forgetting. This is the first certainty of the work; that I am a fable, remembering its own origins, kept vibrant by retelling.

The chronicle of my origin, of my family's origin, came into my possession after my grandmother's death. The pages are filled with precise, careful script, and have been photocopied from an obviously much older volume. The capitals are sharp and clear, the connections between letters fluid. Likely a feminine hand, though no one knows who wrote the material. The most recent events described in the narrative took place around 1700, but the language describing those events is modern in character; late nineteenth century, probably.

The chronicle, which begins in the thirteenth century, was given to my grandmother perhaps fifty years ago by an American relative with whom none of us has maintained contact. He was not the author but had received the book from more distant relatives. In its pages are myths and dreams and tales: a man held captive in the hold of a ship, breaking the manacles with his own strength; a woman hunting with wolves in the forest; a young girl born among exiles. I read of war and memory and of what my ancestors were compelled to preserve. There are no artifacts from the time of the chronicle; only worn stories, threadbare, freighted with the symbolism of our clan.

Where this chronicle ends – the exile of the Protestants from France, the Salem witch trials – another begins, written by my great-uncle Dave in his youth, after the First World War, after he wandered the mountains and then returned to Scotland, his ancestral homeland, to make sense of his origins. He was, I think, trying to understand why he had survived. His narrative – typed neatly, bound in black, precise and scholarly – describes among its first events an accusation of witchcraft brought against one of my ancestors. The last entry of my grand-mother's chronicle describes another ancestor, an inquisitor, and the witchcraft trials initiated by him. I find this strange and intriguing: these two events took place at the same time, on different continents, and were enacted by people who knew nothing of each other. Yet their descendants came together in my own family. Perhaps we continue, even now, the mythological struggle between heretic and inquisitor.

Dave's family journal details his trip to Scotland and his visit to the ancestral lands of our family. He discovered what he thought were a few relatives, and he found references to our migration in the parish journal. At the site of the derelict homestead, he wrote, "The old house has been torn down, but its site is visible, and we took away several stones as souvenirs."

Stones, particularly igneous stones – resistant to erosion, implacable and enduring as the gods themselves – were, for the Kem, a means of embodying ancestral narratives, tales of beginning, chronicles of family and culture and individuality. Every stone sculpture was itself a hieroglyph, a rebus, a talisman imbued with esoteric meaning. During the reign of Khafre and his contemporaries, the Kem transported millions of tons of stone, shaped it, carved it, rendered it the expression and lasting imprint of a culture discovering the soul.* They brought stones from all over the Middle East and Africa: by boat, by sledge, by the power of words, if the old tales are to be believed. They transported blocks of seventy tons to Giza from as far away as Aswan, some five hundred miles. The Kem devotion to stone was matched only by the Inca and the Maya, whose similar achievements in craftsmanship came thousands of years later. For them also, the sacred stone arose from the waters. The title of the Mayan book of origins, the Popol Vuh, means "the light that came from the sea."

In the Kem society of the third millennium BCE, replicas of the black stone of origin – the *benben* – were kept within temples and atop obelisks. They were also used as capstones for pyramids. The most famous of these, the capstone of Khufu's pyramid (the Great Pyramid), has long vanished. The question of who walked off with it is not insignificant. How – not to mention why – did a band of marauders, or an invading army, remove a massive capstone, likely made of fifteen tons of meteoric iron,* from a summit almost five hundred feet off the desert, without leaving a trace?

Khufu's capstone, made of a metal the Kem considered sacred, was taken from the Great Pyramid perhaps four thousand years ago. But its image has persisted through myth narratives and thrives even today. The Washington Monument, deliberately designed in the tradition of Kem obelisks and intended – like the Great Pyramid – to be the largest monument in the world, is crowned by a 3,300-pound marble capstone at the summit of which sits a nine-inch-tall aluminum pyramid. During the period 1848–1885, when the monument was constructed in a series of halting stages, aluminum was a precious metal, and the small pyramid was the largest piece ever cast. The Washington Monument is still the tallest masonry structure in the world (about seventy-five feet taller than Khufu's pyramid), and its role in American culture is identical to that of the *benben* stone of the Kem: the Washington Monument symbolizes, in stone, a tale of origins.

The circular blade of the grinder sweeps across the sharp edge of the stone, abrading the corner, throwing off sparks. I work in stages, one edge at a time, easing into the stone, widening my window on its interior. That window, which began as a small incision, grows to encompass the entire top of the stone. The surface must be smoothed, made more uniform, readied for carving. The top edges must be rounded over to accommodate the contours of the face I will try to carve.

I remove as much as an inch of stone from the corners; layers of igneous rock are pulverized and transformed into fine dust that covers every surface of the shop. My dust collector, mounted on the ceiling and guaranteed to clean every particle of dust from the air in my shop every ten minutes, becomes clogged. I can hear, beyond the din of the grinder and through the insulation of my hearing protectors, its motor dropping in cadence, growling, threatening to stall. The white plaster mask of my face is on the bench, in the path of the black stone dust. It first becomes darkened, then obscured but for its contours. I think of Shelley's famous poem about the Kem, "Ozymandias": "Half sunk a shattered visage lies . . . Boundless and bare, the lone and level sands stretch far away."*

As I pare down the surface, smoothing and leveling, I wonder about the black stone of origin in the Kem myth. It too was smooth and level and became the first seat of God, the Unnameable. The Shebtiw came and departed, but the Unnameable remained, shaping the new land with light. The myth relates how the Unnameable encountered a shadow cast by its own corona. This shadow, which is the necessary corollary of every light, meandered through the murk, twisted and labored, swelled into the shape of a serpent: the Great Leaping One, Nehapiwir.*

The island of beginnings was replete: suffused with light, nurtured by a well of souls. But it was not yet animated by time. Within its sphere, a world of becoming was yet to be born. The serpent fractured the boundary of that sphere, during a battle with the Unnameable that is described in the Kem myth in great detail.

This first battle was identical in character to an incident in the First World War, during which my grandfather and his brother, my great-uncle Dave, fought side by side.

My grandfather drove a team of black horses. An artillery gun, bolted to a stout carriage and rolled forward on wheels rimmed with iron, swung behind the horses as they moved from trench to hill. When one of the horses was killed in the fighting, my grandfather and his companions roamed the neighboring farms at night, searching for a fresh black horse. Always black. When they found one, they would spirit it away. The unfortunate farmer would wake the next morning to find himself bereft in another of the many ways of war.

In September 1918, when my grandfather was twenty-three years old, an Allied offensive was undertaken along the entire war front, from the Meuse region of northern France to the English Channel. Four avenues of attack were planned for four consecutive days beginning September 26. On the second day, the Canadian Corps was assigned to the capture of Bourlon Wood.*

During the serpent battle, the Unnameable called upon a host of deities that had crafted the first temples from granite and basalt.* In their animal forms – lions, bears, bulls – they made a protective trench across the headland of the island. They moved slowly, in four groupings, leaving a carnival of footprints in the sand. Along a ridge at the boundary of the headland, where the cries of birds rose from nests in the grass, the divine bull – looking ahead, squinting into a sun climbing over the island's meadow – mistook the scaled eyelid for a boulder, glanced past a mouth curved like a trench in the soil, failed to see the serpent's neck beneath his heel. The bull stepped down with his hoof. The serpent rose up and struck.

The hosts of the Unnameable fell back in the face of the serpent's attack. The snake encircled the seat of the god, pierced its hands and feet with fangs, and crucified the Unnameable at the shore. (In a later age, the Christian tradition adopted this scene in its own tales of origin.) The eyes of the Unnameable were broken open.* The god's form dissolved into every shining thing: its right eye became the sun, its left eye the moon. Below, the body of the serpent unfurled.

On the evening of September 26, the Canadian forces assembled in four divisions along a dry section of the Canal du Nord. It lay like a trench between Sains-lez-Marquion and Moeuvres. By midnight, preparations were completed. The soldiers lay in the open, huddled together for warmth. Across the canal, at the enemy encampment, nothing stirred. Under the camouflage of night and black horses, my grandfather Robert and his brother, David, moved unseen.

"It's a wonder," said my father, "that they didn't go deaf from the sound of the guns." At dawn, flashing across the canal, the horses still – miraculously still amid the thunder – the artillery barrage began. Infantrymen crushed across the canal bridge and fanned out into the forest. From their adjoining gun emplacements on dry ground just west of the canal, Robert and David shelled the Bourlon hillside through the day, targeting enemy guns trained on the bridgehead. Late in the afternoon, as the infantry edged to where retreating soldiers had left a barren hilltop, an enemy artillery shell ghosted across the sky and exploded in the midst of David's battery. My grandfather, perhaps a hundred feet away, watched the soldiers of his brother's emplacement tumble in the flash and roar. And, seeing that the hill had been taken, my grandfather crawled across the shattered ground to where David lay wounded and lifted him from the wreckage of the guns.

The foundation stone was fractured. Fragments fell away from it, into the sea and up to the sky, whirling and turning and vanishing. (Those fragments are still making their way home.) But the serpent was subdued: four phalanxes of gods rushed forward, captured the head of the snake, and wrestled it to the ground.

The brothers moved westward, one carrying the other along the corduroy road laid down by the army. At the field hospital, my grandfather stayed with his brother through the night, watched over him. They settled down beside each other as the night drew on, listened to the cries of the living and silences of the dead. Their words thickened as they spoke, stretched out and took shape in the autumn air, mixed with smoke and kerosene, with antiseptic, and lay upon the world like a blanket of promises. They spoke of mountains, of the west, of a path winding beneath the glacier.

Those words, spoken at the junction where all roads cross, held aloft by two brothers dreaming, remade their world. Later, when they came west and David walked the alpine paths, everything he saw was a memory of that night's reverie. And I, walking those paths generations later, still see the words drifting in the sky, still watch them settle onto a ground of fallen cedars and tiny, speckled flowers.

In the Kem myth, the gods and the serpent together enact the ritual of "settling down beside" one another.* They become one people, one company of gods. The bull fashions a stone marker on the summit of the island's hill as a reminder of the necessary companionship of enemies. This resolution, in which the adversary is welcomed as intimate friend, is one that every subsequent age has fought, and often failed, to achieve.

Breaking the enemy defensive line at Bourlon Wood cost the Canadian Corps thousands of casualties, but their effort helped stall the war's momentum. The day after the battle, the retreating German general sent word to Berlin that the war was lost. The Canadians arrived at Mons six weeks later, in time for the armistice on what was to become Remembrance Day. Today the battle of Bourlon Wood is marked by a memorial stone on the hilltop. When my father was the same age as his father was during the war, they went to see the lime trees nursed back to health and the monument with the stone block at its heart.

Steep steps approach the summit through a terraced garden, quiet now with echoes.

The tale of my grandfather and his brother is one of the more recent origin myths of my family. But myths possess genealogies; they descend from a fabled origin, are steeped in the womb of the earth's dreaming. Poetry is their midwife. Behind them, a web of predecessors stretches back through generations of telling, vanishes beyond the horizon of memory. The fable of the two brothers and the battle for the hill is only a more contemporary version of the much older Kem tale, perhaps archetypal, of the war between the company of gods and the serpent. In our familial myth, the defensive trench of the Kem is replaced by a French canal; but the fable is identical.

Myths are like this: we claim the storied child as our own. Look, he has his father's eyes. Her mother's hands. One of us. We will make a place for you, who have come to the river, the manger, the cave of wonders. We will claim you as our own, we will defend your place among us against those who would challenge it. We will believe the tale that you were born within the circle of our relations. We will forget that we have seen your brothers dancing in the fields of our enemies.

The altar of the black stone – at Bourlon, in an obscure tale of the Kem, on my workbench, damp and bright as I wash dust from its surface – is a pivot around which many things turn. Almost every tale of origin speaks of it, surrounded by bright fire. It is the foundation stone, the eye of wisdom, the grail. Relic of beginnings, it is the nexus around which the scattered forms of creation once gathered. It lies at the center of every myth, and we are caught up, even now – perhaps now more than ever – in its story.

In roughing out the carving, I am chiefly concerned with the removal of surface material. I can experiment here, using different tools and procedures. I need to learn the particular dialect spoken between stone and tool: how hard to press, and at what angle; where the grain of the stone lies, and what its rhythms are; how to cut, and be precise enough not to shear. As I work, the top of the stone grows smooth, and more rounded. It begins to look like a rock from the river. The bottom of the stone remains untouched, and is rough. This duality would not likely arise naturally – stones tend to be either eroded on all sides, or not at all – and for the first time I feel the absolute commitment of this task. I have engaged with the stone as a craftsman; it now bears the unmistakable mark of having been worked by human hands. It lay unhindered for millennia, minding its own business. Now I've taken it from the riverbed and started to chop bits off. I've drawn it into myths and tales, enclosed it within the circle of my own becoming. For its sake, and my own, I need to demonstrate that this has all been more than idle chatter.

Stone carving is an exercise in faith: that the material might yield, gently, its hidden structure, that my imagination and instinct might be sufficient to the task of discovering the stone's inner life. I am unnerved by the prospect that I might get it wrong, that my impulses might betray, rather than serve, the concealed beauty of the material. I go slow.

Too slow, perhaps. I am tentative to the point that the grinder, which is capable of slicing through the stone almost as an ax cleaves wood, makes only small incisions. I prospect, moving to various points on the surface as I try to find a place to dig in. I am uncovering, from the long shadow of forgetfulness, an ancestral face. I don't want to harm it, to scar it, to bludgeon my way through its delicate features. Along the edge of where I think the nose might be, I winnow down carefully toward the cheek.

I look at the surface of the stone, where the diamond blade sloughs off material in clouds of dust. And suddenly, surprisingly, my vision becomes blurred, then doubled. A second image is superimposed on my line of sight: a face, smooth and serene, watchful. It's just a glimpse of something ephemeral – *Yes, start right here, along the deep cleft where the nose meets the cheek* – and then it's gone.

I ease into the work, buoyed by a single, fragmentary glimpse whose origin I cannot explain. My faith is bolstered. My hands feel warm, at ease. I carve a deep furrow on either side of the unformed nose, checking the angle and depth of the cuts against the plaster cast of my face. I think of Khafre.

The origin stone of the Kem promised, for those capable of deciphering its symbolic text, the power of divinity. This is an old story, told and retold in many guises. But it began with the Kem: from the Hebrew God on his first day of creation (*Let there be light!*) to the spells of Harry Potter, words as magical power are a legacy of Khafre and his contemporaries. The religions of the Book (Judaism, Christianity, and Islam) are inheritors of a cosmology – archaic beyond measure – in which books embody divine power. The Kem told numerous myths concerning Thoth and his celestial book of knowledge – called the tablet of destinies by the Sumerians and, later, the tablets of the law by the Hebrews. Eventually, as this mythology made its way through medieval Europe and the Middle East, the sacred book of stone came to be associated with the Bible, with the Qur'an, with the secret books of alchemy. The book of Thoth is the original philosopher's stone, spinning the world's ramshackle tale.[*]

On my workbench, the ridge of a nose begins to emerge from the stone's background. I slough off much of the surface on either side; the grinder screeches, the dust rises, I am covered by a film of pulverized basalt. As I sight down the middle line of the carving, looking for where the nose and forehead might meet, I catch a momentary reflection of myself in the window: a gray visage, hair the color of dark concrete, coat to match.

I work for much of an afternoon in this condition, worrying about my lungs and my health and the consistent clogging of my dust collector. Then I head inside, take a shower, and settle into the den. There, ruminating on books of stone, I take down the old volumes I inherited from my grandmother and my great-aunt. These are my stones of origin, some of them centuries old, touchstones of my own past. I pick up a small German edition of Goethe's *Faust*, dated 1837. The character of Faust the magician is based, in large part, upon a figure in Kem mythology, a man named Hardjedef who sought and found the book of Thoth. Inside the cover of *Faust*, I find a slip of pale notepad paper. On it, written in pencil in the hand of my great-aunt Eileen, I read: "Are we progressing?"

I lift down a book on Taoism, a subject of interest to my great-aunt, and now to me. Folded and tucked inside the flyleaf

I find a typed letter, dated 1968. The writer, a friend and relative of Eileen's, reports, "I am still only semi convalescent, and I do not know if I shall ever get any better. It is now two years since the 'accident' laid me low. I have, however, learned that nothing matters except a gradual understanding that life is a continual loosening of the bonds that bind one to things of time and space, and that nothing matters except a consciousness of what is beyond – the Tao, perhaps . . . Write and tell me you have been among the mountains again."

I find a small sheaf of papers within the leaves of a 1912 edition of Tennyson's poems. The book falls open at that place; the text beneath reads, "I will leave my relics in your land, and you may carve a shrine about my dust, and burn a fragrant lamp before my bones."* The sheaf comprises several sheets of old notepaper, a folded map of Italy, an advertisement for Robson Shoe Repair in Vancouver (address: "the wooden hut near the corner of Robson and Bidwell"), and a university examination package ("Discuss the tendency of the Romanticists to express themselves in imaginative narrative"). On all these pages, in the handwriting of my great-aunt – both intense and languid, somehow – are listed the names of books. Hundreds of titles. Some I recognize, others are foreign. Poetry, prose, plays, criticism, history. Somerset Maugham begins a list at the top of one page. Below, the works of Joseph Conrad are enumerated, and below these, in cramped letters near the bottom, I read titles by someone named Maurice Hewlett. The list fills the reverse side and continues on the next sheet.

The lists are in pencil, and some are so faded that I cannot read what she has written. On the back of the map of Italy, behind an encircling pencil mark at Florence, I see a shopping list and a sum of figures: purse, plaque, hat, pants. Total cost, 135 lire. A plaque? Of what, and where is it now?

I was still a boy when Eileen died, and the love of reading she awakened in me is a boyish love, full of romance and adventure and the heady salt scent of the sea. As I read these notes, which surely she had intended only for herself, I feel as though I am entering into her long-departed heart.

The radius of the grinder blade is large enough that I can shape the hollows of the cheeks with minimal fuss. The contours of the rough nose appear as I press deeper: bridge flat and wide, sides steep. It emerges, unmistakable, from the background topography of the stone. With every stroke I become more confident of discovering the face beneath. But not my own face. The plaster cast, a rough template, is not the image I glimpsed in the stone. I can use my own features to guide the work, to approximate proportion and distance, but the ancestral visage is something else. It must come from memory, from imagination, from the dream of a rock on the mountainside. As I work, I have the feeling that I am digging out, as from a grave, someone buried but still breathing.

Through the last weeks of winter and into early spring, while a turbulent sky fluctuates between sunshine and shadow, I work the stone and I read. I make my way through the family chronicle and the books of my great-aunt Eileen. I read Kem mythology, spliced into the diverse traditions of ancient Egypt and interwoven with many subsequent tales. I'm particularly drawn to the myths inscribed on the walls of the Temple of Horus at Edfu, purported to have been built on the site of the first Kem temple. Old foundations lie beneath the current structure, erected during the second century BCE. The limestone inscriptions – myths of origin, of the Unnameable, of the Shebtiw and the serpent battle – refer frequently to older tales, to earlier temples, to gods and heroes of an age preserved only in fragmentary images. I'm reading chapters and vignettes of the soul's history.

And for every turn in the Kem myths, I find parallels in my family chronicle: in the letters and books of my great-aunt, in the journal of my great-uncle, in the stories told to me by my father and grandmother. Everywhere I look, the old myths are retold. I read of the Unnameable, god of origin, burning upon an altar of fire in the serpent attacks; and I read of Margaret, the most archaic of my Laird ancestors, burned at the stake for witchcraft. I read of a black stone floating upon the primordial sea; and I find a black stone in the oldest family records, in an account of an ancestral home built using the principles of Renaissance alchemy.*

The Kem are now lost, forgotten. And though the skein of their cosmology still glides through the philosophy and spirituality of the West, they themselves have gone into exile. But their trail is not cold. I discover it in the trodden paths of my own family, as though we have been drawn, without knowing, onto familiar tracks. Such tracks are never derelict but run across valleys, through forests, toward distant glaciers, preserving the way.

In the shop, I run my fingers over the stone, searching for contours beneath the dust. The tips of my fingers are stained the color of ash. The sculptors of Khafre would have devoted considerable effort to touching the work in this way: assessing, probing, reaching. But the rhythm of their work would have been incalculably slower. The grinder accomplishes in seconds what would have taken a month by hand. The slow rhythm of the ancients is an aspect of the work I'd like to recapture, though I plan to finish the work in my lifetime. As an experiment, I retrieve some corundum powder from the tool cabinet, a screwdriver from the drawer below the bench, and start in. Corundum powder is harder than sand, the abrasive used by the Kem sculptors, and the flat tip of my steel screwdriver is much tougher than any copper tool; but even with this considerable advantage, I expect the going will be slow.

I sprinkle some powder where it's most likely to remain while I work it: along the deep cleft beside the nose. I sprinkle on a few drops of water and push the tip of the screwdriver into the slurry. I scrape. Back and forth, pushing down with as much weight as I can muster, I drag the tool repeatedly across the surface of the stone. The corundum glitters as it moves. I keep working for about five minutes, shifting my grip, altering my stance, persistent but eventually halted by the growing ache in my shoulders.

I take a short break, to figure out how to work longer before tiring, and then settle in again. This time, I lean forward, place the heel of the screwdriver's handle against my chin, and hold it securely in place with both hands. I rock my upper body, using my weight to keep the pressure and my legs to move the tool. Fifteen minutes, then I have to stop again.

I use a rag to wipe the powder from the stone. The surface is shiny, but some of that luster is from the water. I wipe with the rag again, then wait for the water to evaporate. A couple of minutes later, when the surface hues are uniform again, I see the hatch marks from the grinder. The left edge of the work area, where I had leaned in most aggressively with the screwdriver, has a marginal sheen. Otherwise, I seem to have made no impact on the stone – with tools much harder than those possessed by the Kem. At this rate, I imagine this single face would occupy me full-time for more than a decade. Or perhaps the current academic theory of the Kem technique – copper and sand – is not altogether accurate. Perhaps, as old tales relate, they did sing the stones into shape after all.

But if copper tools and pounding stones and sand and persistence were used, I marvel at the dedication of those craftsmen. So much time would have been required, so much of that precious elixir to make even the simplest objects. Yet millions of Kem artifacts have been discovered: plain as well as remarkable. Many display an astounding level of precision, easily matching the best we can accomplish today. Incalculable stores of artifacts are still hidden: at Saqqara, near modern Cairo, only five percent of the necropolis has been explored. How did those sculptors, whose average lifespan was probably thirty or forty years, find the time to fashion such wonders?

I read, and work, and dream. In one of those dreams, a ship, perhaps a mile in length, lies moored at the shore of the river near my home. Its hull is pale gray, like the wing of a dove. Inside, the cabins and wheelhouse are vacant, the windows layered with dust. It is summer. Along the dirt track of the bank, dust rises and settles as I pedal my bicycle. I gaze downstream toward the ship. It draws me, insistent and implacable.

I climb the ramp, far up to where the deck bakes in the sun. The deserted ship is silent. I cross the deck from the port side, pass through the abandoned wheelhouse, and emerge on the starboard side. The river below, brown and lazy, meanders sternward toward the sea. I look out to the opposite bank. Small-leaved trees shiver in the light breeze. The air is hot. Steel stanchions at the edge of the deck are chalky with corrosion; threaded safety lines loop slack and flimsy in their mounts along the gunwale. In one spot, a stanchion has broken off, taking with it a section of rope. The gap, about three feet wide, opens into empty air. The fall from here would be several hundred feet.

Avery stands on the deck. His hair, straight and white-blond, ruffles along his forehead in the wind. The strangeness of this place, which has awakened in me awe and trepidation, does not affect him. Inquisitive and serene, he gazes down to the surface of the water. He takes a life jacket from my hand, straps it on, holds a stanchion with his left fist. The day slows, an inevitable momentum gathers around him, and though he does not yet move, the impulse to reach for him rises in me. I remember, fleetingly, that his name means "the truthful one." The one who avers, the witness. In that moment of reflection and stirring movement, Avery turns to me, says, "I have to see," and leaps from the deck.

He falls. Horror and terror, those familiar companions of my road, wash through me. Avery falls, spiraling, and I, frozen, watch him go. After an interminable descent, he strikes the water. White water erupts around him, his red life jacket flashes in the sun, and the brown river closes again.

He vanishes. And suddenly my dread of losing him overcomes my terror at his descent. So often it is this way: spurred on by fear, when what I need is courage.

I run forward, cross the white deck, and jump off. I fall and fall. Far below, I glimpse what looks like Avery's head, or perhaps his life jacket, surfacing from the depths. But I can't be sure – the river is too far down, my sight is obscured by the water of tears and the roaring of the wind.

I hit the river some distance from where Avery went in; a long way off, it seems. The speed of my impact takes me deep into black water. I don't see him anywhere. My momentum eases, but I turn my head downward, swimming farther into the depths. I reach the bottom of the river. Below the silt and mud, a column of blackness tunnels into the earth, into nothing. I follow this terrifying and imperative chasm. And there, suddenly, I see Avery. Still wearing his life jacket, he floats past me, traveling toward the surface. He's moving fast, appears conscious, and I let him go. His buoyancy carries him up faster than I can swim. I look up, following his ascent. There's light up there, far off. As I watch from the depths of the black well, the light grows into an eye spread across the waters. It floats, lithe and massive, on the surface of the river.

I turn and swim toward Avery, toward the eye, feeling the pressure in my lungs as my air dwindles. The eye grows as I approach it; but I run out of time, and the aperture of my consciousness closes. I rise, feeble and disoriented. Before I reach the eye, it opens.

I awaken to foghorns in the distance, sounding from the Fraser River as ships pass along the waterway in the night.

On a cloudless day in early March, when the sun's distant warmth fails to pierce the chill, we head down to the beach that fronts the strait to the south. The waterfront shops are quiet, the tidal flats sleek at the edge of the ebbing sea. A fleeting squall rounds the rocky point and kicks up a spatter of whitecaps. We drive the shoreline road, watching gulls rise with shells in their beaks. When they reach sixty or seventy feet off the beach, the birds swing toward the tumbled breakwater and the road. They let the shells fall to the rocks, then skitter down the breeze to pry the mollusks loose from their shells.

We park in the almost deserted lot. When summer comes, this parking lot and its dozens of companions along the shore will be filled to capacity from early morning until long after nightfall. But now, months before the brief carnival of northern summer, I can make out only a few figures along the pier: two companion joggers, a loose knot of tourists with a straggler hurrying from behind, and a lone figure at the pier's end, looking southwest to where the mountains come down and give way to the open ocean.

The kids climb out of the car, excited and rushing. Elizabeth checks to make sure the zippers on their coats are pulled all the way up, their hats secure. We remind them of the beach rules: stay close, be careful, listen. As I lock the car doors and check my wallet for hot chocolate money, I remember the absence of caution in my own childhood. My brothers and I were encouraged – by my father, by a culture that still equates boys with risk – to be adventurous to such an extent that I can hardly believe we survived. We jumped off sea cliffs, hiked up avalanche chutes, hung on to the bumpers of skidding cars along snowy roads in traffic. My elder brother made gunpowder bombs, with my parents' knowledge and tacit approval. He once gave me a Christmas present rigged to explode when I opened it. The wiring mechanism failed, and the bomb failed to detonate. If it had, the small charge might merely have startled me; after all, my brother had used one of his smaller "crushers" (as he called them), intending to scare but not to harm me. Who knows what might have happened if I had leaned toward the box as I opened it, or reached in with my fingers. It never occurred to us that such pranks were dangerous.

As Elizabeth and I follow the kids up the stairs to the promenade, I wonder aloud about the way my family normalized unsafe risks. It seems as though my brothers and I inherited and enacted the tension between my parents: my mother's railing against the cage she had constructed for herself, my father's insistence that everything would turn out all right, his absences when they did not. She had thought to make fresh dreams when she married, as if that act alone was sufficient to break the chain of her own family's despair. But the spirits followed her, and eventually she surrendered to them, as her parents had before her. Spirits with the names bourbon, Scotch, and gin, hidden like genies in bottles above the kitchen sink. My father, the rescuer, the one whose bright future seemed always to be assured, kept trying to lead her out of the labyrinth. But he was frequently away, and when he was home his way of dealing with my mother – pep talks, a positive attitude, goal setting – was insufficient to the task of reclaiming her. Such strategies always are. The lost must guide themselves out, as every recovered alcoholic knows. Support and camaraderie can be of help, but only one person can face whatever lurks in the labyrinth and sends the well-wrapped bombs.

My father's temperament was fundamentally ill suited to dealing with my mother's alcoholism. Subsequently I built my counseling career on the theme of substance abuse. I imagine this to be a common experience: we take up what our parents cannot manage; without knowing it, we assume the weight of their unfinished dreams.

Elizabeth and I follow the kids along the low fence that separates the path from the railway tracks. Rowan and Avery run after each other, dart in and out of the empty picnic tables, laugh and shout with abandon. Rowan, a head taller, her purple coat bright in the clear air, lets her younger brother catch up, then scoots ahead again. Whatever I fail to resolve in my own life will be left to them – I think of those teenage years when my elder brother and I drank ourselves unconscious every weekend – but watching my kids today, their vitality shining unencumbered as we make our way down the shore, I feel the blessing of their safety. They're not caught up in the struggle to make plain the contradictions of their parents' world. They run ahead, free to follow their own impulses, while Elizabeth and I walk behind. We try to carry our own obligations, knowing we will, perforce, pass along some of them to our children. But we will not, I hope, pass along alcoholism, nor the surrender of oneself to empty dreams. Our kids will not be setting fires or smashing windows or blowing each other up to let us know something is amiss. They will find other avenues, no doubt, for the troubles their parents have not foreseen. And we will need to work out those new difficulties as they arise. But now, on a bright spring day, along the edge of an ocean stretching to the horizon, the knowledge that my kids have come this far – through the first and most crucial developmental years – without trauma, neglect, or the sacrifice of their own true natures is the greatest solace of my life. Elizabeth, much more than me, is responsible for this success. She is, both for the kids and for myself, the axis of our turning. I squeeze her hand as we walk down the beach in the wake of our children's laughter.

The breakwater is a mile or more of boulders brought here from the mountains. Igneous stones, most of them: basalt and granite and gabbro. Blue and black and gray rocks, some of them eight or ten feet across. Most of the surfaces show virtually no erosion, indicating that the stones were recently (in geologic terms) cracked from the quarry.* It will take hundreds, perhaps thousands of years for these stones to show significant weathering. I see several stones made of diorite, the material used in the statue of Khafre. After forty-five centuries of burial and abrasion by coarse desert sand, that statue has not even lost its polish.

As always, the breakwater is the principal attraction for the kids. Its easy slope of packed-tight boulders provides ideal scrambling and climbing terrain. We climb over the low fence, cross the railway tracks, and clamber down the breakwater's top edge. There's no danger of falling into the water – the tide is far out – though storms at high tide have been known to pound this shore with waves high enough to cross the break-water and flood the street behind. Not today. The breeze is quiet, the water calm, the sun warm. The serpent is quiet. The eye of the Unnameable watches, serene.

While the kids climb, Elizabeth and I make our way down to the beach. The sand under our feet is moist, and small glisten-ing outlines appear around our shoes. Fragments of kelp from the tide's last flood lie scattered around a cluster of hoary stones embedded at the shore. White gulls and black crows squawk and caw at one another along the tidal flats, jousting in the air for morsels of starfish and the odd unfortunate clam.

Days like these will be a part of my children's legacy: climb-ing on stones, scanning the waters for ships and birds and whales. I choose this as their inheritance, leaving the other at the roadside, where perchance other of our descendants will pick it up and let the genies out again.

Avery gets stuck trying to cross a span wider than his out-stretched legs. He asks for help, and I climb up to him, stone by stone, in the way my father taught me when I was Avery's age: always secure at two points, hand or foot, relaxed, leaning away from the rock. The maximum fall from anywhere along this breakwater is about three feet; even so, that's enough to break a leg or crack a skull. I'm gratified to see that Avery is anchored by three points of contact – two hands and one foot – as he waits for me. He keeps trying to stretch himself across to the next boulder. This is healthy risk-taking: at the edge of skill, pushing the limit but not careless.

As I come alongside, take Avery in my arms, and carry him over the gap, I think of my own childhood experiments in climbing, one of which involved my friend and me scrambling up a high sandstone cliff without ropes. Halfway up, a couple of hundred feet above the road, we got stuck. No way up, no way down. We clung to the face a long while, debating what to do. For an hour, maybe two, we planned and talked and grew more afraid. A driver passing below slowed his van, rolled down his window, and yelled at us to get down: two kids had fallen to their deaths from this cliff a few weeks earlier. We eventually became convinced of our own demise. But we made it down; slow, tentative, terrified. At twilight, safely back on the road, the climb – which had been my idea – seemed to me more a brave achievement than a senseless, irresponsible blunder. My friend, a year older, was more reserved about our prowess as mountaineers. He understood better than I did, not only because of his age, that such risks were as likely to get us killed as to make us feel wholly alive.

I never saw him again after that climb. A few months later, along the road my father and I had driven to find the black stone, my friend was run down by a drunk driver. He returned, the Kem would have said, to the west, where the ancestors wait and dream. But I have not forgotten the way in which his encouragement and calm, when I had lost courage and begun to lose hope, guided us both home that day.

I check with Avery to make sure he's feeling safe, then look ahead to the terrain he's making for. The boulders are smaller, more manageable. Rowan hops from one to the next, careful and assured, her feet landing squarely with each stride. Avery moves on, almost before I'm ready to let him go, and grabs the next stone. He leans forward, jumps with both feet onto a flat-topped slab of black rock with a single vein of white running through it, and is off again.

I climb back down to Elizabeth, who has found some pebbles washed bright by the turning sand. Apricot and bronze and lustrous black. She holds up a small stone the color of jade, points to a web of lines circling within it. Thousands of years, probably, were required for the sand to render the smooth shape of this mandala. All that time, lying beneath the waters, indifferent to the tracks of travelers along this shore.

At the fringe of a shallow pool carrying the last of the ebbing tide shoreward, we find many polished pebbles. We look and touch and show them to each other. On the breakwater, the kids call out to ask what we're doing. Elizabeth tells them of our find, and they scramble down to where we are. Rowan lets out a gasp – "An amethyst, Dad!" – and Avery finds a fragment of smooth quartz the size of his fist. He brings it to me, breathless with excitement, and shouts, "It's a diamond!" into my ear.

We move slowly down the beach, two rambling kids with their parents, hunched over and looking. For Avery and Rowan, every rock is a gem, and they quickly fill their pockets. I remember the lines from my great-uncle Dave's journal: "We took away several stones as souvenirs."

We dawdle for an hour or more. The kids scavenge, asking us to identify stones. Whenever they find a black one, they bring it over to show me its similarity to the stone on my workbench. Avery asks me again about my encounter with the bear: was I scared, did the bear have big claws, were there any baby bears. By the time we approach the pier, the kids have twenty or thirty rocks each. Before we climb the stairs to the boardwalk, Elizabeth and I tell them they can keep two each; the rest must be left here, on the beach, for others to find or to be carried off by the tide. Rowan keeps a shard of pink quartz and a chunk of granite. Avery chooses a smooth black stone – basalt, I think – and a pebble with a golden vein of pyrite snaking through it. They throw the remaining stones back onto the tidal flats. A few gulls swing down to inspect this sudden movement on the sand. One of them seizes a pebble in its beak, lifts off a few feet, then drops it, disconsolate.

We ascend the wide stairs to the boardwalk. Secured by hundreds of black pilings sunk into the beach, the pier extends five hundred yards into the bay. At the end, where the tidal flats give way to a sloping bottom, a second, more modest breakwater protects a score of sailboats and fishing trawlers moored to a finger of dock. The bottom is visible at low tide, and we see a cluster of crab traps on the dark sand, some scattered shells, and a colony of starfish gathered round the base of a piling.

Rowan climbs onto a bench and grabs the rail of the pier. She points southeast, to where the white flanks of Mount Baker rise in the distance. That mountain and the one to the north upon which I found the black stone of origin are the two pillars of a volcanic belt that stretches through this region. The forces concealed beneath the forests could remake the land in a single day. Along the eastern skyline, the Coast Mountains, jagged and formidable and remote, march off into the wilderness.

Turning, looking shoreward, Rowan sees the White Rock from which this seaside town takes its name. At almost five hundred tons, the boulder is a dozen or more feet high and can be seen from anywhere in the wide bay. Spanish explorers first documented it during their travels through here in 1791, though it has lain on this beach since the retreat of the last ice age. A glacial erratic, it was carried here by sheets of moving ice and deposited, conveniently in view of subsequent tourists, precisely at the shore. It probably came from the north. The rock is painted every year now, to erase the graffiti of high school graduates.

The White Rock is a mythological artifact. Local legend relates that a divine prince, son of the sea god, was prohibited by his father from marrying his beloved, a mortal princess. In defiance of this injunction, the prince of the sea hurled a white boulder across the waters; where it came to rest, he and his bride made a new home. They became the first ancestors of the People of the Half Moon, the Semiahmoo, who reside here today.[*]

In myth, black stones and white stones are the same article. A white stone is often paired with a black stone, as in Hebrew legends of the black and white divination stones, the Urim and Thummim, used by high priests until about the sixth century BCE.[*] A black stone is sometimes thought to have been white, such as the meteoric stone that lies at the eastern corner of the Kaaba, the holiest shrine in Islam. This black stone is said to have once been a pearl, gifted by God to Adam, cast out from the garden, as a sign of forgiveness. Another Islamic version tells that God gave Abraham a white stone from paradise, preserved now in a silver setting in the shape of a three-foot eye, that has turned black by its absorption of human experience. Black stones and white stones are each other's disguises.

We walk back along the pier, past the boys fishing for perch, past the joggers heading back out for their third lap. The kids run on the planks, skipping every other one, finding the rhythm of their steps. Some of the planks are new – they still display the green hue of weatherproofing treatment – while others are ashen, smoothed by decades of rain. At the shoreward end of the pier, we turn east and follow the trail to the white rock. It rises from a bed of pebbles a few feet above the high-water mark. Driftwood logs fringe the stone's enclosure. Elizabeth and I sit down on one of these while the kids run around the stone, looking for a way to get on top of it. White and black shells of clam and mussel lie on the beach among the tide's flotsam: broken crab legs, slivers of wood, worn green glass. The air is fragrant with the smell of sea stones drying in the sun.

The kids find a tripod of thin logs, no doubt pressed into service by previous climbers, leaning into a hollow on the boulder's southern face. The wood is worn free of slivers, rough but slippery. Rowan wraps herself around the largest log and shimmies upward; Avery follows. I wander over and stand beneath them as they go. Five, seven, ten feet off the ground. In front of me, on the surface of the stone, someone has written, "Grad 2002 ACS," with a wide felt-tip marker.

Rowan and then Avery stop at the top of the logs, where the wood meets the hollow on the stone's shoulder. They're anxious about being so high, but they want to keep going; to the summit, another five or six feet above them. I don't let them go that far. If either of them fell and slid down the back side, I wouldn't have time to make it around before they rolled off the edge and down to the ground. They're high enough; they shout and whoop and point.

Avery asks, with a big grin, if he can jump down. I tell him, No, sit down, enjoy the view. But I recognize his impulse. When I was a boy, my brothers and I climbed boulders and bluffs and trees for the express purpose of jumping down. We leaped from the high cliffs at Pu'u Keka'a, the Rumbling Hill, timing our descent to the rhythm of the incoming swells. Pu'u Keka'a is a volcanic spatter cone, called the Black Rock by tourists, that is the westernmost point of land on Maui. In local myth, it is where souls of the deceased dive into the ancestral waters. We jumped from its ledges, avoiding the troughs of the swells and the shallow bottom, striking the water where the waves rose up and doubled the depth at the shore. We did not know, at the time, that we were following the tracks of the spirits on their way back home.

Rowan climbs down, placing her feet carefully upon knots and ridges on the logs. Halfway down, when she is low enough that I can reach her, I gather her up in my arms. She's only seven, but it won't be much longer that I will be able to carry her with such ease. Avery comes down next, not wanting any help, halting and sliding all the way to the ground.

We amble back to the driftwood bench. Elizabeth looks out onto the tidal flats and the strait; I sit down beside her. The kids head down to the shore, tossing stones into the water. We watch them coming and going, looking back for acknowledgment, running down the beach into their own dreams. Their voices, echoing and filling out the day, make the substance of our world. They will depart one day, to be the authors of their own myths. But today we share the creation: black stones and white stones along the shore of the sea, an eye of fire ghosting across the sky, errant sand in the grain of a worn driftwood bench.

I work in layers, peeling back the grain of the stone. When it was molten, on the threshold of its beginnings, fresh from the volcano, the turbulence of the heat mixed the minerals in the stone the way cream mixes into coffee. By convection, by the flowing of currents at different temperatures, by virtue of air and ground and its own persistent, blazing heat, the stone was made into many interwoven layers of texture. But unlike wood or sandstone, in which the grain is typically obvious and distinctive, the grain here is subtle. It runs diagonally through the stone, from bottom left to top right, easing toward the vertical as it goes, with the result that my work on the left side is easier. I feel as if I'm slicing through material on the left, whereas the right feels tougher, requires a persistent and repetitive stroke that amounts to almost twice as much work. These layers are like the pages of a book. I read as I go, opening the volume.

I try to imagine the first figures described in my family journal, ancestors who lived a thousand years ago. Priests, clan chiefs, and farmers. A band of warriors, glimpsing a crucifix in the sky. I read of a man captured by pirates at the heel of a dark shore, a minister who died at the pulpit while preaching from the Book of Malachi. ("But who may abide the day of his coming, and who shall stand when he appeareth? For he is like a refiner's fire."*) I read of two women burning, one as heretic and one as exile, and of a man gored to death by a bull. From the Middle Ages, through the Renaissance with its devotion to alchemy, to soldiers and wanderers and writers in the nineteenth century: I read the myths of my own origin, in the leaves of a volume penned by an unknown hand.

I have inherited the last of the old books in my family. But as I read the journals, I discover that my small collection is part of what once was a great library begun by the grandfather of Cotton Mather, the Salem witch-hunter who is my distant ancestor. Much of this library, at one time the most diverse in North America, was brought to Canada when Mather's great-nephew, a loyal British subject, fled Boston after the American Revolution.* Since then, all but the ragged volumes on my bookshelf have gone: to collectors, to other libraries, to fire and rot and apathy. A 1790 edition of *Robinson Crusoe*, tale of the wandering mariner, is the closest I can come to the oldest books.

A series of Kem myths speak of forty-two books of stone, among them the Book of Struggling, the Book of Guardians, the Book of Protection of the Body, the Book of Traversing Eternity, the Book of Gates, the Spell of the Twelve Caves, and the Book of Illumination. The authorship of each volume was attributed to Thoth, the first magician. The myths say that the secrets of the books were forgotten, soon after the age of Thoth and his companions. (Five thousand years ago? Ten thousand? Twenty? No one knows.) The esoteric formulas were enacted in rituals of the Kem temple, but the means of embodying the magic had been lost. The words lay in ruin.

One narrative thread of this bibliomythology, about five thousand years old, tells of the magician Hardjedef, brother of

Khafre, who walked in the library each morning, tracing his fingers across chiseled inscriptions on the walls.* He was drawn by the shadows of vanishing light. Hardjedef was a scholar of the glyphs and of the power of voice. He knew of the book of Thoth which fell from heaven: one book, containing all the secrets, the one secret. Lost, hundreds or thousands of years ago. By reading the oldest glyphs, Hardjedef learned that Thoth had hidden the book of stone – in the river, beneath the black cliffs, protected by a series of nested boxes.* The innermost box was forged of gold. It lay within a bronze box, which was enclosed by a box of palm wood. The palm box was inside a box crafted of ebony and ivory, and this lay within a silver box. Last of all, a box of iron: heavy and glimmering, concealing the mystery; around it, a host of serpents, scorpions, and crocodiles. The largest of the serpents was immortal, and invincible.

I work the stone, easing the grinder down, trying to see what I'm doing through the dust. It spins off the surface with such dense forcefulness that at times my view is entirely obscured. It renders the air into what looks like a liquid texture, thick and viscous as mud on a river bottom. I think of Hardjedef, and the way in which his story, one of the oldest of the Kem, has been reinvigorated and revised by subsequent mythmakers. The tale of the Hebrew ark of the covenant likely begins with him, as does the tale of Alexander finding a stone of wisdom at the gates of paradise.* The Grail legends build upon the legacy of Hardjedef. He is a primordial Gandalf – who in turn is the mythic father of Harry Potter. Between these two, acting as their intermediary, is the Mickey Mouse of *Fantasia*, reading spells in a magic book. That vignette, which I remember with terror and wonder from childhood, is an adaptation, by way of the Greeks, of the tale of Hardjedef. Myths are never fashioned anew, out of whole cloth, by the storyteller. They are adapted, modified, edited, recast into forms sufficiently specific to a given culture as to permit the claim of authenticity. But the thread goes back, always back, to ancestral bards, claimed or disowned, who themselves borrowed the tales from a well of souls that has no bottom.

Myths come in layers, in nested boxes. This is one of the things I come to understand as I sculpt the broad cheeks and jawline of a concealed face.

The myth of Hardjedef tells of him forming, from wax, models of workmen, tools, and a barge.* Speaking words of power, he brought the figures to life (like the brooms in *Fantasia* and at Hogwarts). Their animated forms grew, and they began dredging the river bottom. For three days and nights they worked, tireless, drawing up buckets of sand, sloshing them onto the deck, diving for more. Beneath the slow current, on the cold floor of the river, the well deepened. Hardjedef watched.

The workmen found the lair of the guardians on the fourth day. The iron box was visible behind scaled and seething ramparts. Hardjedef stepped forward and spoke; the scorpions and crocodiles dispersed, and the serpent, coiled around the box, rose up. Hardjedef killed it twice – once with a sword, once with a spear – but each time it returned. During the third battle, Hardjedef wrestled the serpent toward the shore, across the bank, and toward the desert. There he cut it in half and placed a mound of sand between the two halves. Unable to reconnect itself, the serpent lay sundered on the hot ground. Its coils, stretching across the desert in the pattern of the dunes, can still be seen today. Sometimes the serpent moves, or grows invisible, or raises its head into a dune that can be seen for miles. Eventually it will stitch itself together again.

One night, after working on the junction between the nose and brow and finding a small sliver of intrusive red minerals, almost like a capillary, I dream that I'm driving along a country highway with Elizabeth and the kids. We see a water-filled quarry at the side of the road and pull over to take a look. There are tourists and rock hounds and a man selling stones and carvings. Beneath the water, we glimpse beautiful formations of jade and red jasper. I amble down to the water's edge, looking for a stone to carve, and I see a man hidden beneath a pile of rubble, digging and singing.

With a companion – a shadow, a shifting amalgam of many people I have known – we search. After finding many good specimens, we head back to the car along a wooden pier that stretches across the quarry. Suddenly a giant snake – thick as my own height, jaws opened, body disappearing into the murk – twists itself up one of the pilings, seizes my companion, and slithers back into the water. The pier begins to crumble. I jump into the water and follow the serpent down. As I descend, I look toward the surface and see a host of smaller gray snakes pursuing me. The mineral formations lie all around: tourmaline and jade and agate and serpentine.

I seize a sword – was it one of the gray snakes? – and slash my way down into the waters. I see a glint ahead, of something that fades as I awake, heart hammering, into a night made bright by the passing moon.

Nose and cheek and chin drift up from deep within the stone. Along the jaw, where the contour of the face tapers toward the chin, I remove the stone's squared corners. Instead of abrading them, as I have with the surface of the face, I choose instead to slice through the rock, about two inches in from the edge. I cut diagonally, as though removing a pyramid-shaped corner from a block of cheese. The diamond-tipped blade whines into the stone. I brace myself, watch the angle of the cut, prepare for disaster. If the body of the blade strikes the edge of the cut, or if it twists and binds in the opening, a number of dramatic and unpleasant things could happen. The blade could jam and transfer all its torque into the handle of the grinder. Faster than I could react, the handle would spin forward onto the top of the stone. I'd break at least two fingers, the ones holding the upper half of the handle. The blade might also shatter: held tight in the kerf of the cut, spinning fast enough against the stone to glow with friction, bound and vibrating and with nowhere to go. Or, like a hot rod doing a brake-stand, it might seize up momentarily, coil its energy into one big thrust, then skitter across the bench. In this case, my hands would be jerked forward, likely into the blade.

Slow. Easy. Careful. The body of the blade slides into the first cut, with perhaps the thickness of a fingernail on either side of the leading edge. Half the blade, almost to the edge of the arbor, disappears. The motor slows. Then the spinning edge emerges on the far side, the motor speeds up again, and with a rattle the corner falls onto the bench.

Flush with confidence, I start cutting the second corner without shifting my position. Midway through, when my back starts to feel awkward and I rotate on my heel, my hands shift the blade slightly, and it twists in the cut. There's a high-pitched sound as steel meets stone – a ringing, pealing, grinding clamor. I edge to the right, a tiny increment of movement, and the sound stops. Along the edge of my right hand, resting upon the secondary handle above the blade, a wave of heat pulses up, glides past my tight fingers, and drifts into the cool spring air of the shop. The second corner cracks loose; a shard with rough sides, a peaked summit, and smooth base where the cut was made. A ribbon of dark stain shows where the steel spun against the rock.

Hardjedef's workmen raised the box from the well and brought it onto the deck of the barge. The polished iron lay like a silvered ingot in the sun. Hardjedef opened the bolts of the iron box, removed the silver box, and cracked its lid. Inside, ebony and ivory captured and returned the light. He lifted out the box of ebony and ivory, opened it where an emerald bolt lay across the hinge, and found, inside, a plain box of palm wood. He opened this box; inside, there was another – bronze, like a muted ember. He lifted it out. Along its sealed edge, he could see the flash of gold.

Hardjedef placed the bronze box on the deck of the barge. The bright seam shone through his hands, and he could see the fine webbing of blood vessels and muscles within. Out of the corner of his eye, he saw the shore, rising and falling as the barge drifted on the river. The workmen were still. He raised the bronze lid. A flood, a blaze of brilliant light washed over him, and he was momentarily blinded. He could not look directly upon the golden box inside. But by turning his head, as though listening for a sound, far off, Hardjedef could gaze askance at the box. Its brilliance burned him. To gaze, even sidelong, upon the veiled mask of God – not the face, even, but the mask – is to burn with endless beginnings.

I release the power switch and the grinder stops. The blade keeps spinning for a few moments, winding down, marked by a blue swirl of discoloration between the arbor and the edge. I remove my earplugs. Suddenly I hear sounds: a car turning at the top of the hill, a skateboard running across the joints in the sidewalk – *thwack, thwack, thwack* – the creak of the shop door as Rowan peers in and asks if I know where the scissors are. The shop is a mess. An orange extension cord snakes across the stained floor and past the old records I promised Elizabeth I would store out of harm's way, now grimed with a quarter inch of stone dust. Bits of sandpaper and loose tools are scattered across the bench: a couple of chisels, a multihead screwdriver, a small hammer.

In the midst of this detritus, rough and rudimentary upon the bench, are the beginnings of a stone face. Without eyes and a mouth, anonymous, but unmistakably a face. Emerging, unhurried, furrowed by scratches and hatched grinder marks, splashed with white, blue as the deep sea.

I touch the stone and feel its warmth. The pads and cuticles of my fingers are streaked with dark dust. I explore the ridges and hollows of the face, searching for the hidden shape beneath.

Hardjedef removed the gold box from its bronze enclosure. He sensed the weight of the stone of origin inside: the weight of every moment of the world's unraveling, and the lightness of its departure. He sat on the shifting deck, placed the box in front of him. His hands, transparent in the liquid air, moved forward to the center of the lid.

PART II

THE JOURNEY OUTWARD

EXODUS

Avery asks Elizabeth if we can visit my mother's grave. The request comes suddenly, on a cool morning filled with errands, and I'm surprised to hear about it. My mother died before Avery was born, and the tales he's heard of her are not, for the most part, appealing. After all, at the end she was so thoroughly consumed by alcoholism that all trace of her previous charm – a lovely, honest, and passionate charm – had fled.

The days of my mother's grace are slim in my memory: a summer-camp care package, her generosity with gifts and conversation, her love of music and dancing. But these were overshadowed, later, by the emotional corpulence that infests the drinker. Elizabeth and I have tried to give our kids a balanced view of my mother's ailment: that she was ill, sometimes difficult, but also gregarious, and often kind. The only known photograph of her as a child hangs in the hallway alongside our den. It shows a little blond girl, about three years old, a blue ribbon in her hair, playing intently with a toy rabbit. She's looking down, away from the camera, shy perhaps. It's a picture of innocence, of a world not yet cracked open. I hope this is what my kids see, as well as the later, darker vision of a woman utterly lost.

Avery asks frequently about my mother. His request to visit her grave is not a fleeting impulse. He's following something, trying to piece it all together. So we go, on a blustery day with ashen clouds rushing along the southern horizon. The grave-yard rests on a hill overlooking the city and the mountains to the north. From the access road, I can see the flanks of the far-thest peaks, crowned with glaciers stark against the sky's blue. Just beyond them, along a gravel track meandering into the wilderness, lies the mountain my father and I climbed to find the stone.

Some of the graves are somber and unkempt, while others show signs of being well tended: fresh flowers, a white slip of paper folded inside a crack in masonry, pine needles swept care-fully away. We see tombstones of white, of muted gray, of black with moss growing in the cracks of the letters. There are gated enclosures and wooden crosses and wide verges with black crows perching. I haven't been here since my mother's inurn-ment, when my young nephew grabbed the box of ashes and ran with it, away down the avenue. He too was trying to follow something, to piece it all together.

Eight years, one visit, and I can still spot the grave from a hundred yards off. It's there, beneath that small cedar with the slender trunk. We park beside the tree. The four of us trundle out of the car, fasten our coats against the wind, and cross the grass to the plot. Avery is intrigued, curious, but Rowan is old enough to know that graveyards can be spooky. She wants to go back to the car. I ask her about it, and she tells me she's imagining all the dead people buried in the ground. I talk to her, about what remains and what departs. She holds my hand, and together we wander over the bones of the dead.

There are two family tombstones at the gravesite. The one on the left is white granite, hewn roughly, streaked with black. *Black fire on white fire.* I recognize the several names inscribed upon it as ancestors from two generations back. I note, in particular, the name of my paternal grandmother's father, who was consumed by fire. The other tombstone is made of black granite, also rough, also with letters carefully inscribed. My grandfather is here, whose father was gored to death by a bull. And my great-uncle, the war-wounded, who once tamed a wild bull, is here also. It must be strange to tame an animal of the kind that killed your father.

The names of my great-aunt and my grandmother, her sister, occupy the lower portion of the black tombstone: Eileen, meaning torch, and Bernice, the name of a queen from the twilight of the Kem, during whose reign the Temple of Horus at Edfu was constructed.* That temple, perhaps more than any other artifact of the Kem, has preserved their mythological legacy. Bernice, beside whose grave I stand with my family, was the keeper of our family legacy: myths, dreams, memories. Without her, I would know almost nothing about my forebears. She constructed the temple of our endurance.

The black tombstone, flecked with moss, feels cool to my touch. It reminds me of the stone of the Kem – swirling in the waters – which is also the Hebrew stone of foundation: "The construction of the earth was begun at the centre," says Hebrew folklore, "with the foundation stone of the Temple, the Eben [or Even] Shetiyah, for the Holy Land is at the central point of the surface of the earth, Jerusalem is at the central point of Palestine, and the Temple is situated at the centre of the Holy City."*

Avery wanders round to the back of the gravesite and inspects the rear of the stones. Elizabeth stands on my one side, Rowan on the other. These three are my foundation, as are the others, named upon the headstone as the Unnameable is named upon the foundation stone. They are the center of the many tales by which I stitch myself together, motley and haphazard and entirely inconsistent. This mythological and spiritual nexus inhabits all fables; it happened here, whether it happened here or not. Black and white fires meet at these interstices.

Scattered family tales ghost into my memory. This is where the heretic among my Scottish ancestors was burned, where the inquisitor spoke to a crowd gathered at the gallows. The château of my French ancestors once stood here, though its chapel doors with their carvings of the foundation stone are long gone. This black headstone is the cornerstone of the colonial church, perhaps the oldest stone building in Canada, laid down by my ancestor more than three hundred years ago in Quebec City. The site of mythical origin, of the world's foundation, is every place of homecoming.

At the base of the black stone rests a small horizontal slab of polished marble. It lies slightly to the side, at the level of the grass. Upon its surface, gold-colored letters are inscribed and painted: my mother's name, and two dates. The polished surface is still clean and fresh. Beneath the slab lie her ashes, retrieved from my nephew and placed here at the well of origin. Elizabeth calls Avery over, shows him the spot, answers his question about how a human being is rendered into ashes. He's quiet, thoughtful. He frowns, then smiles at a ladybug skittering across the marble. Then he's off, down the aisle toward the cenotaph nearby. A flag flutters from its pole in the crisp breeze. Snap, flutter, snap.

My mother's people were jewelers. This is almost the only thing I know about them. My grandfather died when I was an infant, and my grandmother, persevering until I was in my early teens, came into my life so infrequently that I can hardly recall her. All but one of my memories of her are fleeting and indistinct. The sole exception: her lying in a cot, at the far end of our living room, stretching out the last of her days. I don't know how long she was there – a week, a month – before she negotiated the terms of her own end. But I recall that on every one of those days, a bottle of amber liquid lay on the floor within arm's reach of her trembling hand. Now, in the light of my memory, the bottle glows with a russet sheen. By the color of steeped amber: this is how I remember those days (was it late autumn?). I recollect them as though looking through lenses tinted the hue of single malt whiskey.

The jewelry store had been closed by the time I was born, and there was nothing left of the stones except what remained in the family. The language of that trade, with its practical esoterica still echoing from the Kem, from the Hebrew high priests with their jeweled breastplates, was no longer spoken in our home. But my mother's brother, the exile – he alone of his family who stopped drinking before it killed him – stayed in the business.

He worked at a small jewelry store downtown, a place of hushed formality, as though the glint of polished metal, the shimmer of stones alive like eyes of every color, as though the wonder of those fiery fragments could be tamed and subdued with sufficient decorum. There was carnelian and ruby and opal. And lapis lazuli, stone of stones, and emerald and sapphire.

During my teenage years I visited him at the store each time I was downtown. I brought my friends to see him, my only maternal uncle, about whose life I knew almost nothing. He showed me all the stones. He named them in his soft, almost reverent voice. His movements were careful and measured, giving the impression, though he was not an elderly man, of pervasive fragility. His hand trembled slightly as he drew out a disk of jade from the display case. He seemed old and gentle, and the tenderness I felt toward him was entirely distinct from the conflicted intensity of my relationship with the only other member of his family that I ever really knew: my mother. It wasn't until much later, when my professional life brought me into contact with those in recovery from substance abuse, that I finally realized the source of my uncle's brittleness. He was a man snatched from ruin but forever burned by the heat of his struggle. He had redeemed himself from his particular shadows, but he would never again be physically healthy. Like my mother, he died young.

Those visits were almost the only times I ever saw him. I can remember him at our home only twice: at Christmas one year, when he was a sufficiently foreign presence that my younger brother was unable to approach him, and one summer afternoon when he appeared, unannounced, pulling up in his El Camino, a vehicle which has ever since been an emblem, for me, of mysterious journeys.

He taught me no stone lore when I visited him. He wasn't trying to teach me anything, so far as I know. He was just visiting. He didn't tell me that amber, one of my favorite stones, is not actually a stone but fossilized tree resin, or that its peculiar electrical properties have earned it a reputation for possessing talismanic powers. He simply held it up and let the light reflect and refract through it, so that I could see the colors – honey and gold and sunbeams. Amber is the color of those memories, of the bottle beneath the cot, of my uncle's stones, of my own wonder of secrets.

Stones are all that remain, in my own life, of my mother and her brother: stones on the third finger of Elizabeth's left hand (given to us by my mother, set into a ring designed by my uncle), and a green stone – emerald – I inherited from my mother after she died. Emerald is the stone of prophecy, and is reputed to be capable of protecting the wearer against every kind of enchantment. My mother had need of protection from enchantments; though in the end, she seemed not to have had protection enough.

In the Jewish tradition, small stones are placed on gravestones as markers, as symbols of memory preserved. A friend of mine once told me that her father, returning to Europe after long absence, found stones laid on the crest of her mother's gravestone. Who had visited, he wondered, who of those that remained had come here – those not exiled, not fleeing, not fractured and lost by the war. Who had come?

I take a small stone from my pocket: blue, veined with white, smoothed by water. I place it upon the summit of the black gravestone, the way the radiant stone called the *shamir*, in the Hebrew traditions of antiquity, was said to lie upon the foundation stone of the world. My blue stone rests in a tiny crevice on the gravestone's rough, dark shoulder.

Elizabeth walks with Avery toward the cenotaph, and Rowan tags after them. It's quiet, but for the wind and the sound of my children's laughter. I touch the two gravestones and the slab of marble, take a last look at the pebble I've left here, and follow.

The cenotaph is at the highest point of the graveyard, along its western edge. Smooth, precisely jointed white marble slabs are inscribed with crisp letters:

They shall grow not old, as we that are left grow old.
Age shall not weary them, nor the years condemn.
At the going down of the sun and in the morning
We will remember them.

I recognize the lines from Remembrance Day services; they're from Laurence Binyon's poem "For the Fallen," written during the first months of the First World War, just after my grandmother and her sister saw a vision of savage horsemen in the sky, before anyone knew how terrible things would become. My grandfather and his brother had not yet gone to war. My grandmother's brother had not yet been shot down, had not yet died, like so many of his forebears, in the sweet countryside of northern France. I think of him, on his first reconnaissance flight, gliding above the fields upon which my grandfather and his brother would, much later, cradle their heads as artillery shells flashed among the black horses. He never saw them in the muck, never met them. He floated into the sky like a red balloon and was lost.

The kids run round the cenotaph, chasing each other. Elizabeth and I watch them circling, then Rowan heads back with me to the car. Avery takes Elizabeth's hand and walks over to my mother's gravestone, to say farewell. I watch them go, and wonder what this visit has been like for the kids. Has it helped Avery make sense of his relationship to the grandmother he never met? While I'm thinking about this, Elizabeth bends down beside Avery at the gravesite. He pauses for a moment, then turns to her, exuberant, and says: "I got it! The stone stays here with the body, but the spirit goes with us everywhere."

Myths are untethered dreams, rising like red balloons into a cerulean sky. Breath – warm and simple and filled with longing – inflates them, and they expand, ascending into a firmament inhabited by relics and departed gods. Eventually, the balloon breaks open, and the dream merges with myths stretching across every horizon.

The Kem are gone, their dreams risen into the sky. They became myths, drifting across the field of time, exerting a persistent and sometimes invisible influence. Their science and philosophy were passed to the Greeks, who freely acknowledged their debt. The sudden flowering of classical Greek culture, commonly thought to be the origin of Western civilization, was a legacy and not a unique development. The

Greeks adapted much of the Kem wisdom: in geometry, art, mythology. And long after the Nile temples were left derelict by a world marching resolutely away from its past, the teachings of the Kem persisted; in hiding, traveling in disguise. They persist even today. The ancestral eye and the stone of origin, united into the single symbol of an eye atop a pyramid, are displayed on the most powerful economic symbol of our age: the American dollar. In the contemporary world, every financial transaction in American dollars owes a debt, in spirit if not in currency, to the Kem.*

I follow the stone of origin, searching for it in later tales of the Kem, finding the wake of its passage in legends of chambers buried beneath the sand. I read of the battle between Hardjedef and his rival for possession of the stone book, and of its eventual return to the island of beginnings. I remember going to Edfu, where the Kem temple rests on a foundation older than history. I sculpt the stone on my bench, shaping the contours with the grinder before switching to a rotary carver for finer work. I think of my mother's face, and my grandmother's.

After the age of Khafre, twenty-five hundred years before Christ, the radiant stone faded from tales of the Kem. It went underground, as the mythic landscape came to be populated by warriors and ghosts. But the stone did not disappear: it migrated instead, taking with it much of the archaic Kem mythology. It rose from its foundations, like the wandering stones of the desert, and followed the people of the exile. They took it in, sheltered it, and made it a part of their tangled history.* They cradled it within their own legends of origin, though it was a child of their enemies, and delivered it to the center of their own cosmology. Those wanderers, the people of the dream, were the Hebrews.*

At twilight on the sixth day of creation, five days after the foundation stone had risen from the ancestral waters, when the tasks of crafting mountains and iron and cedar had been completed, the virescent earth floated like spindrift in the sky. Fireflies gamboled across the quiet hills. In these final moments of unfolding, the Unnameable spoke words that flowed across the landscape and rendered the shapes of creation. The mouth of a well, its location now lost to us, was fashioned from the earth. The first and infinite rainbow was made. The words – recording the secrets, and that which must be remembered – were inscribed in tablets of stone. These are things we have forgotten.

The demons were also made during the peculiar twilight of the sixth day, as was the sepulchre of Moses, whose name denotes a son of the Kem.

Finally, there came the *shamir*, the radiant, living stone. Small – the size of a barleycorn – but bright, like a shard from a star. It is a tiny eye, a fragment of the foundation stone. The light it emits – its gaze, as the craftsmen will come to call it – slices through the hardest stone. The gaze of the *shamir* is terrible and wonderful; sharp enough to sunder the world, clean and smooth. Its cutting action leaves no flakes, no dust, no trace of its passage. The rock is simply cracked through.

The *shamir* cannot be kept in a container of iron or bronze; it will blaze through them. It must be wrapped in a woolen cloth, placed in a lead basket, and surrounded by barley bran.

The *shamir* was hidden in paradise, secreted in its nested layers of protection, while the world spread outward from the garden.*

The Hebrews, like the Kem, were a hinge upon which human consciousness turned. The Kem faced forward into the past; the first Hebrews faced backward into the future. For the Kem, everything rolled toward the origin. Their vision stretched deep into the well: ancestors, a stone, a god whose wing covers the sky. The Hebrews were different. Their destination lay in the future, in a new world not yet manifest but already made by the hand of the Unnameable. Memory was the most important aspect of Kem spirituality – the art of memory, as it would come to be called.* For the Hebrews, by contrast, prophecy was theurgy. Promised land, covenant, Messiah, kingdom of heaven: these are the touchstones of a future-oriented religion begun in the wake of the Kem's decline.*

During the formative age of the Hebrew religion (the first and second millennia BCE, roughly), the consciousness of the Kem gave way to something entirely opposite. Relics passed away. In the Hebrew tradition, every object fashioned at twilight on the sixth day of creation is a tool for the future. With these objects – ram, *shamir*, tablets – the arc of prophecy was begun. "Behold," says the Book of Isaiah, "I create new heavens and a new earth; and the former things shall not be remembered, nor come into mind."*

After thousands of years of history and tradition, the Jews today are steeped in the past; the existence of the country of

Israel and the turmoil that surrounds it are based on the pedigree of that past. Upon the mountain, the Unnameable appeared to Jacob and promised to his people possession of "the whole of Palestine." Furthermore, "God promised that Jacob should spread out to the west and to the east, a greater promise than that given to his fathers Abraham and Isaac, to whom He had allotted a limited land. Jacob's was an unbounded possession."* This Hebrew prophecy is one mythological source of the enmity between Jews and Palestinians, those intractable enemies who are, in fact, one people.

Genetic studies have shown the obvious: that peoples who reside in the same geographical area share the same biological heritage. From a genetic point of view, Middle Eastern Jews and Arabs are essentially identical. This is consistent with their shared mythologies; Jews and Arabs both trace their ancestry to the patriarch Abraham. The war between them began first with a stone – of foundation, of boundary, from which all lands issued – then with a dream, and finally a myth.

I work slowly, sensing and listening to the rhythms of the stone. Unlike wood, which provokes me – with subtlety, with a mysterious coercion – the stone is in no hurry to be shaped. Wood creaks, cajoles, gives off the heat of its insistence; this stone is sedate, seems content to while away the time in my workshop. A black stain of embedded dust digs its way into my workbench.

I start working the chin and make the outline of the mouth. I feel the stone's inertia absorbing my motivation. A year in my shop is not even a moment of its time; why should it rush? I

search along its cracks and contours and fissures for something
to hold my attention, to keep the work vibrant. But I slow,
drifting into the work for a few minutes here and there, wondering about the shape of the face, wandering through old tales
in books. I return to my touchstone every few days, tracing its
texture with my hands. The pressure I so often feel when
working with wood – to push through the tricky spots and get
the work done – fails to rise. Instead, I continue to dream: of
water and coves and sand and hills. Of sounds swishing across
sandstone, of tunnels and a bright cobalt sky.

As spring spins itself into summer, I start to feel out of sorts.
My forehead hurts; fleeting aches migrate here and there
through my body. The work slows, though I manage to rough
out the chin, mouth, and forehead in a series of halting stages.
The slow rhythm feels right. I have time to see the contours
change in tiny increments. I develop a feel for the stone's
roughness, its seeming insistence that it not be too thoroughly
smoothed. It seems to prefer its primitiveness to anything more
precisely sculptural. This dialogue between us results in the
slow awakening within me of a modified plan for the surface:
not elegant and precise, as I had originally thought, but simple
and primitive. After all, the foundation stone of myth is neither
refined nor rarefied. The stone of beginnings is a simple block,
cut rough, worn by tumbling.

I put away the plaster cast of my face, choosing to forgo even
the convenience of measuring my work against its proportions.
Instead I wait for directions from the stone: in dreams, in reveries, in daily moments spent with my wife and children. I don't
try to work the stone but rather let myself be worked. I think

about the cargo of myth, making its way across the landscape of memory.

A prophecy is a dream halfway to becoming a myth. It hovers above the earth, rises on currents of air, meanders across peaks and over a restless ocean. The dream lifts the dreamer, making the old world new again, new for the first time. Prophecies, dreams, and myths suffuse the first nine books of the Hebrew Bible, the scriptural core of Judaism (Genesis, Exodus, Leviticus, Numbers, Deuteronomy, Joshua, Judges, Samuel, Kings). These narratives trace the history of the Hebrew people from creation to the end of the Babylonian exile, in the sixth century BCE, when the myths were first rendered into written form by an unknown editor or editors. These myths were crafted by exiles who had survived invasion and the destruction of their temple. They had lost almost all their sacred artifacts: ark, *shamir*, foundation stone. Only the eldest among them even remembered the temple. They were bereft, in the way that many of the world's aboriginal peoples are today: removed from the sacred land, relieved of the artifacts of memory, tethered by the conqueror. In this situation, a culture must choose either to surrender and be subsumed by its surroundings, or to remake the mythological world with itself as the first and chosen people.

The emergent myths crafted during the Hebrews' captivity in Babylon establish, perhaps for the first time in the history of the West, the conception of time as linear – as an arrow, a metaphor later popularized by the Greeks. In the Hebrew cosmology, the Kem's rolling wheel of time is pierced by a stone at the crossroads, then unrolled into a single line that stretches toward the infinite. In this conception, each slice of time occupies a unique point on the line; there are no overlapping rhythms and overtones, no resonances from previous cycles. For the ancient Hebrews, the bull's-eye of this arrow of time was the celestial kingdom – far in the future, held aloft by prophecy and a covenant.

Time as a linear construct is so integral to the modern Western consciousness (though not to aboriginal societies) that it is impossible for most of us to conceive of it any other way. Of course time moves in one direction only; we are both its witnesses and protagonists. But linear time is a cognitive construct, not a physical law. It has developed, like every tale we tell, from a dream into a myth.

The Kem invented individuality, but the Hebrews invented time.

For Rowan's eighth birthday, my father gives her a new bike. She gallantly offers Avery her old, tiny, pink bike, and he accepts with pleasure. Elizabeth and I take them first to the park to practice, then to the Serpentine Greenway, a ribbon of grass and asphalt near our home that wends its way across high ground above the river and slopes down toward the sea. Avery sweeps back and forth across the path, singing, head held high, almost as though he would lift the bike into the air. Rowan is quiet, tentative, her bike too large even for her gangly legs. Her pedaling is measured. As she glides off into the high grass with a whoop, rides the sinuous hide of the serpent, I experience a long moment of gratitude. It's Father's Day.

The mythology of the Hebrews hinges upon three tales: of the patriarch Abraham, of the exile from the land of the Kem (*exodus* means journey outward), and of the struggle to establish a new homeland. This last motif is still working itself out. The struggle of exiles forms the mythological core of the Hebrew experience, today as much as ever; and in this sense, the Hebrew tales are universal. Every culture speaks of a desert crossing, an ocean voyage, a migration that sunders old connections and forges new tales of beginning. Myths of exile are the creation stories told by travelers. They are shared, in diverse and numerous versions, by most of the people of North America.

Like many others, my family came from Europe in a series of staggered stages. In our case, the migrations took place between 1635 and 1820.* They came, Puritans and Catholics and Protestants, some fleeing the Inquisition, some in search of land, others wandering, seeking a new foundation from which the four corners of a fresh world might spread. They arrived from across a wide sea, carrying with them their allegiances, buoyed by hope but shadowed by conflict. They did not know that their descendants would join with their enemies, that their own unresolved struggles would be taken up by subsequent generations, negotiated by the simple means of shared hardship, and put to rest.

The Scottish descendants of Margaret Laird, heretic, burned in 1698, were joined to the French descendants of Diane de Poitiers, champion of the French Inquisition, by the marriage of my grandparents. A century earlier, the marriage of my grandmother's forebears had joined the exiled British and American sides of the family, a recent war between those two nations notwithstanding.

Exile is the means by which we learn to settle down beside one another, to enact the ritual of the old Kem tales by which hostility surrenders to community. It is not a rapid process: the chronicle of my family describes more than a thousand years of migrations, battles, and intrigues, of descendants returning to ancestral lands to fight among the same forests and fields as their forebears, stumbling upon scattered bones. This period of my family history is also the chronicle of every fractured region of the world today – Israel, Bosnia, Rwanda – in which combatants struggle to decide who remains and who departs.

Typically, a stone lies at the center of the conflict: in Israel, it is the stone of foundation on Jerusalem's Temple Mount, the Eben Shetiyah of the Hebrews. It now lies beneath the Dome of the Rock, within the enclosure of al-Haram al-Sharif (the Noble Sanctuary), third-holiest site in Islam. In Islamic myth, that same stone is believed to have been the point from which the prophet Muhammad ascended to heaven. Both sides claim the rock as their own, as they claim the land that surrounds it. In the myths of Scotland, where my ancestors fought the English for uncounted generations, the Stone of Scone, or Destiny Stone, played the same role.* For seven hundred years, from 1296 to 1996, the Destiny Stone symbolized the struggle for ascendancy and autonomy on a small archipelago in a northern sea. That conflict still simmers, in Ireland, as it does everywhere that people are divided by turmoil and joined by ancestry.

In my family chronicle I read of a battle in France, during the Wars of Religion, in which members of my family fought on both sides. Two brothers led opposing charges. In the midst of chaos, when victory seemed remote to each company, the soldiers looked skyward to see a vast crucifix, formed of rushing clouds and light from a hidden sun. Every soldier on the battlefield saw this spectacle, and took it as a sign of divine favor. *God is on our side*, they thought, then thrashed back into their godless work.

I'm surprised to discover this fragment of mythic history, to find that the battle took place in the territory where my grandfather and his brother fought near the end of the First World War, where my great-uncle Dave was wounded; where my father, years later, saw the stone monument on the hill; where I spent a summer as a teenager, not knowing about the unseen and crossing paths of my many forebears.

The appearance of a celestial crucifix is a recurrent motif in my family history. During the evening of June 27, 1914, three and a half centuries after the Wars of Religion, my grandmother and her sister walked along the shore of a Scottish loch. Two girls, sixteen and twenty-one, on holiday with their parents. The day was blustery, the sky alive with scuttling clouds. The girls paused to rest on a bench overlooking the lake, gazed up at the vault of rushing blue and gray. It seemed to them, as they watched, that the clouds slowed, opened a clearing. The ragged edge of the clearing boiled with turmoil. Along the rippling edge of blue, four immense bastions gathered together – one at each point of the compass. From within these – billowing, rising, growing ever more distinct – four figures emerged: horsemen, lit by the fire of evening.* The sky was drawn up into their forms. The horizon darkened, the clearing grew dim. The world was quartered.

My grandmother and her sister heard a dog, barking far off among the brakes. The horsemen paused. Then they hurtled forward, racing into the clearing, chased by a turbulent wake of clouds.

The figures merged at the still center of a cerulean sky, rampant, twisting into a single eye. The girls, transfixed by wonder, stood together, hands clasped, voices mute. As they gazed upon the tempest, the horsemen folded in upon themselves, twisted their four roads together and spread themselves back along the way they came. A cross remained: an immense crucifix, poised, motionless. By now, my grandmother and her sister were afraid. They did not know the tale of their ancestors glimpsing similar specters in the sky. They did not perceive the presence of divine allegiance, as their forebears had. They ran back to the hotel, haunted by a feeling of ill omen. Their parents could not explain the incident, nor assuage the girls.

One of their ancestors, Cotton Mather, would undoubtedly have pronounced the event an example of "spectral evidence," by which demonic forces press their way into the world. My grandmother and her sister were, after all, young girls of similar age to those who had been so troublesome at Salem: sensually adolescent, carefree, feminine, and fatally threatening to the pious (whose secret is shame).

No conclusions were drawn that day, no one was burned or canonized. But the next day, in Sarajevo, Francis Ferdinand and his wife were shot dead, and the rough beast of the First World War was loosed.

I return to the work, in fits and starts, carving and grinding. I complete the broad brow, the nose, the eye sockets, and the chin. I follow lines, wrinkles, and cracks in the stone. I smooth the rounded cheeks and winnow down a sharp edge where the throat draws back from the chin. As I labor, I become certain that I'm not crafting a reproduction; something else is at work – primitive, atavistic. I have deliberately evoked old myths, tales of beginning, and I should not be surprised to find that the work resists a modern cast.

The mouth is tricky, particularly at the seam where the lips join. This takes some finicking with tiny diamond cutters mounted on the rotary carver. The rough contour of the mouth is straightforward, but the slope and angle of the lips takes me almost a month. During this time, I become aware that I'm responding, in ways subtle and curious, to the themes I'm exploring. The stone's forehead, to which I return again and again, trying to get it right, becomes equated with my own brow. I experience a persistent ache between and above my eyes. The discomfort spreads, and I find myself almost continually uncomfortable in my skin. I don't feel ill, exactly, just out of sorts, as though the sun has begun to abrade me.

I complete the mouth, and the general roughing out of the work comes to a close. The features are in place, the contours are shaped, and the rudimentary face is now unmistakable. It's a primitive face, wider and flatter than my own, with heavy brows and eyes not yet formed from the substrate. The cast of my own face looks small and pinched in comparison with these simple, robust features.*

I'm gratified to see that progress is being made – only the eyes now and the brow, and final work with small burrs to smooth the rest – but I feel fatigued, as though I've been wrestling with a stubborn and intractable adversary. Which, I suppose, I have; after all, basalt is an extraordinarily hard stone. But I'm making headway, and I'm beginning to understand – in my body, in my bones – the speech of old tales.

For the Kem, history was myth. In their chronologies, the reigns of gods as well as kings are listed (Thoth ruled for thousands of years; Khafre ruled for twenty-six). They spoke of invincible pharaohs, of architecture devised by magic. Every historical moment was projected onto a mythological ground in which facts, as we understand them, were subsumed by a mythogenic vision of return. This vision, which endured from before the third millennium BCE until almost the time of Christ, existed outside time. Time requires a beginning, and possibly an ending; the Kem possessed neither. But around 550 BCE, slightly overlapping the decline of the Kem, the emergent Hebrew consciousness invented an entirely novel, and opposite, conception: myth as history.

The writers and editors of the early Bible, exiles working in Babylon, hundreds and thousands of years distant from the events they described, interwove myth, dream, and memory. The prophetic visions of Jacob, the burning bush, the parting of the Red Sea: these are asserted as historical facts, devoid of invention or embellishment. Where the Kem would have told these tales as magical fables – and would likely have been unconcerned about the veracity of their storytelling – the Hebrew storytellers were adamant that their myths were true to fact. In an age when magic was vanishing from the world, their authority depended upon it.

From an archaeological point of view, evidence of the

historicity of the Hebrew myths is slim (though, as historians are fond of saying, absence of evidence is not evidence of absence). Archaeology has failed to corroborate many of the events described in the early Bible: the life of Abraham, the exodus, the conquest of Canaan by the Hebrews, the confederacy of the twelve tribes. From the perspective of the minimalist stream of archaeological research, the Old Testament is a mythopoeic document with tenuous connections to actual events. On the other hand, many researchers find circumstantial, indirect, or fragmentary evidence that biblical accounts are substantially true to fact. This debate between minimalists and traditionalists – likely never to be resolved, as it involves the blending of myth and history – is complicated by the fact that the modern identity of the Jewish people, of their statehood, depends upon the historical veracity of their mythic accounts.

The native peoples of North America face the same conundrum: how to resolve the contrast between their own myths of origin – as the first North American peoples, the First Nations – and evidence of anomalous remains such as Kennewick Man, who differs greatly from all modern human groups. The archaeological record of the peopling of North America shows – from as early as twenty thousand years ago – multiple waves of diverse, commingled Asian and European immigrants. No single culture is the first people.*

When myth is equated with history, the truths of the past always conflict with those of the present. To which truths should we be subject: those of the heart, and the community – or those of the mind, and the state?

The Hebrews were the world's first historians, and their god was the first deity to operate within human time. The Hebrew scriptures speak of time's beginning, with creation by the word, and of time's ending, in the final judgment. This apocalyptic view is the antithesis of the Kem conception, which is epochalyptic.* The Kem were devoted to time's circular rhythm; the Hebrews looked toward time's completion.

We hear tales of the enslaved Hebrews building the pyramids of Pharaoh (they did not*), of a coat of many colors, of a man on a mountain bearing tablets made of emerald. These fables – adapted, invoked, invented – lie at the farthest threshold of cultural memory: intact enough to be taken at face value, arcane enough to be gilded and vague. They are like recollections from early childhood: kaleidoscopic, fragmentary, yet somehow whole. The most archaic tales – the creation, the garden, Noah searching the waters – are beyond the memory horizon. Today most people view them as fabrications or allegories; this is easier than believing in magic. But in the later tales – of exodus, of an ark and a temple – myth and history seem entwined enough that we can take one for the other. This is how time, in the personal sense, comes to exist: by virtue of dreams, borne aloft into myths, glimpsed in a sky of visions, and reflected back as self-evident truth.*

According to Jewish folklore, the angel Samael, the exile who would come to be identified with Satan, was a friend to Eve in the garden.* They grew close over long years, while Adam sojourned with the hosts of the Unnameable. Their intimacy deepened, was distilled into devotion; and Eve gave birth to their child, a luminous boy.

In the late fall, when the infant had grown into a lad, Samael was called away on far errands, and he left the boy with Eve. She let him wander in a landscape not yet shadowed by peril. He followed the sweeping light of evening as it migrated across leaves turned toward the sky. Black furrows punctuated the white bark of birch trees. A wolf called in the distance, waited, called again. The boy saw the dark shape of a bear moving through the brush. But he had no fear of animals: they spoke with him, ate from his hand, showed him hidden hollows where birdsong echoed among fractured stones.

He came to a crossing. To his right, the path was overhung by a yellow wood and sloped up toward a gallery of light. On his left, the way wound down, toward a valley and a road of forgotten days. The old road was a relic. It meandered back into prior ages, toward realms of the Unnameable now hidden in the sea. The other path, climbing into a future of contradictions, was wild and ragged. He smelled the scent of apples coming from there; and something else he could not identify.

The boy, filled with exhilaration, began to sing. The surrounding forest grew still, listened to his celestial voice, watched this fragile, gangly creature whose music was a caress in the air.

At the crossroads, where every myth begins, there is always singing. It spreads with the fiery horizon, moves out along four roads, echoes back from where my father walks ahead into bright autumn air on the mountain. In myth, singing is the means by which words remake the world. Sometimes it is mistaken for the patter of rain, or wind in the trees, or the bellow of breath and the rhythms of blood. But it is singing.

This is what I think of as I shape the final contours of the forehead, above and between the eyes, the location in human anatomy where resonant structures surrounding the frontal sinus assist in the perception of sound. I think of the many traditions and fables in which the brow is said to be the center of illumination, the nexus from which arcane knowledge derives.

I work up from the nose and in from the temples, smoothing the grinder marks with a sphere-shaped cutter on the rotary tool. Unlike the grinder, which screeches and whines and kicks up a flurry of dust, the rotary carver is relatively quiet. With minimal fuss, its tiny motor spins the cutter at as much as thirty thousand revolutions each minute. Small puffs of dust rise from the stone's surface as the tool etches its way. The cutter abrades without chattering or stalling, though my progress slows. The grinder is capable of deep incisions, of paring away the stone, but it's no match for the rotary cutter in finishing the surface. The cutter's diamond burrs, much finer than those on the blade of the grinder, impart to the stone a muted sheen through which I can see interlocking layers of the mineral matrix.

I dip my fingers into a teacup filled with water, hold them above the stone brow, and shake off a few drops. They fall onto the surface, immediately brightening the underlying colors: slate and aquamarine and storm clouds scudding. I dip my fingers again and place them directly upon the stone. A small rivulet advances down the brow and slides into the hollow of the right eye. It leaves a clear track of bright rock. On the brow, a tiny pool forms.

I dry my fingers, thumb the power switch on the rotary carver, and start in. The water swirls, mixes with the grit, kicks up fragments of slurry. But the airborne dust is gone, the cutting action of the tool is more efficient, the song of its work now melodic; no more grating and labored coughing. The tool spins, its cutter vibrating like the wings of a hummingbird. As I work, listening for changes in the soft tone to guide my movements, I ruminate on the brow, on the third eye. I think about the scar on my own forehead, the one that runs upward from between my brows and disappears into my scalp.

Over lunch, I pontificate to Rowan about the third eye. Starting with its emergence in Kem mysticism, tracing my way through the Greeks and medieval alchemy, mentioning an intriguing connection to India, I explain the esoteric belief in the third eye as an instrument of illumination.[*] I show her an American dollar bill with the eye gazing from atop a pyramid. I tap her forehead, above and between her eyes. She regards me with weary patience, lets me get a few minutes into my oratory, then dismisses me: "Dad, everyone knows this stuff. Don't you read Harry Potter?"

Adam came upon the boy singing. And he knew, by the child's lovely features, who his mother must be. They stood, facing each other, across a widening gulf. The singing stopped. The world's hinge creaked, and swung closed. Adam, suddenly possessed by a feeling he had not known before, struck Samael's son upon the brow with a stone, and killed him.[*]

Death entered the world. Samael returned from his travails, found his son – lying, serene, on the damp earth – and his lament was a shadow of the child's soft song. Samael, a spirit of impeccable wisdom and knowledge, perceived the cause of his son's demise. He raised his face in supplication, turning, like the leaves of the yellow wood, toward the light, and he foresaw his infinite tragedy: following dark roads in search of a lost boy, calling, listening, trapped between rage and despair. He saw the world's last day, when finally he would round the bend of a mountain road and find a nimble boy at the edge of a river, drinking from the waters. But he foresaw that in the long, intervening time, during the full age of this world, the enmity between himself and the progeny of Adam would not be diminished. Samael would take his darkest form, the serpent, and provoke discord in the garden. In his grief, he would incite violence and wars and blindness. He would be the harbinger of catastrophe.

The spirit of the boy, rudderless and lost, entered into the hearts of Adam and Eve. And they grieved. Adam, knowing contrition for the first time, dressed in sackcloth, poured ashes over himself, wandered the paths of paradise without looking up at the spreading branches of magnificent trees. He did not eat those rare fruits.

If not for his discovery of the magician's book, Adam would himself have been lost. It lay in the waters of the river that issues – even now – from the tree of life. Raziel, the angel of mysteries, had left the book there for Adam to find, in the hope that his grief might be assuaged by revelation. For Raziel's book contained all the secrets, the single secret. The words were written in black fire on stone of white fire. One stone, one page, wrapped in a binding box of gold.

None but gods read, or were permitted to read, the book of Raziel. Because of this injunction against Adam and his kind – the reading of sacred words, after all, frees the divinity of the reader – angels stole the book from Adam and tossed it into the deep ocean; but the Unnameable, wishing that Adam awaken into his own holiness, dispatched Rahab, the angel of the sea, to retrieve it.

Thereafter, without thievery or interruption, Adam read as redemption. The lost boy, residing in Adam's own unsettled heart, read too. And his spirit resolved to remain with Adam and Eve, with their children, to inhabit the hearts of every generation. This choice, by which the child of Eve and the angel Samael provides the seed of every human soul, is also the source of Samael's desolation; for his son resides, until the end of days, in the hidden place.

The words of the divine book, read and remembered by the spirit of the boy, are the source, in each writer and reader, of every subsequent sacred volume. Those words – imaginal, dreamed, or set down in type – are the prayers and divinations of the soul.

When Adam and Eve died, they were laid to rest side by side in a cave hewn from the mountain. The book lay at their feet. The prophet Enoch found it there aeons later; he read the words, and grew radiant with knowledge. It was by virtue of this reading that Enoch became the first and holiest of ancestral sages. He ascended through the seven worlds, through all the gates of becoming, to the very throne of the Unnameable. There he received the task of distributing his wisdom, in the form of books and family chronicles, "from generation to generation and from nation to nation."* And it was promised to Enoch that these writings would not be destroyed in the flood to come, but would persist, as tales spiraling through time.

When Enoch returned, he wrote of his celestial odyssey in a journal, which his son Methuselah inherited. As for the celestial book: foreseeing that one would come, in time of need, seeking its wisdom, Enoch returned it to Adam's cave. He then departed again, leaping from the black stone of the world's foundation, traversing the seven realms one final time. As he soared through the firmaments, Enoch was transformed into a flame bright and terrible. He flew as a storm of fire, and thunder was his herald.

As I work the stone, as I read the ancestral Hebrew chronicle, as I gather up the tales hidden in my great-aunt's books, everything begins to blend. Myths never disappear but are passed through countless hands, sometimes misplaced or discarded, retrieved by a lucky chance, by memory, by what the eye of intuition perceives as fate. There is only one myth. Its many versions are fragments of a unified tale, its characters one people. The one myth is true – irrevocably, absolutely, unquestionably – and it is a fable, false to fact, conjured for the means of massaging history into a noble countenance. It is a metaphor, an invitation, an indication of divine sleight of hand. Each of its versions is a turn in a labyrinth of meanings. At the center of the labyrinth waits the elusive and essential author.

I read, in the tales of the Edfu temple, of a deluge; and of a man, in the Babylonian Epic of Gilgamesh, who will build an ark to withstand the waters. I follow him to sea, with my ancestors who fled the shores of France in 1686. Like the Jews who were evicted from Spain two centuries earlier, the exiled French Protestants took with them most of the craftsmen, artisans, and scholars of the republic. In the age of our diaspora, fleeing the land of our twilight, we became exiles, unraveling across a wide sea, collected together and scattered.

Long into the night, far from shore, my ancestors could see their homes burning like beacons. I navigate with them in their wandering, find them in the hold and upon the sheltered deck. I see a bright flame on the brow of the ship, and a man standing watch. A raven flutters in his hand. His face is burning. My head aches. I can no longer separate the threads of the tales.

I wonder if I'm like the dumb brutes at the beginning of *2001: A Space Odyssey*, mumbling and screeching as they dance around the black stone monolith they cannot understand. I fall into dreams that peel away into other dreams, cascading backward. I tumble into them, swimming.

Dreams figure prominently in Jewish folklore. In one tale, two brothers slept, and in their sleep, replete with dreams such as came to those before the deluge, the world surfaced into the light of their seeing. Hiwwa and Hiyya dreamed together of a stone covering the earth, inscribed with lines of black fire and white fire, resting upon the waters.* The lines upon the stone were a text; the words shifted and changed as the twins gazed upon them. Letters rose up from the depths of the stone, strung themselves together into words, and then were consumed by a shifting and fiery texture. On each of five nights, the book of splendor lay open before the twins in dreams. Their eyes were burned by it. They yearned to hide its brightness, wished for boxes within boxes to conceal the terrible fire.

Noah was of the same clan as the brothers, and he too dreamed of waters and a stone. But he also saw the resting place of Adam, where the stone book of the ancients was concealed. And in the morning, waking from the shadow of premonition, remembering the way of his dream, Noah traveled into the mountains. He followed high paths, crossed old but not derelict roads, saw the Great Bear loping across the sky.

As I make my way through this fable, reading several of its many versions,* reimagining it, finding traces of the Kem and of myths older than history, I am drawn into reverie. I remember that evening twilight, when the sea was kicked up by a west wind, brusque and mercurial. I see, in my mind's eye, the boat and the shore, far off, and my teenage self at the wheel.

Into the wind, fast, thump and thrump across the waves, the pitch of the motor rising and falling as it alternately pushed the boat through troughs and then crested, surfing down the sliding swells. The wind carried spray across the starboard quarter. My clothes were sodden, my hands cold, my eyes stinging from the salt. The sun's last flare, directly ahead, flashed out from the horizon. The sky was clear in the west, but clouds overhead stirred themselves into fantastical shapes. I steered the boat forward, into the weather, and looked ahead to where I saw the black pilings of the dock, two miles off. To my left, along the lee shore, a ribbon of sand meandered along a beach tumbled with boulders. In half an hour it would be dark.

A row of fenders lay inside the boat, still tethered to their stanchions, made ready in advance for a solo docking. They bounced on their ropes, a chorus of flailing orange and white rubber. The bottom of the boat was slick with water, and the bilge at the transom was full. But everything was secure, I was at home in a place I knew, and the waves were a welcoming rhythm. I navigated through the swells, zigzagging, easing the bow away from the face of a wave, then swinging it back the other way, correcting my motion as the wave swung away behind me.

Every seventh wave carried with it a freight of white water growling upon its peak, striking the starboard bow, making the hull shudder with its impact. A cascade of fine droplets washed the boat. I steered, watched, counted. On a seventh wave, from whose summit I could see the rocky beach and a sailboat heading north, the percussion of the water knocked one of the fenders over the side. Its rope jerked tight, and the fender fell against the outside hull, splashing and thrashing along the side. I held the wheel with one hand, reaching forward toward the stanchion. If I could grab the rope, I could pull the fender in without stopping. In this kind of weather, stopping is a hazard: the wind pushes against the hull and slides the boat parallel to the waves; from this position, swells of moderate size can easily swamp a small boat.

The fender rope was two inches from the tips of my fingers. I assessed the oncoming sea, saw nothing of concern, and let go of the wheel. Working quickly, I scrambled to the rope, grabbed it, swung the fender up toward me, and brought it into the boat. It settled onto the deck with a *thunk*. I turned to make my way two steps back to the wheel, and felt my feet leave the deck. What was the wave count? Five? Six? It had taken me longer than I thought to capture the fender, and the boat had already begun to climb the face of the seventh wave when I turned toward the wheel. The boat had reached the summit of the wave and plummeted down the other side. It was not my feet that had left the deck; the deck had vanished beneath my feet. In other circumstances, this would have been fun. My brothers and I used to stand on the foredeck of our family sailboat in choppy seas and jump upward at the precise moment the boat reached the crest of a swell. If the timing was right, we could jump as high as ten feet off the deck. Usually, we'd anchor a halyard on the deck and use it as a guide both to break our fall and to prevent us going over the side.

I did not have a halyard, or a life jacket, or a moment to consider the sporting possibilities. I went over the side.

Noah found the relic, and it revealed to him all that was necessary to build the ark. He knew the number and order of the animals, foresaw his arguments with the raven, paced out the ship's dimensions in a field on the hillside: three hundred cubits long, fifty wide, thirty high.[*] When the work was done, and Noah had begun the sea journey, he placed the radiant book within a gold box and carried it with him, bound upon his brow. Its light opened the way. "The sun and the moon shed no light . . . The ark was illuminated by a precious stone, the light of which was more brilliant by night than by day."[*]

I fell headlong into those ancestral waters, that sea which has been the home of my family of mariners for three hundred years: drifting, departing, wandering in our long exile. Beneath the surface, yellow light scattered. It was as though the setting sun, retreating beneath the land's horizon, had pierced the depths with brilliance. I heard the pitch of the motor, now suddenly high and loud, as my momentum rolled me beneath the hull.

As my somersault slowed, and my face, an arm's length beneath the surface, was turned upward once again, the boat passed over me. I looked up. On the brow, says the Book of Illumination, your vision of the veiled god opens. The propeller sliced me open, from between my brows to my hairline. There was a flash as the bone of my skull was struck. The water bloomed with red, and the yellow light grew too bright to bear.

Through the deluge, Noah held the stone before him, its radiance upon his brow, and he was a surpassing mariner. He glimpsed – as though in a dream – the root of the earth, a mountain ascending, and a peak, tiny and remote, that broke the surface of the waters. This, he knew, would be the site of landfall, and the crossroads of every future age. He saw the building of a temple upon the summit, glimpsed the intractable war of the descendants of Isaac and Ishmael.* All around the black stone of foundation, Noah saw the rhythm of time, blossoming and withering.

I surfaced, gasping, struggling. Saltwater washed into my mouth. But there was another, secondary taste: also salt, but not that of the sea. It was the taste of my blood, washing down my face from the wound in my brow. I brushed my hand across my forehead and felt a gash electrified with sensation. My fingers came away crimson. The boat was gone. Far in the west, in line with the dwindling sun, I saw its outline pounding across the waves. The whine of the motor rose and fell with each swell, whining and growling. I knew it would turn back; the centrifugal momentum of the motor and the steering would turn it in a slow arc. I waited. The water was cold, my shoes made swimming awkward. The shore appeared, vanished, then came into view again as the swells carried me. I thought of swimming to the beach, an hour at best. But I didn't want to leave the boat. I looked west, and saw it coming around: first to the north, parallel to the waves, then nudged farther east, until it ran far down the bay. I lost sight of it for a while, and I drifted, wiping the blood from my eyes and mouth.

After forty days, when the deluge had abated and the ship of Noah drifted upon the face of the waters, he thought to send Raven to seek for land. But Raven, believing that Noah coveted his lovely wife – who could resist those sleek black feathers? – refused to depart. Besides, among the thirty-two species of birds on the ark, there were some who had brought fourteen members (seven pairs) of their species. But Raven and his wife were the only black trickster birds on the ark; if he was lost, his species would be no more.

Raven gazed with his glittery eyes at the wide sea, at the lightening sky, at Noah. And Raven, the creature whose gift it was to divine the future, concluded that the errand to find land was a ruse.* Raven would leave, another storm would come, and Noah would descend to the belly of the ship and seduce the lone black bird who waited there. Raven, who had shown Adam how to sanctify the dead, who alone among the creatures was capable of calling down the rain, was stung by the magnitude of this injustice. He called his wife, and together they flew from the ark, westward to find a new home.

Noah was bitter at this loss. As for Raven: he became a wanderer, whose tales do not come into this telling. He and his mate traveled far, into the north, vanishing from the knowing of Noah and his kind. But he did not perish. In the end of days, Noah and Raven must meet again, to settle their differences.*

By the time I heard the motor again, the day was gone. By its last light I saw the white hull of the boat heading my way. It had come full circle, and would pass directly by me. I knew if I waited long enough, through two or three circuits of its circular path, the gyre would tighten, and when the boat ran out of gas it might settle near enough to swim to. But as it approached, it occurred to me that I might be able to grab the gunwale and swing aboard. It did not occur to me that such a feat is almost impossible; about as difficult as it would be to lie at the roadside, reach up to grab the side mirror of a car passing at thirty miles an hour, and swing through the window.

I was not concerned with physics. I wanted to get back in the boat. And I imagined, as the counterpoint to my chagrin at being tossed out of my own boat, the tale of my prowess that I would later tell. I would be the equivalent of a Wild West cowboy swinging onto a rampaging horse. Then, as now, imagination was my primary means of coping.

The boat bore down on me. I treaded sideways to line myself up with the side of the hull. I pulled my legs back, out of the path of the propeller, and lifted my arms from the water. The boat was moving awfully fast. Bow spray splashed hard against me, forcing me to close my eyes. When I opened them again, the side of the hull was directly in front of me. It was like the flank of a white whale, slick and smooth and freckled with algae. I opened my right hand, kicked upward, and reached for the midship stanchion. It raced toward my palm. But before I touched it, the path of the boat shifted slightly upon a swell, and the speeding hull hit me in the chest with such force that I was slammed back into the wake. The boat sped into the night.

I lay half submerged in the buffeting water, ribs throbbing with each indrawn breath, forehead bleeding. White foam drifted upon the dark swells. The sea was green in the flanks of the oncoming waves. I turned, searched the horizon, then kicked my feet and gazed up at the darkening sky.

FIVE

I'm tired. The insistent, repetitive motions of my work, the heat of the spinning tool, the exertion required to press upon the stone – these things are beginning to wear me down. But it's more than that. Something is migrating through me. Its movement causes the tremor in my hand, the heat on my face. My eyes feel as though they no longer quite touch the world. I'm worried about completing the work. My energy feels diffuse, lethargic, diminished to the point that when I take the kids cycling I can hardly keep up. The forestry road that we ride on winds along the shoulder of a mountain, keeps going far past the spot where we turn back. I want to know what's at the end, just as I want a glimpse of the finished stone, an indication that indeed I will get the work done. A bit of prophecy would go a long way right now. And it occurs to me, back in the shop with the dusty bikes hanging on the rear wall, that I have a means of accomplishing this, of seeing what the work might bring.

I experiment with a slurry of corundum powder on the polishing wheel of the rotary carver, trying to create a preliminary view of the stone's final surface. Along a rounded edge where the jaw fades to follow the contours of the rock, I press with the felt wheel, slick and black with abrasive. Corundum is a common abrasive material – about two hundred times harder than tool steel – used in polishing wheels and sandpaper. After diamond, it is the hardest known natural substance. In one of its mineral forms, corundum yields gemstones in a variety of colors: red rubies, blue sapphires, yellow, pink, green, and white stones. If corundum contains a sufficient amount of two forms of iron oxide – hematite (bloodstone) and magnetite (lodestone) – the result is a black, blue, or brown stone with vitreous luster. Such stones provide outstanding wear as abrasives. On the island of Naxos, in Greece, and in Turkey, which is the world's main producer, corundum mixed with iron oxide has been used by craftsmen since before history.

I push the slurry of corundum back and forth across the stone's edge, remembering my previous experiment with hand polishing. But this time I have the advantage of a spinning wheel whose revolutions reproduce, in a few seconds, what might take a day using my own mechanical force. I watch for a change in the surface texture. It takes a long time for anything to happen.

The common name for the mineral combination of corundum and iron oxide is *emery*. The word has an interesting etymology. The English form derives from Old French, *emeri*, which in turn descends from a Latin word, *smericulum*. The lineage continues back into Greek, with *smiris*, and finally to Hebrew: *shamir.*°

The *shamir* was the relic that Noah bore upon his brow during the sea journey. It was a stone book, inscribed with black fire on white fire. Its letters, perhaps its one letter, peeled away the skin of the world to reveal a well, and old voices singing, and a mountain rising from the depths.

This mountain was sought by Noah after the deluge. The land would rise again there, as it had in the beginning. And since the raven had departed, Noah chose instead a dove to fly high above the waters, searching. She flew out from the ark, far into the gray morning, circling wider and wider. Eventually, when she could no longer see the ark on the horizon, the dove discovered the peak of the foundation stone – an island in the midst of an infinite sea. Calm waters lapped its shore of dark pebbles.

The dove followed the crest of a ridge, found an old tree growing, brought a single branch back to the ark. Noah, who had kept watch for the bird, saw her flying low in the northeast, and when she returned with the branch, he turned the ark in that direction. He first saw the summit of the island, a smudge on the horizon, then glimpsed the dark shore, then saw the beach widen, as though a tide were ebbing.

But Noah was unsettled, even after the ark had slid onto the beach and its inhabitants were released. The flood had been an unfathomable calamity. Seven hundred thousand people – among them Cain, the first human child – had perished. The burial cave of Adam and Eve had been inundated by the waters. In the heavens, which had been opened to release the waters, the stars themselves had been changed. The deluge had been so fierce that the Unnameable was forced to remove two stars from the Great Bear and use them as plugs to shore up the leaking Pleiades. "That is why the Bear runs after the Pleiades," says the Jewish folklorist Louis Ginzberg. "She wants her children back."*

Noah prayed for solace, for a token of safety. Would not the flood, which is the herald of the end of every age, return to drown the world again? The ancestral spirits, the hosts of the Unnameable, listened to Noah's supplication. And they resolved, although the cycles of the ages cannot be stayed or reversed, to grant Noah a talisman. As he walked along the shore of the island, he looked up to see a roiling sky. The clouds turned, spun upon themselves, and formed the shape of a bow. This was the bow that had been created, along with the first words, the well, and the radiant *shamir*, at twilight on the sixth day. It lay brightly within the clouds. And as Noah gazed upon it, he understood that the earth would persist through travail, that its creatures would flourish as long as the clouds speak in such shapes.*

Exiled from the old lands, Noah set up a new altar on the summit of the island. It was here that the stone had risen from the waters in the days of the earth's creation. Here Adam was formed from dust. Cain struggled with Abel upon this flattened peak. Abraham would later come to weep for Isaac in this clearing. And Jacob, dreaming of a ladder, would raise up the stone here, long after Noah's altar had fallen.

Noah returned the radiant book, itself a fragment of the foundation stone, from its long exile. He placed it within a natural enclosure in the rock, entrusting its care to Shem, his eldest son, a priest in the manner of the ancients.* The book descended through Shem's family: to Abraham, to Jacob, to

Levi, to Moses, to Joshua, and finally to Solomon, who would build the Hebrew temple.

The oldest book in my inherited collection, the 1790 *Robinson Crusoe*, tale of the shipwrecked mariner, traced its way to me through the generations of my family. Working backward along the track, the names of the book's previous owners are Eileen, Merrill, Alexander, and Solomon, whose name means "the peaceful one."

The front cover of the book, mottled brown leather with a golden filigree stamped around its perimeter, has cracked off from the rest of the binding. The spine, ornamented with botanical designs, is stripped to the underlying backing along the top. This damage, I imagine, is from three centuries of my ancestors pulling on the edge of the spine and easing the book from the shelf. The back cover is speckled with the hues of parched leather, scraped in one spot, dented near the bottom by some sharp, small object.

Inside the front cover, where crimson facing pages are thick with the grain of handmade stock, someone has pasted a family crest unfamiliar to me. It shows griffins, a ram, and three sets of white wings. The Latin motto reads *Spes Sibi Quisque*: "Let each man's hope be in himself."

The frontispiece shows young Crusoe before his departure, in counsel with his aged father, the two men clasping hands gently. A leaf of tissue paper separates the engraving from the title page, the contents of which are considerably detailed: "The LIFE and Strange Surprizing ADVENTURES of Robinson Crusoe, of York, Mariner, who lived eight and twenty years all alone in an uninhabited Island on the coast of America near the Mouth of the Great River of Oronoque, HAVING BEEN CAST ON SHORE BY SHIPWRECK, wherein all the Men perished but himself. With an account how he was at last strangely delivered by pirates. Written by himself. VOL. I."

Through how many hands has this book passed? How many sea journeys has it undergone? I wonder if its faint smell, of aged leather and dust and long-ago damp, still preserves some of the scent from its passage across the prairie, from the mountains where my grandmother was born, from the eastern shore where my great-grandfather was run down by the charging bull. I close my eyes, place my nose against the stacked pages, dark with age, and wonder if there's anything left of the fragrance of this book's first home, the library of the Old North Church in Boston, or of that night in 1775 when Paul Revere's lanterns hung from the steeple to signal the Boston patriots of the British approach: "One if by land and two if by sea."

I turn the pages of the book, past the advertisement for the publisher, the list of illustrations, the catalog of booksellers ("Ogilvie and Speare, 3 copies"), and the request for orders of an edition of Shakespeare ("In the Press, and speedily will be published: Price Five Guineas, in boards"). I find the beginning of the text, set in elegant type still clear and black against the white paper. I leaf through the following pages, looking for Crusoe's definitive calamity. I find it on page 55.

For the sea, having hurried me along as before, landed me, or rather dashed me, against a piece of rock, and that with such force, as it left me senseless, and indeed helpless, as to my own deliverance; for the blow, taking my side and breast, beat the breath as it were quite out of my body; and had it not returned again immediately, I must have been strangled in the water: but I recovered a little before the return of the waves, and feeling I should be covered again with the water, I resolved to hold fast.

I drifted toward the dark, listened for the sound of the returning boat, wondered if I had the strength to swim to shore. The water was cold, and though the light from the setting sun was gone, the depths below me seemed to glow. Traumatic experience often evokes such hallucinatory shifts in perception, though the mythological cultures of antiquity would have offered a different explanation. For them, such experiences offer a glimpse of the world's true face.

I saw a slender mast rocking in the swells. As it approached, I glimpsed a white hull and several small figures: one on the deck, peering ahead, another at the wheel, two or three clustered in the cockpit. They came forward, I raised my arm, and they found me drifting. The skipper turned the wheel, the boat slowed as it approached, and I climbed on board from a ladder at the stern.

Hours after my rescue, when my boat had run out of gas and drifted at the center of its spiral, the Coast Guard towed it back to the dock. The night was well gone, and I lay in the hospital – safe, but cracked open, caught still in the brightness of that rough opening. Caught in it now, all these years later.

The fictional Robinson Crusoe was rescued from his island, after much travail and adventure, in 1686. This was the year of my ancestors' exile from France, the year that we were fractured. The Huguenot branch of the family set sail for Holland, thereby avoiding massacre, along with thousands of other Protestants whose faith was no longer sanctioned by the church. They were deprived of their lands – forests and farms and châteaus whose foundations were a thousand years old – and banished from the country.

But not all my ancestors departed. A few were Catholics, which conferred upon them the right to claim the holdings of their exiled relatives. In this way, Jacques-René de Brisay, tutor to France's royal family, patriarch of my Catholic ancestors, gathered to himself a legacy of wealth and favor. But like the fleeing Huguenots, he too set sail from France; in a ship called *Diligente*, on a sea crossing during which half the passengers were lost to storms and fever, west toward the New World. There he took up his post as governor of New France, in what is now Quebec City, then a desperate outpost along a knife-edge of wilderness. Exile, it seems, was his unavoidable fate.

To the west, south, and north of the colony, the landscape could not have been more foreign to the European sensibility. It might as well have risen from the oceans, pristine and terrifying, inhabited by ghosts and strange gods and men of the forest – who could tell the difference? Jacques-René took up residence in ramshackle quarters, spent his first years navigating the labyrinth of relationships: between the French settlers and the Iroquois, the Iroquois and the Mohawk, the Mohawk and the Seneca, the Seneca and the English, the English and the French. They were all enemies, and all allies. In such a labyrinth, he knew, there must be a center, a place of beginnings and endings. Accordingly he initiated construction of Notre-Dame-des-Victoires, the first cut-stone building in Canada. He laid its foundation stone, of black basalt, on May 1, 1688.

The stone rises from the center, beckons the god. For the Kem, the site of this rising was the Temple of Horus at Edfu. In Hebrew cosmology, the Unnameable was (and still is) beckoned from the temple of the mountain in Jerusalem. Nothing is now left of that first temple, but the structures built upon its foundation – an old wall, a dome, an enclosure of scattered buildings – still exert memory's gravity.

The site of the god's manifestation is never a fixed axis; it moves, as cultures and families migrate in their long wandering. The site of the first Kem temples was not at Edfu but farther north, along the sweep of the Nile Delta. In Hebrew culture, the spiritual center was first located at a now-forgotten mountain – perhaps in the Sinai Peninsula, perhaps in what is now Jordan – but not at Jerusalem's Temple Mount.* In each culture, in each family, the well and the stone of origin exist at the site of memory's farthest grasp. But these locations are temporary. They are rolled under and forgotten by the living. Only the dead remember the first days.

In my own family, the first nexus we remember is the Château Anet, constructed in the Middle Ages and decorated with symbolic motifs ultimately derived from the Kem. For the exiled Huguenots and Catholics who came to Canada, that nexus became the church of Notre-Dame-des-Victoires. Later still, in my own generation, the spiritual center was moved again: to the residence of my grandmother, of which no trace now remains.

The corundum powder spins upon the stone, mixing with the water droplets that I scatter on its surface. The slurry is thick and dark, like clay – of which, in the oldest tales of Sumer and Egypt, the first human being was made. Almost every subsequent culture of the Middle East has cribbed that motif. I work the edge of the stone first, refining my technique – hold, skim, return, twist – then move toward the right cheek and nose. I want a glimpse, an opened patch of finished stone, before I move on to the work of shaping the eyes. Beneath the layers of slurry, I feel the polishing wheel speed up as the surface smooths out. I hear it too; the motor notches up its cadence, the vibration quickens. I stay on the cheek, drifting across the surface, grateful that I don't have to work too hard. "Let the tool do the work," the common refrain of modern craftspeople, is something of a myth – most craft work, even with power tools, is accompanied by grunts and swearing and strained muscles – but for the moment, my exertion does indeed almost vanish. The wheel slides, and I follow.

When I can no longer feel any resistance beneath the polishing wheel, when it slides over the stone as though it were oil on water, I stop. I put the rotary carver down, clean the slurry from the stone, and look at the cleared patch on the right cheek. The color is darker than elsewhere on the surface: a deep blue, scattered with fragments of black and aquamarine. And flecks of white, now bright with reflection, hard-edged and crystalline. They contrast with the dark background like stars in a depthless sky.

The Hebrew exiles came across the sea, from the land of the Kem, bringing with them only the most practical of their belongings. They wandered, nomads and travelers not yet reconciled to their destination. At the foot of a mountain in the desert, on a day when the sun failed to set, they waited as their leader conversed with the Unnameable. He descended from the summit, carrying sacred stones inscribed with laws like ones they knew from the Book of Illumination.* On his forehead, a radiance burned, and his face was scorched by it.

The people crafted an enclosure for the tablet stones, called the tabernacle, and an ark in which to carry them.* The ark consisted of three nested boxes: gold, wood, and gold.

They meandered during the period of their exile, transporting their relics and stories, adapting myth into history. They were led by a pillar of cloud and a pillar of fire: "For the cloud of the Lord was upon the tabernacle by day, and fire was on it by night, in the sight of all the house of Israel throughout all their journeys."*

They related tales, as refugees and wanderers will do; to preserve their memory, to understand the past which had brought them out of themselves, to shape the future with fables to redeem the catastrophe. At night, when the pillar of fire swept the horizon, when the sentinels huddled with wonder at the edge of the plain, they told one another the old tales: of a lost garden, of a stone hidden in paradise, of a burning man. They spoke often of the burning man, Jacob, and of his night odyssey, which in many ways was like their own.

Jacob came from the south, wandering a long track of travail, following the river. Along his right flank, the shoulder of the mountain rose toward a dark and flattened peak. The sun rode across the mountain's highest ridge, flashed in and out of hollows shaped by the serpent's hide. Jacob saw a stand of fragrant cedars high on the hillside; lower down, the twisted trunks of olive trees stood skeletal against a background of black earth. A falcon screeched far off – *ka, ka, ka, ka* – and Jacob thought of the spirit double, the *ka*, which is always calling the self. He turned, seeking the source of the sound, and saw a flash of wings low against the western tree line. Jacob looked back toward the mountain; blunt shadows, high up, hollowed out cracks in the stone.

It seemed to him that as he watched, the sun moved with unaccountable speed. Within the span of a single breath, it rose into the expanse of the sky, sped across the face of the world, and slid toward the horizon. Then, where Jacob stood, the night descended.

There was a black and radiant stone; of this much he was certain. It lay at the summit, wrapped in tales: a man holding liquid fire, a roiling ocean calmed by a living star, a book with words so secret not even the gods would whisper them.

Jacob climbed. Long into the night, scrambling for signs of a trail, backtracking, hearing the sounds of the river near. He peered into the dark, searching for direction, for a footprint.

His father, Isaac, must have felt this way, coming here all those years ago, led to sacrifice by the eldest one, Abraham.* Jacob thought of his father and grandfather on the mountain, their feet finding the same holds, their hands grasping the same branches on the slope.

*Father, make haste, bind my hands and feet securely. For I am a young man, and you are old. When I behold the slaughtering knife in your hand, I may begin to tremble, and push against you, for my desire of life is strong.**

Jacob pushed through a thicket, ambled across a meadow of high grass, and lifted himself onto a stony ledge. He rested for a moment, searched the indigo sky for a trace of the falcon he had seen earlier. In the north, the Great Bear chased after her children. Jacob remembered his father telling him that tale, and many others. Isaac had spoken of a sacred stone kept by Abraham, called the Kaaba, that could cure any ailment. Isaac had tried to explain to the child Jacob why he had been willing to die at his own father's hand.

I implore you, father, make haste. Delay not. Stand fast, and after you have slaughtered me, burn me until I am fine ashes.

The ground cover was growing sparse, and Jacob came upon wide tracks that blended, ever upward, into other paths. The tumbled scree underfoot was peppered with sandstone, feldspar, and basalt. He heard the bird call again, this time from ahead, up where the broad summit leveled out. River sounds echoed softly across the terrain, and the smell of moisture was in the air.

As Jacob climbed, he remembered the story of the angel's tears, falling onto Abraham's knife, and the intervention of the Unnameable in the firstborn sacrifice. Jacob knew that he would not have been able to untangle the threads of his love – *Whom do you love more, your creator or your own son?* – but Abraham, perhaps wise and perhaps blind, had followed the old edict into the well of his own suffering.

Jacob crested the ridge, cantered down the slope, gathered momentum, and rushed up the far side. The summit lay just beyond. Through a cleft in the ridge, he saw the river for the first time since he had left the valley. The waters were subdued, somnolent. He stepped down to the bank and cupped his hand into the moving waters. The water was cold, as though it had flowed up from deep inside the earth. It tasted – faint and subtle – of wildflowers. Jacob drank.

On the peak, where Isaac and Noah and Adam had come before him, where the sea had parted for the risen land, Jacob wandered a spiral track toward the stone. He saw its enclosure, out of the corner of his eye, but he did not wish to approach it directly. There were too many secrets here, a weight of memories and dreams. He moved slowly, as though in a reverie. He gazed at the still sky.

Abraham sprinkled the blood of the ram upon the altar and said, "This is instead of my son, and may this be considered as the blood of my son before the Unnameable." And whatever Abraham did by the altar, he said, "This is instead of my son." And the Unnameable accepted the sacrifice of the ram, and it was accounted as though it had been Isaac.

Jacob remembered his father telling him the prophecy: of a temple built upon the mountain's summit, its destruction by fire, the many exiles and wanderings of his people, the horn of the ram blowing as a trumpet on the day of redemption. On that day, Jacob's father had told him, whirlwinds will appear in the sky.

As a falcon gyres ever inward, Jacob's path tightened in upon the stone. But weariness began to overtake him, and he slowed. Ghosts washed across his vision, and by their reflected light he saw many things: a well ringed by a dark island, a man walking in a library of stones, a fierce woman hunting in a forest of wolves. As though from far above, he saw two figures perched at the edge of a precipice, gazing down a cliff of black lava into a ravine of rushing water. He glimpsed something red and round, climbing into a sky of terrible brightness.

Jacob was consumed by the fire of these visions. He surrendered to them, allowed himself to be taken into the womb of the earth's dreaming. He came to rest, finally, at the feet of the relic.

In the span of a single night, he dreamed the world's story. He saw two angels, twins as it seemed to him, ascending into the sky. They were departing, as the old gods had departed. But they called to him, saying, "Lift up the stone of fire. It will be the foundation of the temple, and though the temple will burn with its flame, will be lost and forgotten, the stone – which cannot itself be lost, but is made anew with each generation – will remember your true home."

He opened his eyes from the dream. There, before him, lay the golden box. It was too bright to bear, and he turned his head to look upon it sidelong, as the magician Hardjedef had done. Here was the relic, source of all prophecy.

Jacob, foreseeing that this stone – the *shamir*, fragment of the world's foundation – would be used in the construction of the temple, lifted the box from its enclosure and placed it upon the summit. Fire ran through the seam where the lid and the base joined. Knowing that he would not have another chance, remembering his father's tale of the name of God written upon the stone, Jacob reached with tender fingers – slow, fearful – and removed the lid.

I look down into the layers of the stone, black and blue and radiant in the afternoon light. The face I've sculpted on its surface – rudimentary and robust, emerging from rock made by fire on the mountain – is eyeless and intriguing. The stone does not move, but the elements within it constantly vibrate at the pitch of their atomic signatures. The stone's solidity is, in fact, an illusion caused by this vibration; like images on film, rendered by frames clicking by twenty-four times each second. Nothing is actually solid; at the quantum level, even the most dense materials are mostly empty space.

In myths of the stone, a radiant fire burns away the masks of the world. Behind those masks lie the ancestral well and the archaic ocean – mostly empty space, hanging on the backbone of the void. In this respect, the old tales are not much different than the new. In both cases, one who touches the elemental stone is burned: by radiation, by a pillar of fire, by the experience of coming face to face with the numinous.

I start in with the work of the eyes, so that I might free that burning gaze.

Jacob heard someone approaching in the night: a skitter of pebbles, a snatch of indrawn breath, the muffled slap of a heel coming down on the flat top of a boulder. He replaced the lid of the box, called out into the darkness: "Who are you?" A man came into view, suddenly, as though he had just crested the final ridge that Jacob had climbed long after the sun had set. The figure came closer, and Jacob called again. The man slowed, paused a dozen yards from Jacob, and, without speaking, touched his finger to the earth. Fire blazed from the ground, and by its light Jacob saw a young man's face. The firelight pulsed across it: bright eye, dark chin, flicker of playfulness on the brows. Jacob held the golden box with the stone secreted inside and sang back to the crouching figure: "Do not seek to frighten me, for I am made wholly of fire."

The man laughed, turned his face toward the sky. But when he brought it down again, he rushed forward. He caught Jacob at the waist and spun him to the ground. Jacob, surprised and angered, fought back. He rolled to the side, and, using his oldest trick (the name Jacob means "he takes by the heel"), caught the man's heel, and pulled.* Then they were both on the dusty ground, scrabbling and struggling. They tumbled across the scree, tripped each other in the dirt, locked elbows and knees and shoulders. Neither of them prevailed.

The night wore on. The trickle of water from the river and the breathing of the contestants – labored, hushed, and held – were the only sounds on the mountain. But travelers far away, restless in the night, looked out from their encampments and saw a pillar of fire burning on a distant peak. They were amazed, and they were comforted. Since the sun had gone down at midday they had sought to buoy their hopes of a new day to follow. Surely this, the fire in the night, was a sign of divinity at work in the land. Fire, bringer of the light, is also the faith keeper.

The combatants, twinned fires circling each other in the dark, beckoned the sun with their struggle. It climbed into the eastern sky, suffused the indigo horizon. Seeing this, the laughing man paused, and asked that Jacob let him go. Jacob said, "Are you a thief, that you should fear the daylight?" The man did not reply but instead struck Jacob on the inside of his hip. Jacob fell, and the struggle was over. Then the man spoke, saying, "I must go. My companions are singing the old songs. Do you not hear them?" He offered his hand to Jacob and helped him from the ground. Jacob saw, by the glow of oncoming dawn, that the man's features remained dark. His body was a living shadow of concealed radiance. Jacob remembered the midrash taught to him by his father: "The Lord has said he shall dwell in thick darkness."

The sun's light swept down the mountainside and across the desert to the east. In the valley grove, falcons were waking and leaves uncurled from sleep. The day rolled forward with momentum. Jacob, falling into the world but sustained by the night's wonder, asked the man his name. The man laughed and blessed Jacob instead, saying, "You, who struggled with me, who were consumed but not destroyed by fire, shall be called the God wrestler."

Jacob felt the warm sun, turned toward it. Footprints, left by the struggle in the night, lay across the open summit of the mountain. Whorls of settling dust, ocher in the light, made interweaving patterns on the ground. The sky was clear. Jacob turned back, knowing the man was gone, and walked toward the valley.•

My lethargy grows, but the work continues. The dreams and memories evoked in me by the stone are becoming thick. They fall over and around me, growing in size and substance as I carve, their ephemeral forms resolving. I move through liquid air, shaping the eye sockets, smoothing the temples (where the anatomy of mysticism is made manifest), forming the eyeballs. This requires careful attention: the sockets taper inward, but the eyeballs bulge outward. Blending the ridges and hollows of that terrain keeps me busy for two careful weeks. The background expanse of blue and black seems to stretch itself taut, like a settling sea. Flecks of microcline drift across the matrix like flotsam upon restless waves. I read Jewish folklore, in which the ocean is identified with the white of the eye, land with the iris, and Jerusalem with the pupil. The Hebrew temple, now destroyed, is the elusive image mirrored in the pupil of the eye.

By the time the eyes are shaped to their preliminary proportions, I ache all over, all the time. My body feels too warm, fevered. In my dreams, I see fire: stone and fire together, tumbling and reshaping the world. I dream of my exiled ancestors, and the Hebrew refugees, and the temple to which all wandering peoples are drawn. This temple is always the center of the new land, the crossroads from which all subsequent journeys are navigated. It is dreamed into form by those who relate the old tales; at night, while the pillar of fire burns on the horizon, as quiet settles upon the broken ground.

In the autumn of 1918, at the field hospital where my grandfather and his wounded brother spent the night, in a tent with a red cross on its roof, they spoke into the darkness: of future visions, of home, of the means by which two young men – my grandfather was only twenty-three, his brother twenty-seven – might make their way in the world. While the sounds of artillery fire thundered across the river, my great-uncle spoke of his romance with learning. As it turned out, he would spend the rest of his life as a teacher and scholar. My grandfather, by contrast, was more practical; he wanted to raise a family, to fashion for himself a home of refuge. When such a conversation – of dreams and goals and hopes – takes place under the shadow of the world's duress, every word is absorbed by fleeting and persistent spirits, by the ghosts of what has not yet been. And it happened that both my grandfather and his brother were granted their most pressing wishes.

They wandered after the war, in the way of their ancestors. They traveled west, as far as they could go, to a seashore fringed with mountains. My great-uncle walked, for the length of a long summer, then returned to Vancouver. He taught in the Soldier Civil Re-establishment program at the new university. There was as yet no permanent campus for the eight hundred students; classes were held in tents, churches, and a cluster of ramshackle buildings adjacent to the hospital. On the other hand, students paid no tuition. (Sixty years later, when I was a student at this university, thirty-five thousand students were enrolled, and the campus grounds covered many square miles. Tuition, however, was still cheap.)

My grandfather went into business, married my grandmother, built a Tudor house on a tree-lined street and raised three children: two daughters and a son (my father). This sanctuary, in which I spent much of my childhood, was the center of our family life. It was a temple crafted by exiles forging a new home.

This is how I remember my grandmother, with twelve-year-old eyes: in her quiet den, overlooking the front garden. The fire on the hearth is low. She sits in repose, her head reclining on the back of the sofa. Her white hair – wispy, coiffed with care – lies against the embroidered fabric, brought from India in the days of her traveling. Her face is in profile, the webbing of lines soft and deep. Light from the window streams across the contours of her nose and left eye. Her face looks both regal and simple, like a worn and ancient statue. She laughs gently, but in my memory I cannot recall the reason for her laughter. The sound is like green leaves in rain. And in the moments of my watching, my grandmother becomes what she has always been, what her ancestors made of her: the huntress, the old woman, the keeper of aged secrets.

When I was a boy, I'd remain at home when things were stable between my mother and me, then escape to the safety of my grandmother's house when the situation got out of hand. When, for example, my mother (drunk, upset over an altercation with my father) retrieved a set of Dresden blue teacups (delicate, translucent, a wedding gift) and methodically smashed them with a hammer in the kitchen sink. Those teacups were among the most beautiful objects our family owned. My mother needed to destroy the past; it was, after all, the source of her despair. Had the archaic books been in our home, the volumes I later inherited from my great-aunt, my mother might well have burned them. Today my brothers and my father and I – the scattered survivors – possess not a single object from my mother's past that is more than a generation old. No heirlooms, no memories, no tales.

My grandmother's home, built from a nocturnal reverie of wartime, filled first with children and then with grandchildren. It became my own true refuge. My grandfather died when I was an infant, and my grandmother lived alone. The house was well kept, its bedrooms maintained as though children might soon return. I slept in my father's old room, with its dark furniture, poor light, and aura of safety. The east window looked out toward a wide expanse of yard and a trellis of grape vines along the garage. In the far corner out back, a rose garden lay desolate in winter and fragrant in summer.

More than the bedroom, or the grounds, the comfort I felt there derived from my grandmother's careful nurturing. Every day, late in the afternoon, we'd sit in her den and drink tea. She told me all the things I desperately needed to hear – that the turmoil would end, that I would be all right, that it wasn't my fault. Often my great-aunt Eileen would come to visit, and the three of us would play card games: two old women and a child of twelve, playing spite-and-malice. It was Eileen who brought the books. In this, as with so much else in her life, she showed tremendous instinct. She herself had no children, but seemed to know exactly what would ignite my imagination: Arthurian tales, science fiction, fantasies of other worlds and times. She also brought Poe and Conrad and Blake, Buddhist sutras, and poems from Taoism. Our library at home consisted of *National Geographic*, a couple of coffee-table books, and the Hardy Boys. Eileen's books helped me create a world for myself in the rarefied air of the imagination. Those volumes, many of which she gave to me, rest now on my own shelves, beside the books I inherited from her.

Between books and tea and gentle care, my grandmother and her sister saved my life. The den in which we played cards, read books, in which I cast off my confusion, became my innermost temple of celebration.

When they settled beneath the peak of Jacob, Noah, and Adam – the summit wrapped in protective magic long ago by the Shebtiw – the exiled Hebrews were an old people restored to new life. But the land required consecration, and this task fell to Solomon – who knew the tales of his forebears, who wandered the mountain paths in search of the footprints of Jacob and the stranger. Solomon found the old tracks, walked beside the river splashing toward the valley. Upon the summit, where he slept and dreamed, Solomon found the *shamir*.*

He did not open the golden box, knowing the tales of what it might bring. Not yet. Though he knew, from the ribbon of radiance around its seam, that the *shamir* was inside. He cradled it in the crook of his arm.

On the heel of the dusty plain, he called the craftsmen of his people, those who worked in stone and wood and bronze. They were led by Hiram, the exile from Tyre, and they followed Solomon up the mountain.* On the summit, Solomon brought out the *shamir* from its nested enclosures: wrapped in wool, within a lead box, surrounded by barley bran, hidden in the golden case. None of them could look upon it. Solomon closed his hands around the stone's brilliance and walked among the tumbled scree of the summit. His hands and face burned. The radiance broke him open.

He passed the stone over the surface of a boulder, and the rock was cleaved through. While the craftsmen watched in fear and wonder, Solomon lifted his hands again, drawing a horizontal circle in the air above the bedrock. Beneath him, a column of stone was split from the ground. Wherever he carried the stone, whatever movements he inscribed, the *shamir* followed. It sliced through wood and stone and metal, manifesting the precise vision of its carrier. The *shamir* was a shard of creation; it embodied Unnameable fire.

In the hands of Hiram the craftsman, the *shamir* fashioned Solomon's temple of celebration. The stone made no sound. It cleaved the foundation blocks for the walls, carved the hollow pillars of the vestibule, smoothed the surfaces of the inner sanctuary. Hiram used it to craft the bronze basin to hold sacred waters from the well. Inside the sanctuary – the holy of holies – the *shamir* made guardians, gilded angels with wingspans of a dozen feet. These would protect the foundation stone, and the ark which would come to rest here. The sanctuary itself, sliced cleanly into a cube stretching thirty feet in each dimension, was lined with sheets of pure gold.

When the work was done, when the temple became a temporal symbol of celestial paradise, the summit of the mountain had greatly changed. The dust whorls of Jacob's struggle were gone, the shrine of Noah was replaced by temple walls. The pinnacle of the mountain was still visible, as a base for the ark in the sanctuary, but the niche that Noah had found for the *shamir*, after the flood, was buried. It now lay beneath the base of one of the hollow pillars Hiram had placed in the vestibule. The temple covered the well and the clearing upon the summit. Bare rock and flowing water, symbols of divine genesis, were woven, by the *shamir*, into the fabric of a new creation. The well of souls lay beneath the sanctuary.

Together, Solomon and Hiram placed the radiant stone beneath the left-hand pillar. In the hollow space of the right-hand pillar, they concealed the oldest documents of Solomon's people: their tales of origin, of exile, of prophecy. The two pillars housed stone and word.*

An arched entryway made of two columns of cherry wood, joined overhead, led from the vestibule of my grandmother's house into her den. Inside this sanctuary, which occupied the northwest corner of the ground floor, a fireplace fashioned from smooth river stones covered most of the east wall. On either side of the stonework, on shelves and in cabinets that climbed from floor to ceiling, my grandmother stored her library. In front of the hearth, on a round table with a shelf beneath, oversized books were stuffed wherever there was space. A long couch occupied the north wall. Two easy chairs – beside the entrance and along the west wall – completed the seating. A single window, crisscrossed with diagonal leaded seams, looked past a holly bush and onto the street.

A tall clock in the hall chimed the hours as the three of us – my grandmother, her sister, and I – read books and talked. They spoke of their youth, of the wars, of family. I was told the precious myths that I never would have known to ask about: riders in the sky, exiles sailing across the sea. These tales bolstered the foundation of my belonging, shaky as it was, infused with doubts and fears and a pervasive yearning to find my true home. The old fables, made vibrant by books and conversation, built up around me, enclosed me within their cocoon, gave me secure footing as I wrestled with my own gods upon the mountain.

I did not know, and did not learn until much later, after my grandmother died, that the den had burned, along with most of the adjoining house. It happened when my father was fourteen, the age I was when I lived for almost a year in that house, in his room. For me, that year had embodied the white fire of the god's script: myths, ideas, the awakening heart. But for my father, though he never spoke of it, that year of his youth carried the black fire of the god's script: death, loss of the old, a return to origin.

It began late at night. A spark of fragrant cedar from the embers shot through the lattice of the fireplace screen and ignited the fabric of the couch. The flames consumed the den, roared out its door, climbed the stairs toward the bedrooms. It burned through the ceiling, lofted through the attic, and lifted off the roof. A policeman on patrol two blocks away saw flames reach into the sky, and radioed for help.

My father heard the sound of rushing fire, of his own father racing down the hall, banging on doors to wake the family. But when the bedroom doors were opened, the flames sensed fresh and beckoning air from upstairs windows propped open for the breeze. My grandmother and my aunt, then a girl of nineteen, ran through the conflagration – down the stairs, across the vestibule to the front door. My aunt seized the iron handle of the door and pulled. The knob, almost molten, came off in her hand. The skin of her palm sizzled. The door opened. They ran into the street. The crackle of timbers and crash of exploding glass could be heard above the fire's bellow. The remaining family members – my father, my grandfather, my great-grandfather, my great-aunt Eileen – barricaded themselves in my father's room. My grandfather pushed a cabinet across the door, barring the flames from entry.

My father clambered out the open window – later, I would look out that window in late summer at grapes bursting with juice – and slid down the roof. He jumped onto the back porch, rushed to the driveway, and ran to the garage. There he found the ladder. He hefted it to beneath the north window of his room and lifted it as high as it would go. His father climbed out the window, grasped the sill, lowered himself slowly. He hung full length from the window, stretched his toes downward, and touched the top of the ladder. He came down, but the distance from the window to the ladder – and the exertion required to find the toehold – was too much for my great-grandfather, ill as he was with cancer. Eileen, the mountain climber, who could have descended from any window in the house without a ladder, stayed in the burning home with her father. My father and grandfather, helpless, watched them from below. Their faces were silhouetted against a brightening glow from behind.

The fire smashed open the bedroom door, flung the cabinet across the room, and ignited the drapes. One moment the faces were there, shadows against the light; then flame filled the room, and they were gone.

Solomon's temple was desecrated and reconsecrated in a series of ethnic and religious conflicts lasting four centuries. Finally, in 586 BCE, it burned. Hebrew folklore speaks of an angel heralding its destruction: "Let the enemy come and enter the house, for the Master of the house is no longer therein."*

Babylonian invaders set fire to the sanctuary. Flames spread to the four corners of the temple. The intruders seized the high priest and his daughter and set fire to them between the pillars. The *shamir*, concealed since the time of Solomon, lay beneath the left-hand pillar. The priest and his daughter fell burning upon the flagstones.

Father and daughter looked out toward those who had been saved, saw the faces clamoring with despair. Then a pillar of flame rushed over and past them, flaying them with its heat. They heard their own screams as their clothes caught fire. Smoke seared their lungs, halted their breathing. Their skins cracked, and blood sizzled on the burning floor. With terror, with relief, they surrendered to the fire's embrace.

By the time the fire truck came, my father had lost hope. But the firemen had a long ladder, and they thrust it quickly up the side of the house. Two of them went up, snaking a broad hose behind them, and they brought Eileen down. They went up again – twenty seconds, maybe, had passed – and they carried my great-grandfather out. Both survivors were badly burned. Eileen would carry a web of scars on her back and shoulders for the rest of her life. My great-grandfather did not survive the night.

When I was a boy, my older brother and I set so many unsafe

fires with gasoline that today we would be earmarked for the therapist's office. My brother made gunpowder bombs. I set the beach on fire at our summer home. And I remember, with equal parts horror and chagrin, that as a child of about ten I once set fire to a stack of old newspapers in my grandmother's basement. I ignited bits at a time, seeing how far I could let the flames go before they got out of hand. Every time I put out a sheaf of flame, a puff of smoke wafted up, and this is what my grandmother smelled from upstairs. She came running, calling my name, feeling the basement door for heat. She opened it to find me at the bottom of the stairs, sheepishly holding a lighter.

She soaked the newspapers with water. For the first and only time, I saw her tremble. In a voice too soft, utterly unlike the sternness I was accustomed to in her reprimands, she told me that I could have burned the house down. Ashamed and jittery and filled with false bravado, I couldn't understand why she was so upset.

I'm not working the stone much. I feel too uncomfortable, too hot. The kids have picked up chicken pox from one of their playmates, and I'm starting to worry that this may be the cause of my malaise. My older brother contracted chicken pox when I was a boy, but I managed to avoid it. I assume that if I evaded such a virulent illness earlier in my life, I probably have natural immunity. Besides, no spots have appeared on my skin. But as I get weaker, more fevered, I wonder.

The primitive face on my workbench – broad, rough features like a spirit of the volcano – is almost complete. I've finished the eyebrows, mouth, and nose. The cheeks and forehead are more coarse, and the eye sockets require final shaping. But there's not much left to do. The days are uncomfortably warm, and stone dust seems to hang in the humid air of the shop.

I work the eyes, deepening their sockets and shaping the ridges of the eyelids. A tiny crack in the stone, invisible except when I'm working close to the surface, runs from the right brow, across the contour of the right eye, and down toward the lips. When I study it with a magnifying glass, I see that it's streaked inside with a filament of red. Not the dull ruddiness of rusted iron, but brighter, almost crimson. I'm not sure what it is. Orthoclase maybe, or some kind of zeolite. It's a small incursion, slender as a thread. It merges with the landscape of the face like a blood vessel beneath the skin.

I shift my working position frequently; not only because I'm uncomfortable, and shifting around seems to help, but because I need to check my perspective on the shape of the features, and this requires that I step back for a wider view. Working in this way – up close, then lifting my head to look from a distance – I begin to have two distinct impressions. When my focus is tight on the eye sockets, my face a couple of inches from the surface, I perceive only the stone and the diamond cutter, whirring away. But when I straighten up to assess my progress, I feel I'm peering down at someone who is reclining on my workbench. The stone face is starting to look real – old and weathered and rudimentary, but real. Once, when I scan the forehead to see how its shape blends with the ridges of the brow, I have the impression that the eyes open, momentarily, then close again.

Maybe it's time to stop for a while.

The captives were taken from the temple of ashes. The foundation stone of the sanctuary was blackened by heat. The ark was gone. The *shamir* and the scrolls of origin, secreted within the fallen pillars, had vanished. The prophecies of folklore say that in the end time the well on the mountain will overflow, cascade into the valley, and follow the path of the captives eastward. It will roll away the sediment and the scree as it flows, revealing the location of all the treasures buried by the angels on the day of the temple's destruction.

The captors and their exiles threaded their way, five hundred miles across an indifferent desert, to the city of Babylon (fifty-five miles south of what is now Baghdad, in modern Iraq). The captives shuffled in chains, their heads bowed by the hammer of the sun. The Babylonian king – the mystic and savant Nebuchadnezzar – watched the horizon for the dust trail of their approach.*

Near the end of the long march, the column of travelers came to a meander of the Euphrates. The captives, deprived of sustenance for a fortnight, kept alive by bare rations of water, fell down the bank to the river's edge. They drank, long drafts of succor and lament.*

That night, a cloud descended onto the plain. On the confused and foggy ground, several captives saw a pillar of fire whirling southward, and they followed. The cloud concealed their escape. They ran, desperate and stumbling, suddenly and inexplicably freed from their chains. The pillar of fire guided them until morning, when they came to a territory bordered on three sides by the sea. As they crossed into this land, a river swollen with tumbled boulders plowed across the desert behind them, sealing off the fourth side and protecting them from pursuit. These refugees, fresh with the vigor of escape, stayed in the land of their salvation. They vanished into what is now Saudi Arabia, what was then the southern desert.* Eventually, after a thousand years, their tale would wander back to Jerusalem.

There were some that night who saw the pillar of fire but – whether out of fear, loyalty, or destiny – did not follow. Among them were four companions, one from each corner of the Hebrew kingdom: Daniel, Hananiah, Mishael, and Azariah. They were secured together by a single loop of chain during the desert journey, and they resolved – come what may – to remain with the captives. On the night the pillar appeared, Daniel gazed upon it, as though transfixed, and fell to the ground, seized by a vision. Later he told his comrades that they must endure their captivity until its conclusion; but what he had seen, he would not say.

When they reached Babylon, its avenues festooned with images of strange gods, the captives were led into a courtyard beneath the terrace of the pagan king. Nebuchadnezzar, supine on a litter, gazed down at the captives with mingled disdain and hope. He was a man haunted by dreams. His own sages and magicians had been unable to interpret his visions or to provide him with medicine to allay his restless nights. Haggard and forlorn in his palace, Nebuchadnezzar had heard of wonders from the west: a man wrestling with a god upon the mountain, a stone that could build as well as heal. Perhaps there was one among the captives who might be pressed into useful service.

Nebuchadnezzar ordered the prisoners freed from their chains. He provided food for them, the first they had eaten since their bondage. It was fine food: dates shiny with olive oil, figs, sweet cucumbers, almonds roasted with honey. They ate grapes and yellow melons stuffed with pearl barley. Many wondered that their situation had turned from captivity to seduction; but such speculations were washed away by the flow of goat's milk spiced with cinnamon.

When the Hebrews had finished and rested in the palm shade of the courtyard, Nebuchadnezzar invited them into his own temple. Inside the sanctuary stood an idol of Marduk, conqueror of the serpent, lord of creation. Marduk brandished a thunderbolt, and his tunic was adorned with stars. The Hebrews were instructed to bow down before this god of storms, for Babylon would henceforth be their home and Marduk their lord. They knelt, some from fear, some from weariness, some from the wonderment of their survival. Some complied because the god of their ancestors had clearly abandoned them or had been defeated by the invaders. How else to account for the destruction of Solomon's temple? Singly, in pairs, in groups of families, the Hebrews knelt. Their silence, and the rustle of their ragged clothing, whispered through the colonnades of the temple.

Four men remained standing: Daniel, Hananiah, Mishael, and Azariah. From the altar, where Nebuchadnezzar stood shakily beneath the thunderbolt of Marduk, he again asked the rebels to kneel. Instead, Daniel called out to Nebuchadnezzar, "We respect your kingship, and we surrender to our captivity. But we do not surrender our spirits, which are sworn to the allegiance of the Unnameable."

The Babylonian king gestured to the guards and replied: "I am told that you worship a god of fire. I will send you home to him."

Behind the temple, facing east, from where the mountain wind hurtled across the desert, Nebuchadnezzar maintained a coliseum of fire. Its flames were nurtured by the trunks of Lebanon cedars thrust in from high scaffolds. Sheets of flame twisted up from the burning ground, curled higher than the ziggurat adjacent to the temple. The fire pit glowed with massive coals, crackling and humming with heat.

The four companions remained quiet – resigned, perhaps prayerful. The guards prodded them toward a platform high above the fierce heat. When they reached it, they looked back toward the summit of the temple, from where Nebuchadnezzar watched. The king lifted his hand, in greeting and dismissal. The guards pushed Daniel and his friends forward, over the precipice, into the fire.*

My body temperature climbs: slowly at first, over several days, then rapidly, frighteningly, until chilled sweat runs off me in rivulets. My skin begins to blister. Definitely chicken pox, the "creeping disease," as it was once called. The first twenty or so blisters – on the back of my neck, on my face, scattered across my rib cage – are dime-sized; the skin on their flanks is swollen and sensitive. The kids, for whom this illness was merely an inconvenience, didn't get many blisters, and I'm hopeful that my symptoms will be similar. They're a couple of weeks ahead of me, well past the fever stage. For them, only a few vestiges of the largest pox remain.

But the course of my illness is different.* My skin erupts alarmingly; by the end of the second day, I count three hundred pus-filled blisters on my face alone. The rest of my body is similarly tattooed, in archipelagoes and chains of red affliction spreading across my skin. Dozens of pox emerge in my mouth and down my throat. It becomes difficult to swallow. Each of these hundreds or thousands of blisters – who could count them all? – is an outpost of discomfort: hot, sensitive, insistent.

The chicken pox virus attacks nerve endings in the skin. The blisters are the body's response. Only the soles of my feet and my palms are spared. Everywhere else is a mess of heat and pain. When I try to cool myself by splashing a little water on my face, the sting is instant and electric.

I cannot sit or lie down; the pressure is too much. So I walk, for a full night. Through the dark halls of our home, circling from kitchen to living room, wandering, saturated with fatigue. By morning, more blisters have appeared. Ruefully, I wonder if I have the same number of marks on my skin as there are fragments of white microcline in the stone.

There's no mistaking what this is all about. I may have been infected by blind chance, but mythological tales of fire have set me alight. How could I immerse myself so deeply in the fiery stone, in the lore of burning ancestors and pillars of fire, without being so affected? Early on, I resolved to let this endeavor guide me in its own way; had I known of this eventuality, I'm not sure I would have signed on. The pain grows, coming in waves of burning heat that migrate up and down my body, scorching me with every pass. I once worked as a pain management counselor, but by the third day my coping is threadbare.

Not since Edfu, I realize, have I been this ill; not since many years ago, after I visited the Temple of Horus, where the oldest tales of the Kem are inscribed, and soon succumbed to an ailment that almost killed me. It took me more than three years to recover; and I have not, since that encounter, struggled with anything remotely as scary. But as the fatigue of rambling around the house and the pain become altogether too much, I experience the same feeling as I did then: the impulse to fight crumbles in the face of an imperative to surrender.

I must sit down, collect myself, try to show some appreciation for my wife and kids, whose ministrations I've been unable to receive during this long slide. I choose a spot in the living room, on the raised marble hearth of the fireplace. The stone is smooth and cold; its coolness is a balm, almost, upon my fractured skin. The irony of my position – in front of the fire screen – is a sliver of torpid humor. It seems I cannot avoid the fire after all; I must go into it, through to the other side. I wonder if my grandmother felt this way, when she dreamed of a fire, then was woken the next night by the clamor of flames devouring her house. I wonder: Is fire the agent of the soul's purification, as the Kem myths claim? "And Isis, queen of all magic, put the child Horus in the fire, that he might become immortal."* What am I to make of Margaret Laird, burning at the stake, or my ancestor Henrietta DesBrisay, consumed when she fell into a cooking fire? Or my great-grandfather, huddled and dying on the floor of my father's boyhood room? Or Daniel, tossed into the flames by a desperate king?

I burn upon the hearth, wondering what unfinished dreams I have inherited.

Daniel rolled through the burnished air, tumbling, falling into the fire. The roar of flames entered him, consumed him. Out of the corner of his eye, as he spun down toward the fire pit, he saw the jumbled forms of his friends somersaulting behind him. The fire enclosed them all. They fell and fell.

But they did not burn up. They descended, realizing with wonder that the flames were not destroying them. The blaze brightened around them, forged a cocoon of fire in which they settled, gently, onto black coals white with heat.

Unharmed, clothed in flame, the four companions met at the center of the conflagration. The intensity of the fire had shaped a clearing occupied solely by sheets of brilliant flame. The ground was blasted smooth. Each of the company came into this clearing from the direction in which he had fallen from the scaffold: Hananiah from the north, Mishael from the east, Azariah from the south, Daniel from the west. They were quiet, each knowing the source of their protection, each glimpsing fragments of Daniel's vision at the riverbank. They stood, an illuminated quaternity within the fire's core, then walked eastward, out of the flames, onto the dark plain rushing with wind. Their cocoons of fire remained with them, surrounded them with radiance. Deliberately, slowly, they made their way far out onto the russet ground of Babylon, and waited for Nebuchadnezzar.

The king watched with terror from the summit of the ziggurat. Now he came, summoned by the mystery. He climbed – with shaky and resolute steps – down the terraces of the temple, between the gardens hanging from its flanks, across the courtyard. He took the trail that meandered onto the plain. Ahead, four signal fires blazed in the twilight. Nebuchadnezzar walked until dark, until the blaze of his furnace had dwindled behind him and the beacons in front were his only illumination. Then, his terror mellowed by weariness, he came upon the comrades. He stood at the threshold of their circle. Daniel motioned to a natural rise of the ground at the circle's center; Nebuchadnezzar moved forward and took his place there. His legs crumpled under him, and he sat on the hard ground. The four companions also sat – as though the king were an honored guest and not a tyrant, the Hebrews hosts and not captives.

Daniel spoke. "You dream of a creature, a colossus of terri-fying stature."

"Its head is crafted of gold," said Hananiah.

"Its chest and arms are silver," said Mishael.

"Its belly and thighs are brass," said Azariah.

"Its legs," said Daniel, "are forged of iron, and its feet are made of clay. But not wholly clay. The bones of the feet are forged of iron."

Nebuchadnezzar's vision blurred, and he was suddenly aware of the cold ground beneath him. He could manage only a whisper: "How is it you know of such things?"

"We have passed through fire," Daniel said.

"We are now the four," continued Hananiah.

"Each of us is one letter of the sacred, unnameable name," said Mishael.*

"Nothing is hidden from us," said Azariah.

The four companions – clockwise around the circle, each delivering single phrases, each following the previous speaker without pause – told Nebuchadnezzar the rest of his dream.

They spoke to him of the stone: radiant, spinning, polished like a jewel but not shaped by human hands. This stone approached the dreamer, filled his vision, showed him shapes of darkness and light swirling. But Nebuchadnezzar could not make out the meaning of these simulacra. The stone turned, retreated from him, and whirled toward the creature of the dream, the colossus of metal and clay. Above its silver flank, the golden head turned, as though in defiance. Nebuchadnezzar heard the thunder of earthen feet with their core of iron. The stone hurtled into the feet of the colossus, destroying them. The beast roared and crashed to the ground. Its monstrous anatomy – clay, iron, brass, silver, and gold – shattered as it fell, exploding into shards that mixed together like chaff on the summer threshing floor.* Then the dreamer saw a wind coming, over the dark plain. It lifted the scattered remains of the colossus and carried them away.

The stone remained. It spun, languid, in the mind's eye of the dreamer. Then it began to grow, expanding across the plain. It broadened into the earth, spread to the four quarters of the horizon, lifted its shoulders and summit heavenward. The sun was blocked from view, the sea pitched with turmoil, the air was heavy. All around the dreamer, darkness prevailed. He stood at the base of the mountain, looked upward, and screamed.

Nebuchadnezzar gazed across the clearing at Daniel, whose face was serene, though flames crackled everywhere upon him. The king tried to listen for the background warble of night birds that he so often heard in his garden. The landscape was quiet, rapt by the spectacle of four fiery beings and a beggar. The recounting of his dream had been exact. Were these men angels? He paused in this speculation, but only for a moment.

Knowing that he must complete the ritual, must know, he asked his burning question: "What does the dream mean?"

"It is a prophecy," said Daniel.

"An omen," said Hananiah.

"An augury," said Mishael.

"It is not only for you," said Azariah.

The speakers told Nebuchadnezzar of the ages of the world indicated in the dream: golden, protected by the circle of time; silver, heralded by the tumult of tongues; brass, crafted with hammer and forge; iron, shaped by the yearning eye; and clay, during which the yearning eye turns back upon itself. Their voices flickered in the dark, sent out tendrils of flame into the clearing, wrapped Nebuchadnezzar in a dream of which he was only a fleeting fragment.

"The stone," said Daniel, finishing, "cannot be forgotten or destroyed. It shall break apart the collected reveries and visions of every age. They will be as wind upon the mountain. And the mountain itself will be what it has always been: the ceaseless transformation of the world's becoming."

Daniel's fire brightened. Above him, flames twisted heavenward. As Nebuchadnezzar watched, sparks from Daniel's corona gathered and jumped, like fireflies in the dark, across to Hananiah. The fiery cocoon of Hananiah blossomed; sparks arced around to Mishael and Azariah. The four companions grew in brilliance, yet Nebuchadnezzar could not shield his eyes. A ring of fire encircled him. It raced around the clearing, scorched the air, spiraled into the sky above. The ring became a column, the column a pillar, and the pillar a radiant cyclone whose distant aperture – opening to the heavens, perhaps – Nebuchadnezzar could just make out, tiny in the far distance overhead.

He could no longer see the companions; they had merged with the fire – if ever they were anything else. His clothes smoked, his skin blistered. But the nightmare had fallen away, and Nebuchadnezzar was again the king he had been. For that, even if these were his last moments, he was thankful. But the conflagration did not consume him. It lifted off into the west, leaving a circle of blackened earth and a lone man, bewildered, on the plain of his homeland.

PART III

PILGRIMAGE

HAJJ

SIX

The blisters on my skin do not abate. I burn, far beyond the typical acute phase of chicken pox. My fever dwindles, and exhaustion yields to tentative movement, but I do not heal. For weeks, during which my complexion is that of a man scorched by flying too close to the sun – a boy with feathers and wax and a long fall – I can hardly muster strength to eat. I think about mortality. My idleness and my dependence are so pervasive that I feel as though I am undergoing a slow, intractable dying. I wait, while my body struggles to subdue the heat, while the damaged nerves in my skin confuse the virus with flame. Along my ribs, stretching around to the hollow of my spine, across a swath where the blisters are blood red, my skin is hot to the touch. The heat is more intense than I would have thought my body could produce. When I place my hand on my flank, my instinct is to pull back, away from the heat, as though my body were a stovetop still too warm after cooking.

I can't read much, or exercise, or keep my recalcitrant moods in check. I sit on the couch, look out at the shaded forest, watch my kids and my wife water the garden, and think about death. I have not yet come out of the fire. I lie on the desiccated ground, sheet around me like a shroud, and I attend the ritual of my own dissolution. I am buffeted along by something – an odd, archaic query, an identification with the lost and the forgotten. This odyssey has consumed me; I can no longer muster the energy to master it. I surrender to it, as one surrenders in faith to the stake. I am carried like smoke upon the wind.

The stone lies undisturbed in my shop, unworked, patient. Though it still shows the marks of its birth, the fire has long since cooled. The rate of cooling determined the size and distribution of white flecks in the stone's matrix. I wonder, as weeks pass and many of my blisters seem to be turning to scars, if the rate of my own cooling will serve a similar function.

Eventually the exiles made their way back home, to Jerusalem, the City of Peace ever haunted by war.* They came singly and in groups, scattered and wandering across the desert, carrying with them nothing but the weight of memory. The temple was gone, the stone of foundation bare, the ark vanished. The scorched peak of the sacred mountain lay like a broken watchtower, black and derelict. Moist air from the western sea carried with it the scent of salt and olives.

For the exiles, whose homecoming will not be completed until the end of days, time had stopped. While the ages unfurled around them, they set to the task of rebuilding the temple, of redeeming their infinite catastrophe. Their descendants, Jews in the contemporary world, are still building it today: in the country of the heart, which is not fractured but still preserves the innocence and promise of lost days.

Today the foundation stone lies within an Islamic shrine, the Dome of the Rock, on the wide summit of Jerusalem's Temple Mount. More than a thousand years after the destruction of Solomon's temple, Muhammad ascended from the stone to meet with the Unnameable. Jews and Muslims share and contest the mythological history of the place, and this is the essence of the conflict between them. Now cracked and worn, imprinted with the quarrying marks of Crusaders, still flat where the ark once stood, the stone lies at the heart of the world's most persistent conflict. The Holy Land is so because of the stone at its center, its oldest and primary relic, the foundation of every subsequent devotion. The keeper of the stone is the guardian of the gate of heaven.[*]

Not all the exiles returned from Babylon. Many remained, made peace with Nebuchadnezzar, settled down beside their enemies upon the verdant fields. (Today, of thirteen million Jews worldwide, about 120 are left in Iraq. Saddam Hussein ensured the exile of the rest.) Some went west, back to the lands of the Kem and farther, across the parched face of Africa, north toward Europe. They were dispersed – *diaspora* – as sand thrown to the wind. In this migration, families and clans and tribes became familiar strangers to one another, wanderers, nomads. Most found their way back, across the swells of centuries, either to the Holy Land or to the communities of Jews that sprang up in every place. There were some who vanished.

When the pillar of fire came at night to the captives at the river shore, and Daniel fell into his vision of fire, those who followed the beacon were never seen again. They crossed into the southern territory and were gone.

As the pillar of fire faded into morning, the refugees scrambled upon scree slopes warmed on their eastern flanks. To the west, the hills were still cool and shadowed. They saw hawk prints on the crest of a windblown dune: a sweeping indent of feathers, the crisp ligature of hollow bones incised upon the sand. They continued south, skirting the western mountains hiding the sea, treading stands of acacia, scavenging dates from dry valleys and sun-beaten plains. They knew the great ocean which encircled the earth lay to the south, along their path, and that eventually they would reach it.* But they knew it was not to be their destination. They were, instead, following the track of Abraham.

Before the exile, before Solomon, before Jacob had wrestled upon the sacred mountain, Abraham came south to find refuge for his son Ishmael. Along the track that the refugees would follow centuries later, Abraham led Ishmael and his mother, Hagar – woman of the Kem, ancestral matriarch of the Arab peoples.

Ishmael was fourteen when his brother Isaac was born. More precisely, they were half brothers: Ishmael's mother was Hagar, and Isaac's was Sara, the first wife of Abraham. Sara was thought to have been barren, and Hagar – the second wife – was sought so that Abraham might not die childless. But when Isaac, a child of miracles, was born to Sara, the resulting turmoil between Sara and Hagar became too much for the family. Now there were two boys, two wives. Who was the favorite? Would the boys share equally in Abraham's inheritance? Who would care for the mothers as they aged? Eventually the family fractured, and Hagar was forced out. She and Ishmael fled into the desert. Abraham led them south.

Isaac and Ishmael, boys who had played together, elder leading younger to find rabbits hidden in the high grass, were lost to each other. Isaac, saved from sacrifice, became the father of Jacob, and thereby the father of all Jews; Ishmael, the exile, became the ancestor of the desert peoples.[*]

When the Babylonian refugees made their way south, when they imagined Abraham threading the canyons and open plains, when they lay beneath the stars on cold nights and watched the bear spin above the northern horizon, they told one another snatches of the tale: how Abraham had set out with Hagar and the boy Ishmael, how they meandered in dry and empty lands, following ravines, how the water in their drinking skins was used up in the paltry shade of thorn bushes.[*]

Abraham's was the first hajj, the first holy pilgrimage into a radiant terrain, bright and sharp with outlines: ocher hills, hardpan streaked with yellow, far-off cliffs hidden with haze. Sometimes, when the wind drew moisture up from the south, Ishmael smelled frankincense. Heat rippled up from the plain, flowed into the texture of water – but only the texture, not the substance – and dwindled into the sky. Reflections ghosted before them, led them across dry gulches that once, in the beginning days of the world, were cascades of clear water. They found no wells to drink from; and as they walked on, haggard and persistent, following the glimpses that Abraham saw of a pillar of fire shifting in turbulent air upon the horizon, Ishmael lost his strength. He stumbled, caught himself, lost his balance again and fell to the ground. Hagar went to him, swept her sleeve across his gaunt and burning brow, shielded his eyes from the hammer of the sun. She turned toward Abraham. He stopped, looked south, toward his vision in the distance, then returned to mother and son crouched in the relentless light of the afternoon.

High up, a heron coasted on a spiral of ascending air. Abraham looked up to see the sacred bird circling. It heartened him, this witness, the immortal bird. In every tale that Abraham knew, its presence denoted wisdom and prosperity. From his pouch, slung sidelong and now almost empty, he retrieved the white covering cloth they used as a sun shield. He unfolded it, placed one edge upon Hagar's shoulder, and let the rest billow across the prone form of Ishmael. The boy reached with one slender arm to seize a corner of the fabric, pulled it to his side, and was still again. The covering lay like a shroud upon him.

Abraham knelt beside Hagar and wondered what to do. The bird wheeled high overhead, promising redemption. It looked down upon three tiny figures, crouched among pale pebbles on the dark sand, a fleck of white upon a desolate expanse of umber.

During my convalescence, when the television is often my only slender connection to the wider world, I watch images of the Taliban attempting to destroy the mythological inheritance of Afghanistan. They attack stone Buddhas with rocket launchers, hack the heads from statues of white marble, crush the remnants of two millennia into shards of broken rock. The rationale they offer to an incredulous and outraged world is that the true Islamic state suffers no infidel idols. Did not Muhammad, almost fourteen hundred years ago, destroy the pagan idols in the holy sanctuary at Mecca? In those formative days of Islam's struggle for ascendancy, the relics of archaic gods shared the sanctuary with Allah, the one who would become the sole god of the deserts. Muhammad cast them out, as the Taliban were now casting out their own history.

I see pictures, before and after, of the world's largest Buddha statue – almost two hundred feet high – reduced to rubble. I hear Mullah Muhammad Omar, Taliban supreme leader, wonder at the umbrage his actions have provoked in the world community. He says, "All we are breaking is stones."

This desecration – of a people's history, of their collective memory, of the sacred faces that have nurtured their culture – becomes for me, in my strange and fragile circumstances, a personal affront. My effort, since before I found the stone on the mountain, has been to collect the remnants of a fractured past, to shape them into meaning, to find my own affiliation with distant ancestors. Now, as I wander in the fugue of my illness, fatigued and confused and immersed in the well of myth, I find that there are those whose aim is to destroy the past. We are at cross-purposes, they and I, and the struggle between us is not an abstraction.

I will fashion my stone, and it will stand in defiance of erasure. I will tell the story of its passage, surrender it into the stream of other tales. It is all one tale, one stone, one face. The impulse to divide that face, to choose fragments and versions of the story, disowning all others, is part of the mythological inheritance. It does not begin with the Taliban. Cultures and religions, clans and families; in every context where the Other is projected outward, differing tales prosper. This is the alchemy of myth; its ferment is diversity and wisdom. Its dregs are the forgetting that comes over the storyteller, the deliberate exclusion of the Other as ignorant, foolish, inferior. Racism is the most pervasive mythic impulse.

But the Other is our own people, our own ancestors. Mullah Muhammad Omar, Taliban leader, and I, writer and occasional stone carver, share the same heritage. We are one family, Saddam Hussein and George Bush and Osama bin Laden and I. Not so long ago – some time between the present and six or seven hundred years ago – our ancestries crossed. Countless undiscovered genealogical threads connect us.

It's simple mathematics: everyone possesses two parents, four grandparents, eight great-grandparents; the lineage of our direct ancestors spreads exponentially into the past.* At some point in the fourteenth century CE – about twenty-eight generations ago – the number of direct ancestors of every person living today equaled the number of people living in the world at that time: roughly five hundred million. The common ancestors of everyone of European and Middle Eastern descent lived just over six hundred years ago.

These threads lead far back, weaving a myriad of links to the archaic past. We are, all of us – every person alive today – direct descendants of Muhammad, Abraham, Khafre, of every mythic character who populates the old tales. The shattered Buddhas, sculpted two thousand years ago by our forebears, were made in the image of one of our shared ancestors.

Race, culture, ethnicity, nationalism: these are fables of difference, of the Other, written in the narratives of conquest, war, and exile. I do not choose that path; instead, I claim the tales as one tale, as my own, as the legacy of nomads and sages and boys lost in the desert. Abraham and Hagar and Ishmael ghost inside me, around the well of my knowing, and their tale – like every other – cannot be untold.

Abraham followed the spiraling path of the heron, out from the huddled forms of Hagar and Ishmael. He walked in widening circles, looking for water. Hagar watched his dust trail rise into the haze of the afternoon. He crested a small rise and was gone.

On the ground, muscles strained by dehydration and contracting in protest, Ishmael began to writhe. The luster of his skin was gone; it lay sunken around his eyes, flat and taut across his cheek. Hagar did not wish to watch him die. Frantic, desperate, she scanned the plain for signs of Abraham, for a miraculous indication that her son – and soon after, she herself – would not perish alone. The sere terrain was punctuated by two small hills nearby. With the last of her strength, Hagar climbed them.[*] Perhaps she would see Abraham from higher ground. Perhaps she had failed to glimpse a well of flowing water, or a river carving deep banks. Or a blue lake, waves playing out the rhythm of solace. She shielded her eyes and walked.

The first hill, five hundred paces north of where Ishmael lay, was bare. A stretch of flat and sandy ground meandered beyond it. Hagar stood on the summit, turned, gazed west and south. No sign, no track, nothing but a jumble of small scree hills on the horizon. She paused, as if by waiting she might invoke nameless redeeming spirits; then she clambered down again. The second hill lay southeast of the first, along the contour of a shallow cleft in the ground. Hagar followed the landscape. Midway between hills, she began running. Quickened by a sense of urgency, desperate and hopeful and terrified, she ran: with heavy strides, coughing, drawing heat and dust into her with every breath. The sounds of her labor broke the silence of the afternoon.

She reached the base of the second hill. Stunted cassia bushes crouched in the slim shadow of the western slope. Again she climbed, this time wavering, pushing down with her arms upon her knees, upward, slow and circuitous. She called out in low gasps, as though her voice might seek and find what her eyes could not. There was nothing upon the summit. The bowl of the hard-baked earth lay round and indifferent. The plain was desolate.

But no – she saw something: a brief shimmer, twenty paces from where the small, white form of Ishmael lay. Like a cloud, low and fleeting, a cartwheeling breeze with a darker shape hidden behind it. A wave of heat moved on the rocks, ephemeral. Then it was gone, and she heard Ishmael cry out from below. A distant sound, pitched high, keening. Hagar ran down the slope.

Ishmael was writhing in water. His movements had scraped away the hardpan and released the flow of a hidden well.[*] Mother and son, redeemed from what they had reconciled themselves to be their final moments, drank the clear water. And Abraham, returning from his errand not with water or with rescue, but with report of a strange encounter, saw his wife and son washing the grime from their faces.

I dream of water and fire, while the routines of daily life encircle me and I drift, disconsolate and desultory. I dream of the holy mountain, of the well of origin, of my hands cupping cool waters. Above me, the lava wall rises skyward. But I no longer know if I am dreaming, or if a hidden door has opened inside me and I have stumbled into the beginning tales.

I'm not sure anymore what's real, what I've imagined, what rises of its own accord, implacable and insistent, from the bones of the spirit. Carl Jung spoke of the collective unconscious, the shared mythological and instinctive history of the human species. I feel as though I've fallen into that landscape of relics and ghosts.

Finding no water, Abraham turned back. He made his way toward the spot where Ishmael lay; but he did not see Hagar upon the hill, nor did he see the boy. Instead he came across the foundations of an old temple made of black and uncut stones. The roof was gone and the walls were in ruin. Three ashlars – the lintel and posts of the portal – lay tumbled on the sand. The black stones, heated by the sun, were too hot to touch. Somewhere near this derelict place, Abraham knew, there must have been a spring or a well of water. Perhaps it had retreated underground and now lay beneath him, out of reach but close enough, almost, that if he clawed his way into the earth he might reach down to it. But such thoughts, he knew, are the mark of one deranged by lack of water.

Abraham walked around the enclosure, unsure what to do, circling and looking and wondering that such a structure would be here, in the empty lands. Seven times he circled the site, ever anxious about his errand and more certain of salvation. On his seventh turn, as he rounded the easternmost corner of the old temple, Abraham saw, from within the curtain of heat rising from the stones, three forms resolving themselves. At first he thought the figures were stones, and that the illusion of movement had come from the turbulent air. But the images did not waver. They came toward him, black shapes, hooded, faces hidden.

The three sisters, guardians of the temple, spoke to Abraham: of forgotten things, of vanished gods, of the rhythms of creation. They told him of the sages, the Shebtiw who had fashioned the enclosure with words, who had called the sisters from their sleeping.* The sages sometimes took the shape of herons and launched themselves, at twilight, into the sky. This is how they had come to the empty lands, from another, distant errand. They remained in the desert, speaking words that thickened into shapes, singing the stones into form on the waiting ground. From three stones, the Shebtiw fashioned the guardians: in appearance like old women, in temperament like fire cooled with water.

The sages had departed, traveling south toward the wide sea and the expanse of other tales: in Tibet, India, Mexico. But the sisters remained, venerated as goddesses, preserving the sanctuary for thousands of years. Pilgrims came: to hear prophecy, to steep in the wonder of the crones, to meditate in the temple. The structure, open to the elements, was shaped by the wild forces of the place. Some of the stones fell. But the cornerstone, at the southeastern edge of the temple, remained solidly in place. This stone, made of basalt, black and radiant, was the gift of the Shebtiw. They had brought it from the well of origin, entrusted it into the care of the sisters. It burned, and there was writing upon it.

When the flood came, and Noah passed over the sunken temple as he searched the waters, the sisters were sustained by the radiant stone. They lay underwater while the deluge buried the sanctuary; and when the waters abated, the temple lay in ruin. The sisters, knowing one would come to redeem the holy place, waited.

When Abraham came, when Hagar watched the indistinct chimera of the temple from the hilltop, when Ishmael cried out, the sisters came forward and drew Abraham into their circle. He was swallowed up by their timelessness, and though he was no more than fifty yards from his wife and son, they failed to see his perambulations. He vanished into the twilight that surrounds every holy place.

Later, as night fell and Abraham lay on the damp ground with Hagar and Ishmael, he pointed northeast and showed them the temple of stones, half buried by the encroaching sands. It lay, mute and manifest, as though it had always been there, beyond the threshold of their encampment, unseen by Hagar and Ishmael until Abraham drew their attention to it. The pillar of fire no longer burned on the horizon.

I slowly come awake. Tentative, uncertain of my direction, I ease myself from slumber. As the Taliban tear down their own ancestral sanctuaries, seeking to do away with their mythic heritage (which is also my own), the impulse for preservation grows in me. I must fight back: by means of the stone on my workbench, by way of tales turning within me. I must sustain the link that joins my children to the well of origin.

I tell Rowan and Avery about an old temple in the desert, a place of sacred pilgrimage that predates Muhammad by thousands of years. I describe to them the Kaaba sanctuary, in Mecca, Islam's holiest site: a flat-roofed building, fifty feet high, walls of mortared blue-gray stone on a foundation older than memory. The word *kaaba* means cube (though two of the walls are forty feet long while the others are thirty-five). The building is empty, save for hanging votive lanterns and three pillars supporting the roof. There is a single door, seven feet above the ground, in the face of the northeastern wall. The sacred black stone is set into the southeast corner of the outer wall. In modern times, the Kaaba structure is draped with black brocade, made yearly in Egypt, embroidered in gold with passages from the Qur'an.* (The holy of holies in Jerusalem, the shrine crafted by Hiram with the *shamir*, where the ark rested upon the foundation stone, was also a cube, of approximately the same dimensions.*)

At the kitchen table, over oatmeal and bagels, I try to explain to my children why the Taliban would destroy or proscribe everything not in keeping with their radical interpretation of Islamic law. The reasons are not complicated: the pious always wish to destroy the Other – the neighbor, the guest, the awkward ancestor – to flood time with their own myths, to scrape the horizon clear of old tales. They never succeed.

Myths cannot be excised from their origins: the Kaaba is a relic of the Other, of the Hebrew Abraham, of the three crones who were once venerated throughout the Arabian Peninsula. The Islamic guardians of the Kaaba sanctuary are still called Banu Shayba, the Sons of the Old Woman.* In the beginning, when Islam was fresh with revelation, when the messenger Muhammad wrestled with the angel Jibril on the mountain, Jews and Christians and devotees of the three crones were all recognized as followers of the Unnameable's many forms. Later, when the scriptures were collected and codified, the old imperatives crept in: racism, exclusion, violence urged upon the Other. This is the shared heritage of the religions of the Book: in the passage from revelation to scripture, from glimpse to certainty, animosities proliferate.*

Prayer is better than sleep, says the Islamic call to devotion, and storytelling is a kind of prayer: for the enduring, for the mythic, for the ancestral and the numinous. The stories of the infidel and pagan past are at once the objects of the Taliban's ire and the foundation of their own religious culture. In telling these tales – stones, fire, goddesses in the desert – I resist the Taliban's impulse for erasure. I rouse myself from the slumber of my ailment and enter the fractured world again.

The blisters on my skin begin to heal, though it looks as though numerous white scars will remain. The most prominent, on my face and brow, are unlike the scars I've picked up by way of various mishaps. The pox scars are not uniformly pale but rather chameleonlike, turning from white to red and back again. They are the texture of parchment. Sometimes they become inflamed, like embers fanned by wind, though frequently they are cool. The rest of my skin remains sensitive, prone to welts and red blotches wherever it is rubbed or touched. Every morning, my body is tattooed with patches of red where I lay against folds in the bedsheets. During the day, blooms and blushes migrate across my chest and neck and face. If I itch or rub, marks remain for hours: traceries, lines, hieroglyphs rising and fading upon me.

Eventually I visit the dermatologist; he tells me I've developed a condition called dermographism, "writing on the skin." It seems I've taken up the old tales after all, in welt and weal. I think of the stone of origin, on the surface of which, in a text of fire, words are written.

The exiles, led by a pillar of fire, fleeing Babylon and the furnace of Nebuchadnezzar, found the Kaaba rebuilt by Abraham and Ishmael. Courses of green stone, uncut and nestled together like the humps of camels,* rose from the old foundation. The ashlars of the doorway stood upright. The radiant stone, bound by a silver frame in the shape of an eye, remained bound to the outer wall; it looked southeast, to where the Shebtiw had vanished.

The nomads who appeared to the exiles – all of a sudden, like mirages from out of the empty lands – called it al-Hajar al-Aswad, the black stone.

Today the black stone of the Kaaba and the foundation stone of the Hebrews are the last of the sacred stones. Their archaic companions – the *benben* stone of the Kem, the *shamir* of Solomon – are gone. (The *benben* stone has not entirely vanished. As mentioned, the capstone of the Washington Monument and the aluminum pyramid at its peak are modern reproductions in the Kem symbolic tradition.) Perhaps it's true that the Kaaba stone, now broken and fragmented, held together by a silver ligature, is a fragment of the original *benben* stone that fell from the sky before the time of Khafre. Perhaps it was part of the foundation stone in Jerusalem, or was the *shamir*. No one knows.* But the two persistent stones – one venerated in Mecca by Muslims, the other in Jerusalem and venerated by both Jews and Muslims – still lie at the center of devotion. Millions of Jews and well over a billion Muslims preserve and cherish these relics. Even the Christian tradition remembers them: the church is said to be founded upon a rock, and it identifies Jesus as the cornerstone rejected by the builders of Solomon's temple.* In the modern age, so removed from ancient practices and symbols, the stone of origin remains.

The exiles were drawn into the circle of the Bedouins. They settled down beside each other and became one people: wandering the landscape, reading the horizon for the approach of sandstorms, each year returning to the Kaaba on their pilgrimage to the holy places. They preserved the sacred rite, begun by Abraham, of walking seven times around the old temple. And when the sisters appeared to them, as to the travelers of previous ages, the Bedouin learned the true names of things.*

The desert people maintained the sacred site. They cleaned its dark stones, swept sand from the lintel, placed boundary markers around the enclosure. They guarded the well that Ishmael had unearthed, made narrow paths upon the hills that

Hagar had climbed, searching for redemption. They worked the stones of the outer court with whispering sand brought from Sinai: made of clear quartz crystals, hard enough to polish basalt, known for the soft songs it made when blown by the wind.*

The Kaaba has been continually renovated since the time of Abraham, most recently by the construction firm of the bin Laden family, of whom Osama is an exiled son.

In antiquity, the Kaaba's most notable caretakers were the desert tribe called the Quraysh; one of their number, Muhammad, assisted with renovations undertaken in 605 CE. At that time, the three sisters were still venerated. They had not yet departed the temple, following the old gods out of the world. During the life of the Prophet, new courses of blue-gray stone were laid down and mortared above the stones of Abraham (themselves built upon an older foundation). The portal was raised high off the ground, the roof replaced by a shipwrecked carpenter of the Kem.* The black stone was removed and cleaned. Tradition attests that Muhammad resolved the question of who would have the honor of returning the stone to its mountings: he laid it upon a cloak, handed a corner to each of the groups who had assisted in the renovation, and together they lifted the stone into place. Muhammad seated it with his own hands.

The devotion of the desert peoples to the cubic sanctuary, to the black and radiant stone, to the surrounding circular plaza and the minarets they added to the enclosure, spread with them in their later religious conquests. Islamic architecture evolved from the rough-hewn temple of the sisters into complex geometric forms based on the cube, to filigrees and domes and rhythms of enclosed space. The Dome of the Rock in Jerusalem, home of the foundation stone and site of Solomon's temple, was their creation. In Europe, Islamic arches and arabesques inspired the Gothic cathedrals. While Renaissance mystics contemplated the philosopher's stone, the spirit of the Kaaba's black stone made its way among them.

That spirit thrives in the architecture of today: in the geometric patterns of the modern, in the rectilinear forms of urban plazas, in the soaring and slender shapes of minarets in the guise of office towers. In one modern example, the Japanese-American architect Minoru Yamasaki's design for a commercial district was intended to reproduce, in proportion and symbol, the Kaaba sanctuary. Yamasaki's towers were based on the geometry of the cube, delineated by arches at the base and extended heavenward. He provided a fountain to represent the sacred well, and a radial circular pattern for the grounds, mimicking the enclosure surrounding the Kaaba. The office buildings were wrapped with steel filigree, as the Kaaba is wrapped in brocade embroidered with gold. Yamasaki's project was completed in 1976 (the towers were finished earlier, in 1973) in lower Manhattan and was called the World Trade Center.*

The black stone in my shop, veined with blue and flecked with white, lies unfinished on the bench. I haven't worked it for almost two months, during my odd and frightening ailment. I've been fatigued, distracted by my discomfort. The destruction of sacred objects by the Taliban urges me toward healing, toward completion of the work, but it's another month or more before I actually return to the shop. I've left too many things for too long – recreation with the kids, time with Elizabeth, the details of my professional life – and it's August by the time I pick up the rotary carver again.

I thumb the power switch; the tool coughs to life, and I press the whirring cutter into the stone. My hands are tentative, uncertain now of the rhythms of the work after such a protracted hiatus. I shift position several times, looking for the best purchase, listening for changes in the sound of the tool to guide me in shaping the final contours of the eye sockets. The cutter skates across the surface, abrading the material in neat furrows; but I have trouble regulating the cuts. My guidance of the tool is ragged; the abrasions are clipped or extended. Along my forearms and across the backs of my hands, this small, beginning exertion evokes migrant flushes upon my skin: a spreading archipelago of blotches, red clouds rushing, parchment stained with crimson ink. Chicken pox scars glow white against the fine tracery of capillaries at my wrist.

I accomplish no actual work for the first few days: I tire easily, my hands are both sensitive and numb from absence, the cutter jumps around as I try to remember what the stone wants me to do. I go slow. I think again, as so often, of the vanished craftsmen who shaped the Kem sculptures, the temple of Solomon, the Kaaba of the desert. These artifacts were crafted by myth and by hand together, one nurturing the other. The hands that formed the black stone of the desert and the hands of the sculptor of Khafre were of one people, settled together in spirit, remembering the same tales. One thread of persistence:

from the carvers of the Buddhas to the masons in colonial Canada, setting the foundation stone of the old church. One defiant negation of erasure.

I pay attention to the sounds of the stone, to the particular timbre of hard minerals worn down by diamond. In this listening, I rediscover the basalt's own fundamental tone, the octave by which it resonates. It's the music of water. In turn, I find the distinct notes of our encounter, and the finishing of the project begins in earnest.

I splash water onto the dark surface and watch it run in rivulets toward the eyes. The cutter picks up tiny droplets and flings them into mist. The black-blue stone smooths out along the careful rises of the irises, the delicate ridges of the lids. The hollows of the inner sockets fill with a tincture of dark water. I see fleeting reflections upon the surface, and I think of the frame of silver that surrounds the black stone of the Kaaba. I round out the sockets, then shape the pupils in small sweeping motions, remembering the old Jewish fable of the redeemed temple reflected in the pupil of the eye. Water splashes back at me; I am soaked in memory and prophecy. My skin cools.

These myths I have stumbled upon, that at times I have wrenched from the bindings of tradition, that I have collected and drawn into my own sphere like wayward ghosts, are fragments of humanity's collective tale, deposited royalty-free in the chambers of the heart. They are not owned by a single group, or by history, by culture, by the academy. They roam, exiled, gathering up the skirts of their foundations and wandering across the landscape. They depart, surrendering the guises of uniformity and consistency. They reinvent themselves, spinning new versions from old, ever moving. We find relics in their wake – a shard of iron, a snatch of cloth, a red balloon rising into the sky – and we claim the talisman as the symbol of our pedigree. We are the chosen people, the ones of whom the whirlwind spoke. Look, the proof is here: in the temple, where the first and timeless stone is kept. But myths move on, old and always new; if they don't, they die.

The origin myths of the Hebrews meandered east and south, followed the captives across the desert, found themselves welcomed into the enclosure of the sisters. By the time of Islam, a thousand years after the exiles followed the pillar of fire in search of the fable of Abraham, the Hebrew tales had become the mythic foundation of the Arab peoples.*

I coast over the cheeks and forehead, smoothing the stone's texture, readying the surface for the minimal polishing that will complete the work. I run the rotary cutter along the ridge where nose and eyes meet, deepening and clarifying the rough scarification. Back and forth, from the summit of one eye socket to the other, I whittle down abraded edges and surfaces pocked by the cutter's facets. I winnow down a crevice on the chin, polish the upper lip with careful strokes. Where the cheeks narrow toward the sensuous sweep of the mouth, the face looks distinctly feminine. All along, as I've been thinking about my own ancestral face, carving instinctively, guided by the archaic dreams of remote ages, I've assumed that the face, like my own, will be that of a man: after Khafre, after the radiant stone of Solomon and Jacob and Abraham. Now, as I look on it in the refracted light of the goddess tales – matriarchs and sisters and crones, languid as birds wheeling above the desert – the cast of the face is unmistakably feminine. Perhaps, as I've eased the rough edges into smoothness, as I've washed the surfaces and made the abrupt planes softer, the contours of the stone have shifted. But it's more than that: from the first outlines that I made of the mouth – using the grinder, a delicate touch, and a surplus of anxiety – the sensuous lines of the lips have been there. The slope of the cheeks has always been slender, the jaw sleek and graceful. It's not simply the polishing that has helped these features to emerge. They were there, and I did not see them; they were there, and not there.

So goes the Arabic aphorism *Kan ya ma kan*: there was, there was not. There was a mountain, and a well, and a stone of fire burning with endless beginnings. And a people, nomads and sages and exiles, who revered the crones of the desert. There was a clan of divine beings who had seeded the world with words, made books from stones, had long since left the empty lands. There was not a true god before Allah, a temple built by sisters of the word, goddesses who remembered a time before history.

Kan ya ma kan is a conundrum of Islamic theogony, symbolized by a putative incident in the life of Muhammad in which he first accepted, then rejected, the intercessory status of the three sisters of the Mecca temple: al-Lat (the goddess), al-'Uzza (the mighty one), and Manat (the other), goddess of prophecy. The Islamic tale of these events is called both the fable of the Satanic verses and the story of the cranes; after all, the sisters were of the same mythological family as Thoth, and as the Shebtiw: immortal, slender birds whose art is stillness amid the cacophony of change. They share the convoluted theogony of the Greek sisters the Fates, the witches of *Macbeth*, and the three sisters of Norse mythology, who live beside a well beneath Yggdrasil, the tree of life. (The Scandinavian myths are not, in fact, as removed from the pre-Islamic tales as might be expected; a number of Arabic words appear in ancient Icelandic literature.*)

Here are the lines that were first included, and then removed from, the Qur'an: "Have you thought of al-Lat and al-'Uzza and Manat, the third, the other? These are the high-flying cranes; verily their intercession is to be hoped for."*

According to the oldest Islamic histories, Muhammad agreed to include the sisters as angels within the pantheon of Allah. This strategic move ensured, among the polytheists of Mecca, a foothold by which the Prophet might spread his doctrine of Allah, the One God. The sisters had been divine mistresses of the desert for thousands of years, and the nomads were not about to betray them for a middle-aged man who had a vision in a cave. After his concession – after Muhammad realized that his compromise enabled the existing theology to consume his own, to migrate into it and subsume it within its own well of tales – he changed his mind. Allah would be one god, without agents, peers, or intermediaries. Muhammad told the custodians of the temple that Satan had tricked him, had taken the guise of the archangel Jibril and decreed blasphemy as orthodoxy.

In the contemporary Qur'an, the Star Sura describes Muhammad's prophetic journey, beyond the stars, during which the Unnameable revealed the eternal message. The sisters have been excised from that message: "These are nothing but names which ye have devised, – ye and your fathers, – for which God has sent down no authority."*

The sisters were banished, and Islam moved away from polytheism. Traditionally this shift is viewed as evidence of a commitment to religious purity, of the absolute ascendancy of Allah. But every tradition of the Book accepts intercessory agents: the prophets in Judaism, the saints (and Mary) in Christianity, the angels in Islam.* No, the abrogation of the crones was an act of religious gendering. The sisters were exiled, and with their exit the age of the goddesses in the Middle East – stretching back beyond memory, back as far as forty thousand years or more – came to a close.* Islam continued to venerate Mary (Maryam), the mother of Jesus, and Aisha (mother of the faithful), one of the wives of Muhammad, as emblems of moral virtue. But the Kem matriarch Hagar is not mentioned by name in the Qur'an; she, along with the three sisters, migrated into the rarefied air of discarded myths. They are banished but not gone, these crones.*

Kan ya ma kan: it happened, it did not happen. Besides, no one remembers, and nowadays the doctrine is beyond argument: Muhammad cast out the idols from the temple and thus proved the falsity of the cranes, crones. Satan's guise was revealed, and the scripture corrected. To suggest any other mythic history (as Salman Rushdie discovered when he wrote *The Satanic Verses*) is dangerous in an age when extremists are still casting out idols (stone Buddhas come first to mind).*

But there they are, slender jaw and soft cheek and bright eye; all three sisters, wrinkled and textured in the stone I found on the mountain. How did I come to find them, through fire and water and forgetfulness? And what am I to make of their most famous prophecy, adapted by Shakespeare in the first lines of a play about war:

When shall we three meet again?
In thunder, lightning, or in rain?
When the hurlyburly's done,
When the battle's lost and won.*

I've been tracking my father's people, their generations like dried leaves in the chronicle they left me. As I've said, I know almost nothing of my mother's people; they are gone with her, burned up with the drink that seemed to be (but cannot have been) her sole inheritance from them. I find my father in all the old tales, Father Sky with his beard in the clouds; but I also find the Old Mother, the crone of the earth, in the story of my own emergence. She is as much a part of my own mythology as my father, who walked ahead last year toward the bright sky on the mountain of the stone. He remains; she has left no clues for me to follow. Her temple is destroyed. She is a spirit of wandering and rumor. But I find the way of her homecoming: in my return from the shadowland of my younger years to the welcoming fires of my wife and her family, who took me in, sheltered me, offered me the blessings of belonging. When I walked in the desert, searching for water, I was redeemed, at every turn, by the soft and resilient ground of the woman who sustains my life, my children's lives.

I remember a story from childhood, of a man whose enemy fills his water skins with wine instead of water; too late, far out in the sands, the man discovers the treachery. He remembers that water flows in the great aquifer beneath the desert, and he digs. He dies digging down, drinking wine. My mother's life was like this. She did not find the ancestral well or the stone enclosure of the three sisters. She was lost. But someone found her tracks, carried on the journey she began but was unable to finish. By virtue of ferocity and gentleness, Elizabeth embodies the spirit of the three sisters, of the Old Woman, of the huntress, and she has carried us all home.

These are the three, in my own life: my grandmother, my great-aunt, my wife; mighty ones, goddesses. They have not been cast out. Their chronicles have not been lost. In the Qur'an, the sura called "Women" speaks of one hundred and four divine books created by the Unnameable.* Only four are now known: the Torah, the Psalms, the Gospel, and the Qur'an. The others have vanished. But the hundred undiscovered books of Islam are not lost; they're in my library, along with the books from the stone temples of the Kem, in the volumes I inherited from my great-aunt Eileen, the fire-tried, the one whose name, in addition to connoting "the radiant one," also means "the great bird."

By the end of August, I'm well enough to travel. Colleagues invite me to New York to talk with them about mythology and sacred dance and the feminine spirit in art. One of my colleagues is a Jewish psychoanalyst, descended from German Jews, who is working with a patient whose parents were Nazis. My skin flushes in the heat of Manhattan and the excitement of our talks; but I do not feel ill, and sunscreen protects me from the last flaming days of summer. We talk about the nature of forgiveness, about what is carried on by generations who defy, who must defy, the injunctions of their parents never to forget. I come back to the question in myself: What must I preserve? For me, for my children, for the sake of the threads of human continuity.

I ruminate on these things, on the sustaining force of the feminine, as I walk the streets of Manhattan. I think of the three goddesses of my own life – whose names mean the radiant, the victorious, the promise keeper – and I wonder about their indomitable spirit, the way in which it cannot be diminished – by negligence, by war, by time spun farther than the grasp of memory.

My meandering brings me, on September 9, past the Kem obelisk in Central Park and into the Metropolitan Museum of Art, where I stand before the only remaining fragment of an ancient sculpture. The body has vanished, and most of the head is gone. What remains is a small artifact, about six inches high: an elegant mouth – smiling, in repose – and the beginning curve of a face, carved from yellow jasper. Between ragged fractures where the stone is sheared off – one just above the top lip, the other below the chin – the mouth has been sculpted with astonishing precision by Kem craftsmen in the age of the Hebrews' exodus. This statue, all that's left of an archaic queen, was fashioned in devotion and shattered by war, almost twenty-five centuries ago. Still, she smiles.

I remain in the gallery a long while, absorbing the details of this remarkable object: bright and smooth, polished to a high sheen. Yellow jasper, symbol of the imperishable, the rain bringer, a stone reputed to drive away evil spirits, has long been associated with healing. Perhaps this mouth, so fragile, the instrument of a forgotten voice, has been preserved by virtue of the jasper's protection. This relic endures, even as the Taliban destroy stone Buddhas in Afghanistan. In many guises, the instinct for beauty prevails.

I return home from New York at midnight on the 10th. A few hours later, hijacked airplanes fly into the World Trade Center towers, into the Pentagon, into the ground. Like their ancient allies, the attackers tear down the standing stones, endeavor to destroy all that is foreign and strange. The old fires have not stopped burning.

I am drawn away from the shop and into my grief for many days. I sit with Elizabeth in the quiet sanctuary she has made of our yard. The first ocher leaves appear, and we wonder how to make sense of such events. Rowan writes a poem about the end of summer, in which birds fly to nice warm places. Safe passage. As the season turns, I pray that I find the wisdom to weigh, in my own small and quotidian life, the will to heal against the wish to harm.

When I can no longer abide images from the television, when the rawness in me must be assuaged, I return to my workbench. My affliction is softened as I cradle my tools and guide them across the stone, polishing here and there, finishing my long effort to restore a shattered visage. The facade of the stone gathers itself into the contours of a resolute chin, a strong mouth, and a cheek rising toward a restful eye.

Rage and tears and a strange dread, lurking and tenebrous, find their way into the rhythm of my work. I strain to reclaim, in the grain of dark stone, the soft faces of those now lost to our sight. I mourn the death, too, of the isolated innocence of my culture. And I try to answer Avery's four-year-old questions: he cannot understand why the hijackers would hurt anyone. He devises surprisingly elaborate plans for talking to them, for asking them to stop.

He watches me work, brings me tools, draws close in this time of elemental fear. My hands trace their way across the smooth contours of the jaw and the rough edge of the forehead. I imagine the craftsmen of the Kem shaping the face of the jasper queen, and I wonder, as I inspect my work during a warm afternoon, if it's her voice I hear, humming among the trees out back. I discover, once again, that the simple work of hands is a guide in my own healing. I am shaped by the work of creativity as a stone is by tools. And I am sustained, finally, by the hope that my one stone might stand with the destroyed Buddhas, with the scattered and the fallen, with those on their way back home.

Creativity can be a deep sustenance – whether in stone or wood or soil. And though my carving is crude, fails utterly to match the surpassing skill of those ancient craftsmen, I persevere; for the work of creation calls not only to the practiced hand. The air is thick with transformations.

I wash dust from the stone. The bright surface beneath appears alive again, as it did during that brief glimpse months ago. But this time I am not fevered, distracted by the creeping fire upon my skin. I am sobered, as are so many others during this time, and I see with great clarity the dark striations weaving their way across the rudimentary cheek, the flecks of white feldspar scattered like snowflakes along the brow. As I gaze on the face before me, collected from the ashes of mountains and the visions of my own troubled days, I glimpse a woman serene and fair. She looks upon our fractured world with an indomitable spirit. And she smiles.

SEVEN

Martin Nordegg, the Jewish nomad who founded the mountain town in which my wife's parents grew up, was led to the site by three birds, flying high on the horizon. This happened before he had designed the town in a radial plan that mimics the Mecca enclosure of the Kaaba.*

We head east toward the town of Nordegg – my wife and I, our children, my wife's parents – along an old road that was first a mountain track and is now a quiet highway. The distance from our suburban home near Vancouver to the destination of our pilgrimage is almost exactly the distance from Mecca to Jerusalem. We're going back to see the derelict homes, the mine of black rock long closed, the summit of the peak above the town. Along the way, we'll unwind old tales from their careless burials, wiping the dust from their eyes. We're returning, three generations of a family whose collective memory stretches back no more than a century. Our fables, like most fables aged with the patina of telling, are not very old. They don't have to be.

The kids listen, rapt and questioning and incredulous, while the old people talk.

On the first day of our pilgrimage, the verdant landscape of the coast gives way to mountain valleys and to glaciers swept clean by tumbling ice. We pass the road where my father, as a boy, ran beside his parents' car as it crept into the canyon. We skirt the shore of a lake where a sacred mask is said to have emerged and led the people in a dance of the ancestors. On a hillside that winds toward a high saddle and a horned peak of polished basalt, ridges and valleys unfold before us like aged fingers laced together in prayer.

The mountains jostle downward, merging into a plateau that widens before us. We follow it, toward the desert we must cross. Clumps of scrubby pine and juniper flank the descending road. We see stands of white birch, trunks long and slender, bark bright as new parchment. Elizabeth and I sit in the front of the minivan; her parents sit behind us; the kids are in the back. As we travel, my in-laws talk about the land, pointing to where the river flooded, to the old ranch that almost became their home, to the sites of mishaps and discoveries and pleasures. They have traveled this road many times, and as they talk – arguing about details, splicing two or three tales into one, wandering off into detours and diversions that sometimes hook up again with the main tale but often dwindle away – I have the impression that the tales reside not only in my in-laws, in their memories, but in the landscape itself. The fables are evoked by our passing. They linger as ghosts in the wake of our departure, become quiet again but can never be lost. The road is suffused with stories. This road and every road.

They talk of the railway, of the spiral tunnels cut into the mountain, of the exacting tunnel engineer, afraid his calculations were off, who killed himself the night before the two construction crews, working toward each other from opposing sides, broke through the wall between them and found the tunnels matched to within an inch. The road follows the railway line, more or less, and my in-laws point out the new stretches of highway, the collapsed avalanche sheds we bypass, the hot springs where Elizabeth's father once thought of opening a medical clinic.

They talk, and we listen. We have questions and seek clarifications. Their stories often conflict. *It was like this; no, it happened another way. Kan ya ma kan.* In the crash thirty years ago, when the car blew a tire and cartwheeled five or six times, when Elizabeth's sister was thrown from the vehicle before it came to rest in a hay field, they could not find her because she lay unconscious in the field and shrouded by her flaxen hair. No – Elizabeth's brother saw her; he did not see her but looked for and found her; he did not look for her but heard the whimpering of her small voice. And though his collarbone was broken, he carried her back to the wreck and waited while a passing motorist ran far down the field, to the homestead where he called for help. I'm surprised to learn that my mother-in-law still hears from that passing motorist; he calls every couple of years, as though he has stayed on the phone all this time, making sure everything is all right, waiting for the ambulance to come and gather up my mother-in-law's shattered bones.

Elizabeth's parents talk in their slow, laconic way of trips along this road, of days still fresh and laid out in their minds.

My mother-in-law and her two sisters figure prominently in every tale: the eldest who is of fire, the youngest of water, and the middle one, she of earth, the grandmother of my children. Within the circle of Elizabeth's extended family, these women are known by a simple epithet: the three sisters.

We travel far eastward, over the plain of the desert and into the mountains on the other side. Near the end of our first day of travel, we pass beneath a massif in the shadow of the dwindling day. It overlooks tumbled foothills and the prairie to the east. Three rough peaks, gray and solid, textured with cracks and fissures. The Three Sisters.

At the temple of the sisters in Mecca, along the desert track where Abraham once searched for water, Muhammad lay in repose at the close of evening. He gazed up at the clear indigo sky, wondered about the unfolding of ancient tales, and fell asleep. It was the end of the 27th day of the month of Rajab, in the 620th year of the Common Era. The Prophet was fifty years old.

In his dream (which was not a dream), Muhammad retraced the exile, the pilgrimage, of Abraham and of the Hebrew travelers who had departed the Holy Land centuries before. From the enclosure of the Kaaba, Muhammad journeyed backward, to Jerusalem, where the stone of foundation – of which the black stone of the Kaaba is a fragment – provided for him a place of ascension.

But wait – he is not traveling yet, he is still sleeping, and the companions of his night journey have not yet opened him up, nor shown him the vessel of wisdom, nor has he yet mounted the winged beast. He is sleeping.

We head north the next day, through hardscrabble towns on the edge of the prairie. The road descends, passing through an eroded landscape with exposed gullies and canyons. These are badlands, geological formations a hundred million years old. We pass hoodoos, spires of twisted sandstone that are said to be alive. Every tradition, it seems, renders its stones into animate shapes.

Along the stretch of road where the car crash occurred all those years ago – where Elizabeth remembers standing with her pet turtle, its shell clacking against the plastic jar as her hand shook, where they waited for the ambulance in the quiet corner of a golden field – we turn westward. I ask my mother-in-law if she can identify precisely where the car left the road. She used to know, she says, by the look of a particular pole standing at the roadside, by the slope of the terrain. But she no longer remembers: it could have been there, where a rusted tractor perches on an overgrown knoll; or farther on, before the pond but after the long hill. She cannot recall the precise location, but she remembers, will always remember, waking after being thrown from the car – her legs broken – waking as though she had been profoundly asleep.

She opened her eyes, saw a world bright and clear as she had never known it. There was a radiance in things – in the grass, in the slow spinning of a wheel on the upturned car, in the sky, in her children, alive, alive. The light rushed into her, opened her up. The world was new again, fresh and new.

Now there are no more junctures, no more exits; just a winding road west, into the mountains, back to the place in which fully half the mythology my children will inherit finds its origin. This is the track of their mother's people. As we travel, they gaze at fields and barns on hills and distant peaks.

At midday, we glimpse for the first time the summit above the town: a flattened peak with cliffs and bastions around its perimeter, a softly sloping forest beneath. I consult the map, to get a sense of the landscape, and find that we are close to the Blackstone River and to Abraham Lake. The town site, now a national historic monument, is a small notation surrounded by emptiness. It's been fifty years since the coal mine closed and the life of the town ended. Less than a century since its founder, a German Jew who changed his name from Cohn to Nordegg to escape anti-Semitism, left Canada during the First World War because his German heritage put him in danger. He never returned to the town that bears his adopted name, to the streets and buildings he designed, to the collieries that supplied fuel for the railway until diesel supplanted coal in the 1950s.

The families of Elizabeth's parents lived in adjacent homes, their patriarchs working the tunnels and the tipple where the coal was screened and sorted. After the mine closed, in 1955, the town died. The families moved on, to Edmonton and Calgary, to other small places scratching the land for sustenance. Their myths went with them, spreading into the curves of roads and hollows of trees, layering the landscape with stories, half-remembered tales, ghosts.

Today the place is quiet, buried, as the Kaaba was when Abraham found it. Most of the buildings are gone. No one walks the streets. We park at the new museum in what was once the school. Above us, on the mountain slope, miles of honey-combed tunnels lie hidden beneath the forest.

The impulse to return to the old places can be a kind of rest-lessness, or an instinct that lies long dormant and is suddenly awakened by a gust of wind, a bit of careless storytelling, the scent of a green apple – anything will do. It doesn't take much, after all, to evoke the desire to partake of one's origin, to glimpse the beginning places of one's family and culture. But such places are provisional stops; they point ever backward, to other foundations, stories, moments too remote to capture. We settle upon the most recent of them, taking the transience of memory as our compass of endurance. Everyone is a nomad, an exile waiting to return home. And home is any place we choose.

For Avery and Rowan, this abandoned town will embody much of their past. It will carry, for them, the weight of their beginnings. It occupies an authentic space they can visit, unlike many of the fragmented and mythological tales of my father's people, which ramble far back but do not provide many sign-posts on the actual land of memory. Nordegg is firmly on the map of Alberta: west from Red Deer, through Sylvan Lake and the farm where Elizabeth's grandmother lived, past Rocky Mountain House. Or east, from behind the Columbia ice field and across the White Goat Wilderness. Memory begins with the land, and here the territory is not quite at the threshold of erasure. Two or three generations hence, this place will be for-gotten by our family. We will spread elsewhere, into terrain fresh with fable. At family gatherings people will reach for the odd name of that faraway place, perhaps snatching it for a moment from the well of tales before it descends again to lie with the ancestors. Our descendants will remember that their people came from the West Coast – where we now reside – as I remember mine coming from the east, and my wife remembers hers coming from a far-off shore. My grandmother remembered other places (whose names she heard from her mother) which are not now remembered. All that's left, as the family chronicle relates, is the mnemonic of the stones: "The old house has been torn down, but its site is visible, and we took away several stones as souvenirs."

Where the town site once unfurled up the slope from the valley, almost every house has been torn down. Where the forest has not reclaimed the terrain, high grasses slowly consume what remains: hewn fence posts black with age, iron gates crumbling, ancient tractors (the denizens of every forgotten place). A spruce tree marks the corner of the adjacent properties occupied by Elizabeth's parents and their families. Beneath it there lies a small, empty, unremarkable field. The houses are gone. A shallow depression marks what might be the remains of the cellar, dug by hand from the hard soil, but no one is sure. Near where the property meets the curved gravel road, and small evergreens grow in the spruce's shade, I find three flat stones, each about a foot wide, lying in the grass. I point them out to my father-in-law, who tells me they are the remnants of a walkway he laid down with his father-in-law almost sixty years ago. These flagstones, brought from a quarry nearby and set with care, are the only firm indication that Elizabeth's family was ever here. The stones persist, all else fades.

This stubbornness of stone, its implacable endurance, explains its importance in the rituals of memory. Stones preserve our reveries of origin. Every pilgrim and returning exile seeks the solace of those reveries, especially in uncertain times. This is why Muhammad slept beside the Kaaba stone: to leverage his dreams into prophecy, into the horizon of myth. He was looking forward, to his remaining twelve years, during which he would be exiled to Medina, would wage war, would unify the Arabian Peninsula. He would first direct his people to pray toward Jerusalem with its foundation stone at the holy center, then redirect them to pray toward Mecca with its radiant stone, gift of the three sisters.[*] There were many details to envision, many rewards to hope for, and he was already weary. So he slept within the enclosure of the past, which is the mirror of the future.

And the tale stretched out.[*] From the indigo vault of the sky, three beings descended: Jibril, revealer of scriptures; Mika'il, angel of sustenance; and Israfil, the trumpet bearer, who will stand (so says the prophecy) on the foundation stone in Jerusalem to announce the day of resurrection.[*]

The celestial trio flew in an arc of fire across the horizon, burning the dross of the stars. They wheeled and plummeted, tumbling like Daniel and his companions in the fire of Nebuchadnezzar. Below them the desert lay still and unsuspecting. Spiraling down, in the way they had learned from their forebears – the nomadic Shebtiw who had been called to the well of ancestors at the world's inception – the angels came to rest by the waters of the spring, found by the child Ishmael in the days of Abraham. The Prophet lay nearby, restless, searching for wakefulness in sleep.

Jibril lifted Muhammad, softly, with care, and carried him to the waters. Then, with one finger of his terrible light, he touched Muhammad on the forehead and opened him to the light of creation.* The Prophet awoke to a blinding clarity, to the shapes of things as though they had been touched for the first time by his sight: a sandstone wall fringed with tussocks of grass, an acacia tree on the edge of the plain, the scattered hue of wildflowers on the mountain to the north. He was awake to the rhythms of things, to the staccato of insect wings and the pulse of the earth beneath him. In the dark wall of the Kaaba enclosure, the radiant stone shone with fleeting forms. Muhammad looked at his own skin and saw fire tracing its way across him, its fine lines racing in the paths of his blood, its brilliance coursing through him.

Jibril reached into Muhammad's body, fire into fire, laid his fingers like the blade of a broad knife upon Muhammad's throat, and slashed downward, opening the Prophet's body to the navel. No blood spilled forth; only light, exiled, migrating, returning, filling the desert with its revolutions. Muhammad saw all this, became this, was lofted beyond himself and into something he had not guessed before.

Jibril removed Muhammad's heart and washed it in the waters of the well, cleansing the remnant darkness. Three times the angel washed: dipping, rinsing, cradling. He filled a golden vessel with water and emptied it into the Prophet's chest, filling the cavity with *hilm*: wisdom, knowledge, impeccability. Then Jibril replaced the awakened heart, closed the wound, and touched Muhammad on the back, between the shoulder blades. The lines of fire upon the Prophet's skin burned brighter, migrated toward the place where the angel held his hand, were drawn up into a single lens of radiance, luminous and glimmering along Muhammad's spine. Jibril removed his hand. The whorl of light remained, the seal of prophethood.*

Muhammad sat up, stretched his joints, gazed at the three angels of fire. He saw that something lay behind the shrouds of fire. Faces and shifting forms and a sound that reminded him of swimming underwater: a high-pitched hum, distant and clear. And he saw that there was a fourth being among them, a winged steed with the body of a horse, neck of a lion, and features of a woman.* This was Buraq, the lightning mount, who had come to carry Muhammad back along the path of Abraham, back to Jerusalem where the stone of origins lay. Buraq had carried Abraham, Enoch, Jacob, Noah – all the prophets – on similar night journeys to the seat of foundation. Every prophet returns there, so that the dreams of the people might be carried on strong winds into the bright skies.

These travelers – a man amazed, three angels trailing fire, an animal strange as the Sphinx – lifted off into the night sky and headed north. They passed the landmarks of the old trails: ashes of night fires left by exiles, worn paths flanking the slopes of mountains, a horizon of rising stars. Muhammad breathed the chill air as he soared between angels of fire. On his back, the spot touched by Jibril was hot. The company flew long into the night, stopping to pray at the sites they knew from old tales. And after each devotional, as they ascended into the dark, Muhammad was shown the secrets: of paradise, of desolation, of the soul unfolding in the rhythms of time. He saw the celestial book as a pearl hanging in the darkness; he saw Moses, praying among red sand hills; he saw the dark one, the Dajjal – the Islamic Antichrist – the adversary spoken of in the end-time prophecy. The Dajjal's hair was wild, like the roots of a tree, and his left eye shone like a star. Muhammad arrowed past these and other sights, among them the Timekeeper, as old as the world, whose death will herald the demise of the current age. He saw Abraham, resting with Ishmael beneath a canopy of bright lanterns.

The companions journeyed far, coming at last to Jerusalem and the temple upon the mountain. They wheeled above it, gazed down upon the stone at its heart. The site was derelict, left fallow during centuries of conquest and religious war. Gone was the sanctuary rebuilt by exiles returning from Babylon. It lay tumbled beneath the scree of Greek and Roman occupations, beneath the stones of Herod's temple that had fallen in 70 CE. The western wall was the only temple structure that remained. Above, on the broad summit where Noah and Jacob and Solomon had come, the stone of foundation was surrounded by debris.

Detritus is everywhere. Near the mine entrance, a boneyard is strewn with hulks of rusted metal. Springs and fastening plates and machinery cores. Tractors and truck frames swim in the rising grass. Black timbers. Bulldozers have been efficient with the town site, burying and carrying away the homes, but here on the hillside things are different. Crumbling structures lie scattered across the wide field; in their shade, machinery parts and underground vehicles punctuate the forgotten landscape.

We pause at a small, flat hillock of grass outlined by a

wooden foundation, where my mother-in-law says her grand-father once cared for the horses. At many other mines, she tells us, the horses remained underground until they died; but at Nordegg they were well cared for and came out into the twi-light with the miners at close of day.

At the entrance to the blacksmithing and carpentry sheds, I see a smattering of blue flowers in the grass. I cross the thresh-old into the old shops, devoid now of their tools and smoke and sounds. I walk past the stained forge, beneath an apparatus on the ceiling for lifting heavy parts, and make my way to the car-pentry bench. There's not much to see, just a long cabinet slumped in the corner and the remains of a ratcheted wooden vise. Someone has walked off with all the tools and attach-ments, and though the bench top is still secure, it is warped and degraded from decades of proximity to the broken windows. I wonder about the men who worked here, craftsmen from Italy and Yugoslavia and Scotland, long gone, their descendants now likely working in cubicles, at keyboards. The air in this shop is fresh from the alpine, clear with the tang of hemlock and spruce in the forest above.

Beyond the shops lies the storehouse, in which a few of the shelves and cubbyholes are still stocked with gear. Clumps of obsolete fasteners lie in bins labeled in fractions, the labels painted carefully in blue and white. I see old cans of paint, a cluster of ax handles, some rubber fittings cracked with age. Rowan and Avery run past me, looking into empty containers. They rush outside, toward the briquette plant, its tall structure stained with rust and repaired with corrugated steel. I look back, toward the entrance to the mine, and it's not hard to envision the bustle fifty years ago. Crews and equipment moving beneath and across the landscape, bringing coal up from the earth, sorting it in the tipple. The sounds of ringing metal, of exertion, of loose machinery crackling and rambling along rails.

We head over to the tipple, where railcar-loads of coal were dumped into a series of sorting hoppers, dried, screened on shaker tables, and pressed into briquettes. The old works are rambling and huge and silent. An errant bird has made its way into the building. It flaps impatiently along the skeleton scaffolding that climbs several stories toward the ceiling. Steel stairs and catwalks thread themselves through the network of conveyors and tanks. We come across the press where the coal, mixed with creosote, was formed into briquettes under the immense pressure of two steel drums rolling upon each other.

One of the stories Elizabeth's parents tell is of a boy, working his first year at the mine, who fell into the drums while lubricating their gears and was crushed by the machinery. The foreman shut off the power, but the drums kept turning under their own momentum for an hour or more. This story is frequently mixed up, by Elizabeth and me and the others of our generation, with the story of the other boy, the violin player who was the finest music pupil of Elizabeth's grandfather. This other boy was killed with twenty-nine other men in the mine explosion of 1941. When they were carrying the bodies out, and the hands of the violin boy shuffled out from beneath the black sheet on the stretcher, Elizabeth's grandfather saw those slender hands and knew who lay beneath. Soon after that, he took no more pupils.

I think of the violin boy as we climb toward the conveyor

that once took the briquettes to the loading dock, and I remember that earlier we passed the graveyard of the miners killed in the explosion. It was a tidy enclosure beside the old school. Twenty-nine somber graves, one of which, that of the violin boy, had fresh flowers laid upon its stone.

We spend a couple of hours in the aboveground structures of the mine, looking around, listening to the remembered stories of my in-laws. It doesn't matter that the grounds are derelict; they are like the old roads we have traveled on to arrive here, inhabited by tales that cannot be lost as long as there are tellers. The tales change as they pass on, and are not changed.

On our way down the hill, toward the fledgling museum at the foot of obliterated streets, we pass again the property where my in-laws grew up. It's now twilight. On the far slopes of the mountain, shadows reach into the valley. We stop once more, and I get out of the car to look at the flagstone walkway, almost hidden in the grass. Overhead, a bird rustles in the spruce tree. I think of the stone in my shop, much like these underfoot: dark, striations of color twisting in the grain. Origin is everywhere.

Muhammad and the angels spiraled down, toward the desolate wreck of the Temple Mount. Buraq's wings rushed in the dusty air; her hooves clattered upon the scattered stones. The Prophet dismounted. Jibril led him forward, through the debris, to where the stone of origin lay. The angel placed his finger upon the rock, pierced it with fire, and motioned Muhammad to tie the slender reins of Buraq through the hole.*

While the angels kept watch, illuminating the summit with their fire, Muhammad entered the fallen sanctuary of the stone.

In the valley below, travelers wandering on vagrant paths gazed upward to see fire upon the mountain; and they remembered old stories, now mixed up and forgotten, confused with other tales, about a man wrestling an angel, a box of fire, a jewel that could crack stones, a bird circling above a flooded hilltop long ago.

The sanctuary was empty save for the flagstones underfoot. The debris surrounding the enclosure did not penetrate into the sanctuary, or it had been removed by someone who remembered the archaic tales. Muhammad walked in a wide circle through the dark, approached the stone sidelong, stole quick glances at it before approaching directly. The rock lay patient and mute.

The Prophet wandered at the fringe of the stone, heard the sounds of trickling water, peered down to where the ancestral well flowed up from the heart of the rock. The well of souls lay beneath him, and he thought he could hear voices in the tumbling of the waters.* Muhammad kept moving, west along the edge of the enclosure. He saw the foundation trenches of Solomon's temple, cut clean and true by the *shamir*, now eroded by almost two millennia of strife and neglect and weather. On the north side of the rock, he saw a rectangular area outlined by worn stone: the resting site of the Jewish ark, long vanished.*

A few impressions on a flattened summit, scorched by fire, surrounded by the mess of history. This was all that remained.

That night, Muhammad met with the ancestral spirits. The fabled and nomadic Shebtiw made their way back to the stone of origin.* The well of ancestors grew bright, and the carriers of dreams ascended. Hardjedef, who had burned while unraveling the nested boxes of the magician Thoth, came from the west, walking along the spine of the mountain. They all came: Adam and Noah and Moses and Jacob and Daniel. Abraham, Isaac, Ishmael, Hagar. And the three sisters, the storm of their arrival wrapping the sanctuary. Singly and in groups, from wherever their errands had taken them, they returned.

And they spoke, gathered around the stone, quiet and raucous by turns, prophetic by way of remembering. Every archaic fable was taken up, passed among them, invigorated by the bellows of old voices. Muhammad's dreams were forged, then carried into the night sky, toward the Unnameable whose abode is beyond the horizon of myth. And the Prophet was also carried aloft, buffeted by the turbulent air. He rose from the stone, traversed the heavens, and was gone.

On the long drive back from Nordegg, I think about the stone in my shop and the stubbornness of tales, through dereliction and neglect and intentional erasure. We stop for the night at the end of a long valley beneath gray mountains. I think of the ancestors I have adopted and of the family that sustains me. We walk to a viewpoint overlooking a lake of glacial water. The kids run ahead, down the path. They are my prophecy, as those ancestors are my memory. Together they lift me toward the Unnameable. I would be rootless, restless, without their solace, exiled and without homecoming. When I have drifted off, following my impulse for the strange, the secret, the esoteric, into my addiction to *elsewhere*, these touchstones redeem me from absence. Beyond the gales and empty stretches of my own horizon, my children and my family raise the wind of my greatest traveling and lead me home.

Late that night, crisp alpine air blows through the valley. Shadows and ghosts inhabit my dreams. Then, in the blink of my mind's eye, I see a man walking over the terrain of my inner life. He moves, purposeful and direct, through an empty enclosure that resembles the rear of a church. I see pillars of pale marble and a floor patterned in lines of white and yellow stone. He is clothed in the colors of leaves burned by autumn. As he passes in front of my field of vision, he glances up at me, a quick and neutral glance, the way one notices but need not react to a broken branch hanging from a tree, or graffiti on a highway overpass. He continues on, and as he goes, toward a destination unseen, I recognize – finally, surely – that the traveling man is me.

My perspective shifts, from observer to participant, and I find myself in the old church. It is quiet. Sand covers many of the surfaces. I wander, rounding a corner to find a tomb of carved porphyry with a Mayan snake writhing upon its rim. Wet sand covers most of the tomb, and I dig it away. More carvings emerge: hieroglyphs, animal forms, shapes I do not recognize. And a box, on an elevated platform. I clear away the sand so that I might see the carvings more clearly. But I do not open the tomb, and I do not touch the box.

When Muhammad returned from his ascension, his light like a star above the plain, he spoke to the gathered assembly, prophesying to them: of the building of a shrine over the foundation

stone where the Hebrew temple had once stood, of the inter-
mingling of mythologies between Muslims and Jews and
Christians, of the eventual forgetting of that ancestral and religious kinship.* Myths would be claimed, he said, as history,
and these myths would become the basis for war. This conflict
would prevail until the old tales were both remembered and
forgotten, their truths made flexible enough to hold the breadth
of human vision.

The final prophecy of Muhammad concerned the stones. In
a low voice, singsong with the cadences of Arabic, he told the
prophets and sages of every age – gathered, as they sometimes
do, to hear the music of the worlds – of the indications of
redemption. On the morning of the day of peace, he said, the
black stone of the Kaaba in Mecca will lift free of its moorings
and return to its origin, to the foundation stone in Jerusalem
of which it is a fragment. The stone of beginnings, the pillar of
the world, anchored to the waters of the abyss and penetrating
the airs of heaven, will awaken at the coming of the black
stone. And the foundation stone will speak, saying, "Peace be
to the Guest!"*

Peace seems a long way off by the time we arrive back home
and I hear about further developments in the Palestinian upris-
ing. I've been immersed in the positive qualities of stones and
their mythology, the way they embody a particular psychologi-
cal and spiritual distillation, and I'm disturbed by the fact that
the *intifada*, planned since the failure of earlier peace talks,
was ignited by the visit of Ariel Sharon, leader of Israel's Likud
Party, to the Temple Mount, home to the foundation stone.

Sharon's visit was an indication of many things: the assertion of Israeli sovereignty over a Muslim-controlled holy site, a deliberate provocation to an embittered Palestinian population, a declaration of a hard-line approach to the persistent question of who controls the *temenos*, the holy ground. His actions won him leadership of the country. He made his stand, as many have before him, upon the mountain of prophecy, wrestling with the angels and demons of history.

The news is full of omens. The debris pile of the World Trade Center is being winnowed away; chaos is spreading in Afghanistan. I discover that one of the September 11 hijackers, perhaps their ringleader, grew up in Giza, beside the monuments of the Kem where the *benben* stone was once revered. And I hear, with increasing frequency, of Osama bin Laden, whose family's construction business renovated not only the Kaaba but also the Temple Mount in Jerusalem. The political situation seems increasingly mythological. After all, the linchpin of the conflict in Israel involves ownership of an ancient rock. Diplomacy has consistently yielded positive results on every other political matter – land ownership, refugees, autonomy, military issues – but peace talks have always stalled over the question of what to do about the Temple Mount. Each side holds a deeply entrenched position – essentially saying that the other has to go – and each side is bolstered by religious myths of exclusion and propriety.

The terrorists, with their atavistic impulses, would have us reverse time, return to an age when the Book and the old stones in Mecca and Jerusalem would be proof enough of divine covenant. In the Middle East, stones are also a symbolic vernacular language for people: in scripture, in politics, in history. In this sense, the last prophecy of Muhammad, that of the stones, is apt: until the stones come together and recognize their own unity, there can be no peace.

I finish working the stone. Now that I've seen the old mine, the flagstones, the fallen debris of the past, I feel more fluid and easy in my body. My skin no longer burns, and I see the red traces only in fleeting moments. I polish, here and there, looking for symmetry in the dark rock, sensing the integration of the piece. I feel it in myself, too; the slow coming together of dualities, a synthesis that began with water and turned to fire and is now cooling within me. The ancestral face is nothing more than my own, and as I gaze at it, matching it eye to eye and lip to lip, my own divisions vanish. I am the ancient and the infant. The devotional and the rational both reside in me. They are not separate, and they need not contest each other.

There is an effort now to rebuild Nordegg, as there is to rebuild the World Trade Center, to forge new myths from the fractured ground of the old. This initiative requires both the devotional and the rational, together weaving the presence of the past. One eye sees forward, the other gazes back.

I've rebuilt my own relic, this black stone that has been my companion and goad during four seasons of awakening. Only one thing remains to complete the circle of unfolding.

EIGHT

The snow line is high in the alpine; lower down, the terrain is wet and dark. Two feet of snow fell in the valley last week, but the rains have laid the ground bare again, making this hike possible. My memory has preserved crucial landmarks – spiral of rock, trunk with a burl, sinew of mountain marked by old lava – that would have been covered by snow. I would not have wanted to delay the stone's return until spring.

My father and I approach from the north this time, down the serpentine road. The overcast sky lightens in the east as we drive: first to sepia, then to citrine, then to the gull-wing gray that is the signature of November. My father remarks that the brightest part of the sky lies far ahead, directly above our destination. We drive the old highway, past a lone fisherman perched at the edge of a creek, through the canyon with its ramparts of sullen mist. I catch a fleeting glimpse of the roadside entrance to the cave we found when we stopped for a picnic thirty years ago. I remember my older brother leading me in, whispering about bears.

We turn off the highway and onto the gravel road, which climbs in a series of switchbacks upward. The forest – logged recently in spots, punctuated by ever-diminishing groves of old growth – is almost black beneath the canopy. I roll down the window to smell the rioting rot. The air is damp, clear, and replete with elusive scents. I can identify the smell of pine, and of wet soil, and perhaps salt from the coast nearby, but most of what's here drifts by unrecognized. We climb higher, through stands of maple and birch. The wet maple leaves smell sweet, sugary. Moss covers most of the lower trunks. Beyond the crunch of gravel and the rhythm of the car's engine, I hear a low, insistent ringing hum.

The road is greasy with rain and mud. We round a tight corner and ascend the final switchback. I feel hopeful about the day, but I'm already tired. My head feels foggy, my vision blurred, my forehead warm. It comes and goes: sometimes I feel fine – cool and relaxed – until suddenly my face flushes with heat and pressure, as though summer sun is bursting from within my head. I think about healing stones – of the Kem, of Abraham – and the stone that now lies in my pack, neatly nestled between a pair of jeans and three extra pairs of gloves. I think of the Tibetan pilgrimage during which stones are carried up a spiraling track to the peak of the mountain: as solace, as devotion, as healing prayer.

We park the car at the clearing, high above the valley floor. The air is crisp, the scent of recent snow still in the air. But there's no trace of white on the slopes nearby. The wind must be coasting down from above, bringing with it the tang of alpine. We gather up our gear, shoulder our packs, take in the view west and south. My father pauses at the edge of the clearing, looking out over the ocean far below. I adjust the straps of my pack, which seems unreasonably heavy, and wait for him. He turns slightly to the side and points southeast, to where the peaks of Goat Ridge, Sky Pilot, and Mount Sheer slice the horizon with jagged peaks. He reminds me that we used to have our own names for those peaks: Bob, Ross, and Bruce, the three brothers. We made this landscape our own, my family and I.

I expect my father to shrug, laugh, and move toward the trail. But he does not. He looks back toward the sea again. I wait. He stands still in his brown sweater. Then he turns to me and says, in a voice softer than I'm accustomed to, "This is our country."

We start down the trail, remembering the alder and bracken and speckled leaves. My pack digs into my collarbone – I've shaved roughly twenty pounds from the stone, but its weight is still considerable. My legs feel jittery. At the first turn in the trail, where we leave behind every sign of human presence, a farrago of multicolored leaves lie strewn across the path. Their vibrancy is startling in this season of encroaching gray: ripe papaya, Chinese porcelain. I notice leaves the color of dried papyrus, thin and dark with moisture marks. I reach down and feel their texture: smooth, webbed with patterned lines, uniform on one side and punctuated by ridges on the other. I pick up a leaf with edges like apricot and a glowing center as deep as the ripe plums of late summer. Near the tip, a neat, oblong hole has been made by some passing insect.

Here, on the forest floor dying away into winter, a second spring of fallen leaves illuminates the landscape. I find all the colors of the tropics: vermilion, maroon, indigo. A slash of russet runs through a leaf bright as mango. I see long, tapered leaves like kris knives; others are almost round, their edges serrated and rough. Along the fringe of an oblong leaf, edge bristling with tiny spikes, I discover an emerald band. It follows the curving contour of the leaf, bright against the pomegranate skin. I step over a root of birch and find a green leaf, almost a foot long, lying face up on the ground. I pick it up; the underside is the color of raw silk. Water drips from the graceful tip. Where the drops splash on the ground, I see a leaf rolled tight, its hide the color of binding on old books. All around: such books, such a library.

We've been on the trail about twenty minutes when I hear something, below and to my left: a rustle among branches, but without the crackle of twigs under foot or hoof. It's as though something is moving through the air, brushing against the trees above the ground. I look toward the sound reflexively. Nothing. I raise my hand; behind me, my father stops. I scan the hillside below, straining to focus. A high-pitched whistle migrates through my ears. I turn my head to the side for a moment, reaching for the forest sound. But it's gone. My father hasn't heard anything. Perhaps, he suggests, it was an echo of our own passage.

I settle into the rhythm of my walk. And though my body jangles with weakness, still unaccustomed to exertion after the months of illness, I brim with enthusiasm. I have rehearsed the route back to the river hundreds of times in my head so that when we returned, exactly one year later, on Remembrance Day, I'd be certain of the way. I have walked this path in dreams and in reveries, I have noted its landmarks along other roads and tracks. The turns of this labyrinthine terrain have spread out to compass all my other journeys. The primal crossroads is here; I walk a straight line toward the center. It is not possible to take a wrong turn.

We take a wrong turn. Where two trails meet – one ascends toward the alpine, the other meanders into the valley – we take the lower path. I know, with certainty, the way we have to go: up, along the steeper trail with the overhanging scrim of branches. To the hidden intersection we found last year. But whether because of illness, distraction, or some presence ghosting through the trees, we bypass the path. We press on, not noticing. Yet something seems not quite right. It begins as a hesitation in my walk, a creeping fatigue which I first attribute to my poor health. Then I become confused, juggling the map in my head, trying to make the parts fit together. There must be a junction in the trail ahead, at which the finger of a small trail leads off toward the river. But how can that be? The secondary trail would be too far down, or else my reckoning is wide of the mark. These ruminations, any one of which would, normally, stop me in my tracks, simply roll around inside, untethered, abstract. The likelihood that I am placing us in considerable danger with such foggy thinking does not occur to me. My feet have been placed on the path, and I walk.

We pass small stands of devil's club, sable stalks bristling. As I push one aside, some of the spines rake against my right hand. A slight stinging sensation warms up the crest of my thumb. A little farther on, orange fungi – wide and flat, edges chewed by tiny predators – lie nestled like misshapen pancakes in the grass. I hear water trickling nearby. The trail narrows between rows of young, wind-fallen trees, their slender trunks crossing the trail like intermittent hurdles. We step onto and over the lowest of them, pushing the branches toward the ground. The larger trunks block the trail at waist height; we snake beneath them. My pack gets caught.

On the other side of a rise tinged with the red of rotting cedar, we come suddenly upon the river. The foreshore bank is steep. Clinging to creepers and exposed roots, we scramble down to the water's edge. In a gravel clearing made by spring wash, we collect ourselves and assess our progress. Out of the closeness of the forest, my head begins to clear. Aren't we going the wrong way? I look upstream, to where white water rushes across red boulders and dark shapes. No, this is right: we climbed up from here last year, following the contour of the far bank. This time, without ice and frost, we can go straight up the river gorge. It will be wet, but fast.

I hop across to a midstream boulder. The surrounding water is loud and frothy. I stand there, poised to make a second, longer leap. My father looks tentative, but follows. I crouch, take a breath, and jump. Water droplets splash my face. I come down on a slanted spur of rock. My shoes slip, skitter, then come to rest. My left foot, which must have brushed the water, is wet. I smell the fresh and damp air, feel the swag and wamble of the boulder beneath me, and suddenly wake up.

What are we doing? We took a wrong turn, way back, and now we're clambering up slick boulders in a rushing river. In running shoes, in cold weather. I'm weak, my father is seventy, and we're climbing a river gorge. I'm not sure how this has happened, but we've forgotten about the shortcut, about the jog in the old road. All the discoveries of our last trip seem to have vanished. Here we are in precarious straits once again.

I pause, breathing chill air suffused with water that has sluiced through falls and a cave high above. I ease myself away from the somnambulism that started with the sound – brushing leaves, a whisper of passage – and has brought us far from our destination. I turn toward the bank, hop across to an onshore boulder, and step onto the bank. My shoes sink into the wet sediment. My father waits, face flushed with exertion. Let's go back, I tell him, back along the trail to where the junction lies. We've come the wrong way. He's relieved, as am I, that we won't be trying to climb the river. And he shares my confusion: how is it that we so thoroughly misled ourselves? Perhaps this place is a labyrinth, and one must be guided by whatever forces govern the terrain. Permission to pass is given, or not.

We track backward, as we did on our previous trip. Then, we also made it to the river – though higher up – before turning back. Detours seem to be necessary here. Small white pebbles and fragments of cedar have been churned up by our passing. We follow these bread crumbs up the bank, along the crest, down again into the forest. I breathe easier.

The day warms, though a faint rain has begun to fall. I wonder about forgetting, and diversion, and necessity. Time passes quickly, and we come upon the junction sooner than I would have thought. We turn onto the ascending trail – my father ahead, my memory replaying his dwindling departure last year – and climb toward the sky.

I don't get far before the heat begins: first in my brow, then down through my body like a red tide. My skin grows hot, and sweat runs off me. I stop to strip off my coat and sweater, continue on in a light shirt. This concerns me: it's far too cold to be running around without insulation. But this sweat is not simply the water of exertion: even in extreme conditions, even in a sauna, I have not sweated this much. No, this is a fevered bath, my own river of fire. I take a deep swig from my water bottle and struggle on. But a dozen steps farther, as I shinny beneath an overhanging branch, my strength leaves me. I stumble. My knees dig into the cold ground. I steady myself against the branch, brush the sweat from my eyes, and take a deep breath. My father is now far ahead, hands in pockets, upright and stalwart.

I place my right foot on the ground, push with both hands against my knee, and try to hoist myself. It takes three tries. I stand, as the alpine wind presses my shirt onto my skin. I'm as wet as if I'd been thrown into the river. The straps of my pack chafe against my skin. One step. Two, three. An aggregated skein of rock from the volcano snakes across the path; I try to navigate across it without falling. I lean forward, drawing the weight of the pack over my lower back. Since we turned at the junction, the stone has been getting heavier. I reach behind me, to feel its contours. As I do so, I have the sensation of being pushed forward. The stone possesses its own mounting momentum, stronger as we edge closer to its home.

Up ahead, where the trail turns out of sight, my father waits for me. Just beyond, last year's forgotten road meanders off the side of the main trail. We're back on track. The incline eases somewhat, which heartens me. But I am weary beyond measure, as though the travails of the chicken pox and my subsequent fatigue have been compressed into a single morning. Heat and fire and the urge to collapse. But there is no going back. The tales of the old gods, the chronicle of my ancestors – these have taught me at least this much: the way lies through the fire.

We find the river again and cross it. Now we are high on the mountain, just below the alpine. The air is chill and sweet. We climb the far bank, fifteen or twenty feet up to where gangly branches offer up their last few blueberries. The soil of the bank is steep and loose. Does the river rise this high in spring? If so, the roar of the waters – which, even now, clamor through this cleft like a storm – would be loud as thunder.

As I mull over spring runoff and winter ice, I notice depressions in the soil of the bank. Some are our footprints, but others, clearly, are made by – what? Bears, beavers, other travelers? I can't imagine other people traipsing through here, but I suppose the bear we ran into last year might frequent this stretch. After all, cliffs and tangles enclose the river as far up and as far down as I can see. This is the only open spot. There's a small gravel clearing and good visibility to either bank. And the bear's den is not more than fifty yards from here. The bears have turned in early this year, which usually means they sense a long winter.

We crest the far bank and cross again into the shadows of the forest. Every year, lost hikers disappear in this landscape.

Errant cars, driven off the shoulder of the highway below, simply vanish. A while back, hundreds of searchers – on foot and in the air – failed to find a vehicle known to have left the road at a more or less precise location. The following summer, hikers found the car (and its unlucky driver) shielded by trees and undergrowth, a few feet from the roadside. This country, wild and inhospitable, unnerves me with its savagery. I feel even more vulnerable now; on fire, soaked in sweat, shaky as hell. Who could survive out here? If we were stranded, the blueberries would last about fifteen minutes. What then?

On two pages, folded twice, inside the front cover of my inherited copy of *Flora of Southern British Columbia*, in her careless handwriting, my great-aunt kindly provides the following:

Edible Plants found at Moderately High Elevation

Wild onions: bulbs may be eaten raw or cooked in hot ashes [with note to page 86, where I find pressed flowers]

Bitterroot: white root is bitter when eaten raw. Palatable when cooked.

Mariposa tulip: should be roasted in hot ashes.

Biscuit root: tubers may be eaten raw like celery, or the ends may be removed and the inner portion dried and pulverized to form a flour. Mix with water and bake.

The fallen trunks are not slick with frost this year. They're wet, but manageable. We climb along them, scrabbling for balance, reaching for handholds in the underbrush. It's not far now: along the bank, past the narrow gorge, beyond the bear den. Anticipation rises in me, counterbalances my exhaustion. Up ahead, hidden by a final rampart of hemlock, spruce, and cedar, I hear the waterfall. Last time, when the river was slowed by ice, the water sounds were muted. Now its full throat is open, and already I feel droplets of mist on my face. I look across the slope, north to where the sky is clearing. The high peak, skirted by a glacier, is bare to the wind. A straggling fleck of cloud falls away from its dark summit. Far off, where the horizon is a monolith of gray, I see the first tendrils of a winter storm. It will be here in four or five hours. By tomorrow, there will be a foot of snow where I'm standing, and all the gates of this place will be closed until spring.

We stay near the river, navigating by its sound, far enough from its edge that we don't tumble into the gorge. We're never more than twenty feet from the bank, but most of the time we can't see the water: the forest is too dense. When I imagine we've come high enough, we turn right and down, crossing a patch of devil's club. A rotten stump, perched on the steep incline, shows a tangle of roots sprawled in the eroded soil. Beyond it, two firs lean away from each other. Between them, in the near distance, I see a stretch of cliff. Black rock, textured with streaks of gray. And a bright summit, veiled by the top-most branches of lone and giant sentinels.

Where the slope of the riverbed eases, and the trunks of fallen and inverted trees offer many handholds, we make our way down to the water's edge. The waterfall, many times louder and more forceful without the scrim of ice we encountered last year, rushes through the cave of boulders. Inside, stones on the floor are washed by clear mountain water. Their colors – alabaster, beetroot, terra-cotta, graphite – reflect across the walls of crushed obsidian, as though the old volcanic fire still burns in lenses of black glass.

White water jostles at the rear of the cave, snakes through a fissure of light from the river behind. This is where we go, up and around, to the place of beginnings. The pool is there. Ripples coast across its surface. I see the stone I struck with my hammer. I follow the imaginary line of the cracking ice with my eye. There, at the back of the pool, is a dark cleft. A boulder of aggregated obsidian, skewed and leaning, hangs over the spot. Last year, when snow covered every surface, the boulder blended into the terrain, looked like another snowdrift hovering above the waters. Now I can see its root, sunk deep into the riverbed, and its rough black hide. It is a mouth, yawned open. The pool slides down the well of its fathomless throat. A delicate sprig of frost, built up from mist flowing and freezing along the shore, lies just above the water's edge.

I unshoulder my pack and place it on the wet ground. I unzip it, push aside spare gloves and the pair of jeans, and reach for the stone. It feels immensely heavy. I draw it out and take two steps to the pool's edge. Behind, to my left, my father waits. I can see that the boulder, cantilevered up from the riverbed, leaning out over the pool, will eventually topple forward into the water. This stone that I have worked, that beckoned in dreams, will be buried in waters of black fire. It will find solace in the waters. It will be lost, and found again by its homecoming. Stones, said Pythagoras, are frozen music. Perhaps it will sing, and I will hear its song, far off, carried on the wind.

Before I can spin the moment out with ritual, the stone moves in my arms, as though of its own volition. It pulls me forward with its momentum, leads my hands out over the waters, and I let it go. It falls through the damp air: turning, the face rising. It descends with a *sploosh* of frothy water. The view clears, and I see the stone far down, in the deepest water. It lies in shadow, contours blurred by the passing river. Just another lump of rock.

I take a long last look, then turn back to my father. Behind him, the forest climbs toward the volcano. I look downstream, past the cave and the waterfall, to where the river sprints around a bottleneck of stones. The air is cooling quickly as the storm front approaches.

The heat is gone from me. For the first time in months, I feel well. Tired, but exuberantly well. My father has a dab of blood on his trousers from our scramble up the steep bank. My shoulders ache from the weight of the stone. We stand at the threshold of the sky – in looming darkness, surrounded by fire. We feel an insistent, inevitable pull. And we begin our journey home.

N O T E S

Full citations for sources given in these notes can be found in the References.

PART I: EMERGENCE

8 *nor bottom*   The ancient Egyptians called this primal water Nun: a universe of singularity, an erasure. The sounds of its name run forward and backward, unfolding and recapitulating. Nun is the first palindrome – expanding and returning, seeing itself in the mirror, searching for its double form. Nun is the template for every uncreated utterance, the word in the beginning. Every movement toward articulation is a re-enactment of this first expression, each word a world created from nothing. This first name is, even now, hidden like a stowaway in our language of the everyday – no one, none, *nada*, *niente* – promise hidden in the skin of absence. By way of a mythological association between the primordial ocean and temporal oceans, *nun* is the Aramaic word for fish. Nun is also a letter of the Hebrew alphabet, symbolizing vitality in faith, the power of divine speech, and prophetic inspiration.

9 *Island of the Egg*   The symbolism of the cosmic egg is an integral aspect of almost every mythological tradition. In the Kalevala, the Finnish national epic, a duck lays its eggs on the knee of the goddess Ilmatar; the eggs break, and the world is

formed from the shattered remnants. Similar tales are found in esoteric Judaism, in Hermetic philosophy, in modern physics. The Big Bang is the most recent version of the myth of the cosmic egg, shattering from nothing into everything.

The mythological association between eggs and cosmogenesis is the source of at least one important technological innovation: the distillation of alum (a hydrated double salt, usually consisting of aluminum sulfate and the sulfate of either potassium or ammonia). Alum was a substance of profound alchemical and practical significance from before the time of Alexander until the nineteenth century. It was used as dye, as healing elixir, as transformer of metals. Its manufacture in England, from 1620 to 1870, involved burning the shales of the Yorkshire coast using brushwood fires on the beach. The rocks were heated for about nine months (though the main shale band at Boulby kept burning on its own for more than fifty years). The resulting powder, rich in sulfates, was doused with water, channeled into alum houses, and mixed with kelp or urine (sources of potash and ammonia) to yield a liquid called "the mothers." This solution was heated until the alum salts crystallized.

The secret of alum's production lay in the precise duration of this process; too much heat, and the alum was ruined by the crystallization of ferrous sulfate. At some indistinct point in the history of alchemy, a moment of divine instinct led to the discovery that a hen's egg placed in the solution would rise to the surface at the precise moment of the alum's optimal concentration. No one knows who discovered this secret, but its emergence is undoubtedly a legacy of the mythological association between creation and eggs. Alchemists, the chemists of every age until the twentieth century, would have known about the various tales of a formative egg emerging from a sea of possibility. In the case of alum, their adaptation of myth into science is a miniature history of the evolution of the scientific method. This method derives not only from reason but from instinct grounded in ancestral myth. For a robust exploration of alum production, see Osborne, *The Floating Egg*.

Modern science emerged from the alchemical (or Hermetic) tradition, which in turn was begun by the ancient Egyptians, the world's first scientists. Hermetic philosophy is named for Hermes, the Greek version of the Egyptian god of wisdom, Thoth. Hermetic doctrines are among the sources of the sacred geometry employed in the cathedrals of Europe. This knowledge flowed first through the temples of Hermopolis along the Nile, arrived much later in Greek Alexandria, and spread from there across the Levant. It arrived in Europe, in the first centuries of the Common Era, as an obscure teaching with an archaic pedigree. As a path of wisdom, Hermeticism is also the source, at least in part, of the mythologies of the Grail, the philosopher's stone, and the practices for refinement and transformation of the base self into illuminated gold.

10 *fire and water*   Unless otherwise stated, the mythological material in Part I is derived and adapted from Reymond, *Mythical Origin of the Egyptian Temple*. Eve Reymond studied the inscriptions on the walls of the Edfu temple, constructed during the Greco-Roman period. These so-called Edfu Texts, written during the twilight of ancient Egyptian civilization, were the last esoteric narratives to be preserved from earlier periods. Reymond makes a compelling case that some of the myths are old beyond guessing.

11 *vanishing*   The Book of Illumination (the Pyramid Texts) is a work of astonishing complexity. Its myths and cosmological speculations, which are likely more than five thousand years old, describe a worldview extraordinarily remote from our own. The symbolic language of the glyphs remains obscure, and though the text has been translated by various scholars, the meaning of many of the words is still unknown. R.O. Faulkner, in the preface to his English translation, *The Ancient Egyptian Pyramid Texts*, concedes that the difficulty of the material requires an essentially poetic approach: "A translator can render a passage only as he himself feels it" (p. viii). Faulkner employed a set of diagraphic marks to help the reader make sense of the more difficult passages. One of those marks, the ellipsis, "indicates that a word or words are untranslatable" (p. xiii). Many ellipses run through Faulkner's translation. Taken together, they are a string of invisible pearls, hiding a tale to which we no longer have access.

Another famous English translator, Sir Alan Gardiner (quoted in Faulkner, p. viii), confirms: "The only basis we have for preferring one rendering over another, when once the exigencies of grammar and dictionary have been satisfied – and these leave a large margin for divergencies – is an intuitive appreciation of the trend of the ancient writer's mind." With the Pyramid Texts, translation is not merely a structural and etymological task; it requires deliberate immersion in a foreign consciousness through which the imagination must find its way by the barest of clues. Reading and reimagining the cosmology of the Pyramid Texts is an unsettling experience. Despite the symbolic obscurity of the texts, their eloquence and philosophical richness are compelling. Yet these texts, and the society which created them, have almost entirely vanished. My local university library possesses a single copy of the Pyramid Texts; while writing this book, I checked out that copy and kept renewing it for almost a year before it was requested by someone else. The religious texts of our age will, no doubt, become similarly obscure – as will our cultures – in the millennia to come.

On page 11, taking the suggestions of Faulkner and Gardiner, I have chosen a mythopoeic and intuitive interpretation. My version is a conflation of several passages generally called ascension texts by Faulkner. Excerpts of his version appear below (ellipses are mine).

> Lines 1004–10: "O my father the King, the doors of the sky are opened for you, the doors of the celestial expanses are thrown open for you ... You shall ascend to the sky, you shall become Wepwawet [Upuaut, the opener of the way], your son Horus will lead you on the celestial ways; the sky is given to you."
>
> Lines 137–39: "Your bones are those of the divine falcons in the sky. May you be beside the god, may you depart and ascend to your son ... The sun-folk shall call out to you, for the Imperishable Stars have raised you aloft. Ascend to the place where your father is ..."
>
> Lines 1682–83: "Stand up for me, O my father ...

for indeed I am your son, I am Horus. I have come for
you that I may cleanse and purify you, that I may
bring you to life and collect your bones for you . . ."

The Pyramid Texts are suffused with references to light, to
illumination, to the seeing eye. The title of the texts should be
more consistent with their content. Therefore I have abandoned
the traditional title, which simply refers to the location of the
texts' discovery, and suggest instead the Book of Illumination.

By the time of Christ, twenty-five centuries after the pyramids
were built, the authors of the Book of Illumination were long
gone. All that remained of their legacy was colossal, mute monuments and buried statues. The divine language, its columns of
glyphs carved into enduring stone, had been forgotten. The
Sphinx lay concealed up to its neck beneath the sand. With the
discovery of the Rosetta stone in 1799 – a black basalt monolith
inscribed in Greek and three forms of Egyptian – the old tongue
spoke once again and the amnesia of history began to recede.
The Book of Illumination is the oldest scripture in hieroglyphics
and the most archaic corpus of religious texts in the world. There
exist older religious myths, symbols, and documented rituals –
some stretching back to the Neanderthal age – but the Book of
Illumination is the earliest preserved example of an integrated
religious cosmology.

Understanding the words embodied by the glyphs does not
yield to us the meaning of the sacred language. The hieroglyph
depicting an eye, for example, denotes spiritual engagement, protection, unity, creation, the sun, balance, time – a long list of
associations that the glyphs, in themselves, hint at but do not
directly disclose. In English, by way of contrast, letters bear no
concrete relationship to the words they spell: the letters in the
word *stone* do not embody, in themselves, any hint of the word's
meaning. They are simply signs which together make a code of
sounds. It is not possible to decipher the meaning of a word by
the shapes of its letters.

The hieroglyphic language combines several distinct levels
and strategies for communication: ideograms, which portray
direct visual meanings; phonograms – sounds, as in English; and

determinatives, word endings that denote the context of the preceding glyphs. Each glyph – image, sound, or determinative – represents a physical object: a mouth, a door bolt, a cobra. Each element provides, in addition to its linguistic meaning, a secondary reminder of its layered context. For example, the hieroglyph for the word meaning "to kiss," pronounced like the word *zen*, shows two phonograms – a door bolt and water, for the sounds *z* and *n* – alongside an ideogram of the human face. The phonograms indicate the sounds of the word, but they may also embody a deeper symbolism: the bolted door of intimacy is opened in the act of kissing, and the waters of affection, which are also the waters of the well and of the river in spring, flow downstream toward the heart.

The relationship between medium and message, which we exalt as a quintessentially modern discovery, was exhaustively explored five thousand years ago. Richard Wilkinson, in *Symbol and Magic in Egyptian Art* (p. 161), contends that Egyptian hieroglyphs "transcended the boundaries of most written scripts in successfully blending symbolic representation and the written word to a degree that no other system of writing has surpassed." The integration of written language and symbol displays a level of virtuosity so profound that we can hardly grasp it. The interconnections of the Internet, for example, in which objects are embedded within objects in almost infinite nested sequences, would have seemed, to the ancient Egyptians, rudimentary indeed. The Internet is, for all its complexity, a nonsymbolic system: each of its elements (files, Web pages, computer keyboards and monitors, cables, and so on) possesses a discrete and single-level meaning. A keyboard can be represented by an onscreen icon, but it cannot mean anything other than a keyboard – unless you give it further levels of meaning yourself (in which case other people may not understand you).

There are, in English, no shared multilevel meanings of a keyboard. But imagine a hieroglyphic keyboard: each key is shaped into a distinctive symbol, and the letter displayed upon it is an expression, in another form, of the same symbol. But not exactly the same: the letter is another flavor of the motif of the key. The placement of the keys is related to the fingers that touch them as you type, and the symbols of the keys relate to the symbolic functions of each finger. Moreover, the key placements are designed to evoke specific movements of the fingers as you type, the order of their action as well as the shapes they make. You animate animals and ideas and gods as you move your fingers. And you have a choice about what you animate, because every expression offers hundreds of ways to type it. You can write forward or backward, or vertically. You can change the order of letters, insert symbols that abstractly or concretely express the sense of your words. Your sentences can interlock like crossword puzzles. You can specify that your writing contain anywhere from two to twelve levels of meaning (but not one level, as in English). Every letter, every phrase, every passage you write is a hologram of your entire communication. From the simplest rebus to the most elaborate phonogram, every fragment is a map of the whole and interconnects with every other fragment by way of a web of meanings so colossal no one can grasp all of it. Besides, the movements of your fingers evoke the gods in unfathomable ways, and they insert further meanings which you do not intend and do not understand. The meaning of the text, finally – any text, from a household budget to a philosophical treatise – extends beyond the world, reaches toward the eternal. Your keyboard has five thousand keys.

The symbolic language of Egyptian hieroglyphic texts employs the dialect of dreams: nuanced, multifaceted, holographic. The glyphs are woven with interlocking symbols and strands of meaning through which reading becomes a devotional act. Word or phrase reversals – palindromes – hide in every text, leading the reader forward and back along a spiraling track of understanding. Every textural path unfolds in at least two directions: two truths, two selves. Palindromes are hinges upon which the attention of the reader turns. *Ben* is the primordial stone; *neb* is gold, the symbol of conscious awareness (and the root of our modern word *nebula*). *Ais* is the brain, *sia* consciousness. *Ab* is the heart, *ba* the soul. These reflected and doubled pairs form a concealed language beneath the pragmatic. They turn awareness back on itself, back to the source.

Passages are strung from left to right, as in English, or in reverse, or even vertically (top down, though never bottom up).

The intended direction for reading is denoted by the orientation of the ideograms: an animal or a god looks toward the beginning of the text. A palindromic glyph passage can be written forward in a section of reversed text, or backward in a section of forward-facing text. Such suppleness of linguistic structure has made decipherment a difficult task.

The thorniest aspect of the language involves the absence of written vowels. For the ancient Egyptians, vowels were the keys to magic and power; to speak them in the glyphs was to be in possession of the means to create a world. Scribes were sufficiently convinced of the inherent power of the vocalized glyphs that they were careful to limit that power: many of the glyphs inscribed on the stone walls in the pyramid of Unas were modified to prevent them from coming to life unbidden. Ideographic glyphs of birds were carved with their feet intentionally defaced so the birds could not launch themselves from the stone. Glyphs depicting humans were often carved with missing arms or legs. Sometimes substitute glyphs were used in place of those thought more likely to animate themselves. For the Egyptians, the Book of Illumination was, literally, a living document.

Nowhere in the thousands of columns of text in the Book of Illumination – nor, for that matter, in any of the early Egyptian sacred texts – is there a hint of a single vowel. Our modern pronunciation of the lost language is a reconstruction, a best guess at where the vowels belong, but it's not the language itself. The authentic voice of the words is gone. We are left to gather up the fragments of a library strewn across a debris field wide as history.

14 *descended from them* Olson, "The Royal We."

The statistician Joseph Chang, in his essay "Recent Common Ancestors of All Present-Day Individuals," demonstrates that everyone alive today is descended from common ancestors who lived as recently as a few thousand years ago. The number of our ancestors increases exponentially with every generation we trace backward (two parents, four grandparents, eight great-grandparents, and so on). If we go back far enough, the number of our potential ancestors exceeds the total number of people who have ever lived. But the number of our *actual* direct ancestors turns out to be almost everyone who was alive a few thousand years ago. This is not limited by culture or geography: *everyone* today is descended directly from *everyone* who lived at that time (if they had children, and subsequently descendants).

Chang's research shows that almost every person in North America is descended from English royalty, and everyone of European ancestry is directly descended from Muhammad. Similarly, everyone alive today – with the exception of those with no surviving descendants – will be the direct ancestor of every human being who will live five thousand years in the future.

For an alternative view, see Rohde, "Somewhat Less-Recent Common Ancestors of All Present Day Individuals."

18 *Father, you know*   Adapted from Burland, Nicholson, and Osborne, *Mythology of the Americas*, p. 148.

23 *immortal sages*   In the Edfu accounts, as transcribed and interpreted by Reymond, the Shebtiw are both twins and members of a larger family of divine beings who do not appear in the narrative. This mythological family of seven members, sometimes called the seven sages or the Shemsu Hor (the followers of Horus), figures prominently in the antediluvian research undertaken by Graham Hancock and others.

23 *Aa and Wa*   In later ages, the name Aa will come to mean, for the Hawaiians, a form of dark lava; it will also, in the Norse cultures, become a word for water. The fiery stone and the sea of emergence, together in a world of opposites. The later meaning of Wa will include an English form, *waw*, meaning wave. In Hebrew it will become the sixth letter, waw (or vav), whose shape – ‎ו‎ – is fundamentally equivalent to the Egyptian glyph *neter*, which symbolizes divinity. In the *neter* glyph, the upper, horizontal line is usually depicted in the shape of a small flag, what some have interpreted as the head of an ax. Similarly, the Hebrew letter waw is typically written with a calligraphic flourish that renders the upper line into the shape of a flag ruffling in a breeze. This symbol also appears, in the oldest Egyptian myths, as the icon representing the perch of the primeval god, the Unnameable.

These ancient names and symbols may be linked etymologically. Through the vehicle of myth, carrier of ancestral memory, many versions of the same tales are told across cultures. The old words, the old gods, are preserved through repeated motifs that may apply as directly to specific words as to specific images. Etymology may be one form of myth. Water, for example, appears in myths throughout the world: as agent of beginnings, as river of life, as fertilizing rain. Its symbolism and iconography are consistent and fairly independent of geography.

The words used to denote various forms of water, in languages spoken by peoples at the utmost extent from one another, are also surprisingly similar. John Bengtson and Merritt Ruhlen traced the words associated with water through the etymologies of various language families. With *aq'wa* as its primary root, *water* is found in Nilo-Saharan (Nyimang *kwe* and Kwama *uuku*), Afro-Asiatic (Janjero *ak-k-a*), Altaic (Japanese *aka*, meaning bilge water, and Ainu *wakka*), Amerind (Allentiac *aka*, Culino *yaku* and *waka*, meaning river, Koraveka *ako*, to drink, Fulnio *waka*, lake), and Indo-European (Latin *aqua*, water). I have reproduced Bengtson and Ruhlen's list from Richard Rudgley's *The Lost Civilizations of the Stone Age* (p. 44), which presents an excellent overview of early language development.

24 *every clay thing* Naydler, *Temple of the Cosmos*, p. 58. This quotation is from the Shabaka text, a granite stela upon which the oldest extant Egyptian cosmology was inscribed. Unfortunately, it was later used as a millstone – the equivalent of using the Bible as kindling – and much of the text was lost. In the surviving Shabaka stone myths, which Egyptologists call the Memphite cosmogony, Ptah is the supreme deity who creates the world by virtue of words of power. He is, in this sense, the mythological peer of the Shebtiw.

24 *whom he procreates* Burland, Nicholson, and Osborne, *Mythology of the Americas*, p. 186.

26 *effect required* Budge, *Legends of the Egyptian Gods*, p. 186. For students of Egyptology, the work of Budge (1857–1934) is considered both foundational and out-of-date. His contributions to hieroglyphic linguistics have largely been supplanted by contemporary research, though his chronicle of Egyptian myth retains a compelling and poetic aura.

29 *surrounded by fire* Hornung, *Ancient Egyptian Books*, p. 11.
The contemporary title of the collection of invocations known as the Coffin Texts is derived from the location of their discovery

as opposed to their content. They are, essentially, a second folio of the Pyramid Texts. This passage has been adapted from Coffin Text spell 1080.

"The winding waterway" is a term common to the myths of many cultures as a mythological designation for the Milky Way.

39 *alchemy* The word *alchemy* derives from the Arabic *al-kimiya'*, the etymology of which is a subject of debate. Possibly it evolved from the Greek *khymeia* (fusion) or *khyma* (fluid), or even the name of Khymes, a Greek alchemist. The words *chemistry* and *alchemy* both descend from a single source, though their meanings have diverged in the last five hundred years. The prevailing view of the source of these words, and the one to which I subscribe in the text, is that *al-kimiya'* evolved from Khemia, the name used by the Greeks for the land of Egypt. The Egyptians themselves called their country Kemi (meaning black earth) in reference to the dark, rich soil of the Nile valley. Modern scholars sometimes use Kem-t instead of Kemi. For the purposes of my narrative, I have chosen the name Kem to denote the ancient Egyptian people. My use of the term, in keeping with my interpretation of the philosophy of that culture, is partially a mythopoeic impulse.

42 *as hardnes* Quoted in *Oxford English Dictionary*, "basalt."

Pliny compiled the first encyclopedia. Our modern word for such a work derives from Pliny's justification, to the emperor Titus, of his own volumes on the grounds that they gathered together the scattered materials of "encyclic culture" (*enkyklios paideia*), the archaic cultures devoted to the rhythm of time. Pliny was overcome by the fumes of the eruption of Mount Vesuvius in 79 CE and subsequently died from his exposure to the ash.

44 *gneiss* Gneiss was a favorite stone of the Kem. They prized the black-banded grain and used it effectively in statues such as the small sphinx of Senwosret III now in the Metropolitan Museum of Art in New York. The pattern in the rock flows along the lion's sinuous flank, as though illuminating the texture of the muscles beneath. In the Kem symbolic language, black denotes fertility and talismanic power (*kem* means black, among other things). For the Kem, the contrasting bands in gneiss were the lights and shadows of creation.

45 *lap of God*   Ginzberg, *Legends of the Bible*, p. 1.

45 *northern Canada*   Six thousand years ago, at the time of the earliest Kem, a culture called the Acasta people inhabited this land. Supreme toolmakers, their trademark was the burinated flake scraper, a stone tool with a sharp edge formed by a single blow. For reasons that will likely never be known, the Acasta people have entirely vanished. Their stone tools, some of them shaped from the oldest relics of our world, are all that remain.

46 *formative earth*   Zimmer, "Ancient Continent Opens Window."

46 *ancestral fires*   In Sumerian, a language recently supplanted by Egyptian in claiming the distinction of having invented writing, words for the past are formed through the use of the word *igi*, meaning eye and face. The Sumerians were close neighbors of the early Kem, sharing mythologies and influences. For both cultures, the past was always ahead; they faced it. In Akkadian, a Mesopotamian language which evolved from and replaced Sumerian around 2000 BCE, words used to describe the past (*panitu*, for example) are derived from concepts of front and face. In both Sumerian and Akkadian, words for the future (such as *eger* and *warka*) derive from words meaning back and behind. The future lay behind those cultures; they traveled face forward into the past, searching.

55 *human consciousness*   Until recently, the accepted date for the appearance of human culture – as evidenced by complex tools and apparent symbolic thinking – was somewhere around thirty or forty thousand years ago. But this threshold has now doubled back – to at least seventy thousand years before the present. Archaeologists working at the Blombos cave in South Africa have found, among other surprises, finely worked weapons decorated with symbolic engravings – within a stratum older than seventy thousand years.

58 *your own becoming*   Adapted from Pyramid Text utterance 81. Many Kem statues depict a serpent uncoiling from the crown of the head to the forehead. This, in conjunction with abundant serpent and eye symbols, has led a number of scholars – among them Joseph Campbell – to suggest that the Kem were the authors of the system of meditation that later became, in India, the tradition of Kundalini. In his *Oriental Mythology* (p. 102), Campbell writes: "There is a problem here of considerable inter-

est, waiting to be explored; namely, the passage of inspiration from both the arts and the mysteries of Egypt to those that came to flower c. 400–1250 A.D. in India, Tibet, China, and Japan."

The "brazen serpent" that Moses received from God in the desert and used as a healing instrument (later destroyed by Hezekiah) takes on a different cast when viewed as an aspect of consciousness rather than a pagan idol. The Kundalini energy has long been associated with remarkable healing properties.

59 *able to cross*   Sharad Master, a geologist at Johannesburg's Witwatersrand University, offers an interesting explanation for the cause of the social upheaval of the Kem's fifth dynasty (which roughly coincided with the fall of the Akkad culture in central Iraq). In 2001, while inspecting satellite photos of the 'Amara region in Iraq, Master noticed a meteor impact crater. The distinctive inner ring of the crater had previously been hidden by a lake, but Saddam Hussein's canal projects, initiated to drain the entire 'Amara region in Hussein's campaign against the Marsh Arabs, had revealed the anomaly. (Master, "A Possible Holocene Impact Structure.")

The crater, two miles wide, indicates an explosion equivalent to hundreds of nuclear warheads. The sequelae of such an impact (around 2300 BCE, when the area was a shallow sea) would have included earthquakes, rampant fires, sunlight blocked by the dust, and monstrous floods. The Epic of Gilgamesh, one of the most famous of the world's old tales, relates that the world was once lit with flame, a storm turned day into night, and the land was "smashed like a cup." Every culture of the Middle East abounds with such recollections.

Most modern scholars now agree that comets and meteors seeded the earth with its first organic life. In the case of the 'Amara meteor, much regional life was also abruptly terminated. The ancients would have discerned poetry in this cycle of creation and destruction, especially as 'Amara lies ten miles from the confluence of the Tigris and the Euphrates, two of the three rivers whose source is reputed to lie within the bounds of Eden. The meteor struck the bull's-eye of the world's mythical origin. An "ever-turning sword of flames," says Ginzberg in his *Legends of the Jews* (vol. 1, p. 32), protects the entrance to paradise from the trespass of the fallen.

60 *first individual*   Considerable controversy surrounds the date of the Sphinx at Giza, though contextual evidence points to Khafre as the monarch in whose reign the monument was constructed. For an excellent overview of the evidence, see Lawton and Ogilvie-Herald, *Giza*. The features originally carved upon the face of the Sphinx were likely those of Khafre, though they were possibly modified later. In mythological terms, the sphinx is also known as a riddler, a creature that asks, "What goes first on four legs, then on two legs, then on three?" This riddle, told long after Khafre by the Greek playwright Sophocles in *Oedipus the King*, is archaic beyond measure. Its solution is simple: human beings first crawl (four legs), then walk (two legs), then use a cane in old age (three legs). But the solution and the riddler hint at more complex themes. The sphinx – part hunting lion, part thinking human – asks, "What is a human being?" In *Oedipus the King*, a play made familiar to the modern mind by Sigmund Freud, the narrative focuses on the contradictions of human experience: passion and taboo, loyalty and incest, heroism and violence, paternity and parricide. Both the play and the sphinx itself explore the nature and paradox of humanity; this is the true riddle.

Because the face of the greatest and oldest stone sphinx is probably that of Khafre, he is the first riddler of human essence, the first to ask what it means to bind together the contradictions of individuality. In this sense, he is humanity's first authentic *self*.

61 *many meanings*   The falcon is the primordial ancestor, called This One (or the Unnameable) in the Edfu Texts. (Later this figure became Horus, the warrior god and national divinity of the Kem.) The orientation of Khafre's hands – left one relaxed, right curled into a fist – symbolizes the receptive left and active right balanced in the monarch. In tableaux of the period, supplicants before the gods are often shown with two left hands. The dais represents the primordial island, rising from the sea of beginnings.

Each of these symbols possesses many overlapping layers. See Wilkinson, *Symbol and Magic*.

62 *unto the children*   Josh. 4:6, 7. Unless stated otherwise, Bible quotations are from the Authorized (King James) Version.

62 *massive and delicate*   Copper appears to have been the hardest tool metal available to the Kem of Khafre's time, though they also possessed some meteoric iron. A fragment of smelted iron was reputedly found inside the masonry of the Great Pyramid in 1837. The sample was lost, then found recently in a cigar box in a drawer at the British Museum. This iron bar is the subject of considerable debate. If authentic, it will revise the start of the Iron Age in Egypt backward by almost two thousand years.

Both copper and iron are softer than basalt and granite, common materials used by Kem sculptors. To increase the cutting action of their tools, Kem sculptors may have used sand as an abrasive. When sand is inserted between the chisel (or saw) and the stone, the soft metal of the tool provides a matrix in which the quartz crystals of the sand become embedded. The cutting action is accomplished almost entirely by the sand. In 1987, a cache of "whispering" or "musical" sand was discovered inside a cavity behind the passage leading to the Queen's Chamber in the pyramid of Khufu. (The cavity may or may not be a hidden passageway; to date it has been explored only by camera, by way of small holes drilled through from the passage adjoining the Queen's Chamber.) Whispering sand, named for the peculiar sound it makes when blown by the wind, is not native to Giza, and was likely brought from the Sinai. It is almost pure quartz, unlike the sands at Giza, which are a blend of calcite, quartz, and plagioclase. Grain for grain, whispering sand is substantially harder than Giza sand and would have made an ideal slurry for abrading all kinds of stone. Today quartz-rich sands are still used as abrasives in sandblasting and other applications.

62 *long dreaming*   In a ritual called "the opening of the mouth," statues were animated in the same fashion as the deceased were awakened to the afterlife. Passing an iron implement across the eyes and mouth, priests read from the Book of Illumination. Several passages, as adapted by me from Faulkner, are shown below:

I am your son Horus, whose eye is opened to infinity.
    I have come in search of you, listening for your voice.

I carry Upuaut, fragment of the god, opener of the way.

Let me release you, gently, that you may sing again, speak with the vanished ones in the place of remembering.

The ritual of opening the mouth was an integral aspect of elaborate funerary rites intended to release, from corporeal death, the "transfigured spirit" of the deceased. This spirit, also called the "body of gold," was luminous and without limits. It was called the *akh*, a partial reversal of *khat*, the body. The *akh* was the migration of form back to the light of beginnings; the wandering self, released from the wheel of time, returning at last to the ancestors, welcomed into the spiral of unity.

63 *which is within* Fulcanelli, *The Mystery of the Cathedrals*, p. 27. The identity of the twentieth-century philosopher and alchemist who wrote under the pseudonym Fulcanelli has never been definitively established (but a rumor persists that he was the symbolist philosopher René Schwaller de Lubicz). The name Fulcanelli is a mythological reference to the Roman fire god Vulcan, a cultural descendant of the Greek god Hephaestus. In turn, Hephaestus is derived from the Kem origin god Ptah. In *The Mystery of the Cathedrals* and in his longer work *The Dwellings of the Philosophers*, Fulcanelli makes the case for an alchemical philosophy, essentially Kem in character, hidden within the Christian symbolism of European sacred architecture. In the preface to *Cathedrals*, E. Canseliet argues that "our ancestors fashioned the *first stone* of [the Gothic cathedral's] foundations, that dazzling gem, more precious than gold itself, on which Jesus built his Church. All Truth, all Philosophy, and all Religion rest on this *unique and sacred Stone*."

63 *God's house* Gen. 28:22.

63 *gods are dwelling* Wolfgang Schramm, quoted in Avner, "Sacred Stones," p. 31.

71 *discovering the soul* The fundamental orientation of every culture prior to the Kem, for seventy thousand years and more (the recent Blombos cave discoveries in South Africa have pushed back the cultural horizon by at least this far), was toward the

rhythms of the divine in nature – the vegetal cycle, the wheel of time rolling toward the ancestors, a world suffused with regeneration and a universal, transcendent order. The earlier cultures lived within a sphere of eternal return, of the moon's transformations and renewal, of humanity as a child of the goddess Nature. This consciousness, which carried humanity for the greater part by far of its development, was spun from the fabric of dreams. Gods walked in the garden. The turning of seasons was a manifest prayer lifted on the wind. Enclosed within a circle of emergence, nothing ever died. And yet the cultures of the Stone Age also assumed the dark cast of a nightmare: human sacrifice, ritual entombment of the living, the absolute abrogation of personal identity. In the Neolithic cultures, the self was subsumed by the inviolable structure of a universe centered firmly on divine order. The edicts of gods and goddesses were absolute imperatives. The odyssey of individual awareness, defined by rebellion against divine edict, was not yet a possible myth. Humanity could not yet eat the forbidden fruit.

Written language appeared around 3000 BCE – probably first in Egypt, then in Sumer – when tokens and symbolic signs were applied in novel ways. Soon thereafter, cuneiform and hieroglyphic scripts evolved to enable the projection of individual thoughts and images. And strangely, suddenly, a world illuminated by fire was ablaze with imagination. Within a few hundred years – by the time of Khafre – it became possible for anyone to claim a destiny equivalent to godhood. And it was written language, essentially, that proved the means of accomplishing this feat. "This is the word which is in darkness," say the Coffin Texts. "As for any spirit who knows it, he will live among the living . . . he will never perish . . . he will never die" (spell 1087).

Nurtured by the gift of written language, the individual self emerged, unmistakably, in the art of the Kem. The eternal halls, once reserved for the gods and the symbolic, sacrificial king, opened their doors. The gate of the garden closed. The gods began to move back along old roads, their vacant places claimed by heroes and warriors and sages of the mythopoeic age.

At an indistinct juncture in the third millennium BCE, a one-way bridge was constructed in the human mind. That bridge, which crosses into the field of the modern self but which will forever prohibit our return to the garden, is the most mysterious of all our creations. It leads, with the audacity of innocent beauty, from a world of cosmic order, whole and ruthless, to a horizon beyond which the gods themselves cannot trespass. Our collective migration across the one-way bridge, over the course of more than two millennia, yielded the consciousness of the West. By the time of Alexander, last of the god-kings, the old world had gone. The Kem were subsumed into the evolving metaculture of the region: Greeks, Arabs, Jews, Turks. Their remaining traditions were driven underground, into the philosophy that would later be called Hermeticism.

72 *meteoric iron*   Bauval, "Investigation."

73 *far away*   Exactly a century later, W.B. Yeats used the same imagery in his poem "The Second Coming," perhaps the single most influential literary work of the twentieth century. Yeats was profoundly influenced by the Kem. "I believe in the practice and the philosophy of what we have agreed to call magic," he said in an essay from 1901. "The borders of the mind are ever shifting . . . The borders of our memories are a part of one great memory, the memory of Nature herself" (Kermode and Hollander, *Oxford Anthology*, vol. 2, p. 1699). Yeats was introduced to symbolist philosophy by the poet Arthur Symons. They both may have known the philosopher and alchemist René Schwaller de Lubicz.

73 *Nehapiwir*   Reymond translates the name Great Leaping One as *nhp-wr* (*Mythical Origin*, p. 113).

For the Kem, as for many other cultures of the old world, the serpent is a symbol of time and transformation. It sloughs off the skin of the past. The fact that a serpent occupied a central, positive place in the cosmology of the pre-Columbian cultures of the Americas was subverted with great efficacy by Christian missionaries during the first centuries of contact.

74 *Bourlon Wood*   The woods of Bourlon are mostly lime, or basswood, a tough yet pliable material that can be shaped by stone tools. Almost every wooden Stone Age weapon – bows and spears and shields – was made from it. In the Middle Ages, lime was called *sacrum lignum*, the holy wood, because of its use in the carving of religious figures. My grandfather and his brother

found themselves in a forest of weapons and gods, all wrapped up together, hushed and waiting.

75 *granite and basalt*   The Shebtiw first created Tanen, lord of the earth, whose name means "the risen land." He was followed by the builder gods, led by Ptah, the supreme craftsman. Ptah's company of artisans is formed from his teeth and lips; other gods are formed from his body. Djehuti, the Measurer, whom the Greeks called Thoth – scribe and magician, keeper of secrets – is the tongue of Ptah.

Kem temples devoted to Ptah were called *hi-ku-ptah*, which the Greeks adapted to *ai-gy-ptos* – Egypt.

75 *broken open*   Reymond, *Mythical Origin*, p. 113.

77 *beside one another*   Reymond, *Mythical Origin*, p. 113.

81 *ramshackle tale*   One version of the tale of the celestial book forms the basis of Mormonism. The Book of Mormon tells the mythological history of Hebrew exiles who left Jerusalem around 600 BCE and migrated to America. Their chronicle was inscribed on gold plates in the language of the Kem ("reformed Egyptian," as the Mormons say), buried, and later revealed to Joseph Smith, the founder of Mormonism.

82 *before my bones*   Tennyson, *St. Simeon Stylites*, stanza 15.

84 *Renaissance alchemy*   This residence was the Château Anet, the ancestral home of Louis de Brézé and Diane de Poitiers (later the mistress of Henri II). The sculptors and architects who worked on the château were alchemists. All over Europe, their brotherhood had erected cathedrals and castles and tombs, each embodying a devotion to Catholicism but hiding, beneath layers of symbol and myth, the philosophy of the "great work" of alchemy. At Dampierre, a castle renovated by the alchemical architects, a carved wooden panel surmounted by the insignia of Diane depicts a stone of fire floating on the primordial sea. See Fulcanelli, *Dwellings*, plate 25.

Alchemy derives – by way of Alexandria, Baghdad, Jerusalem, and Cordoba – directly and unequivocally from the Kem. It is the cosmology and spirituality of Thoth, of the book and the stone, syncretized and translated and adapted to the European cultures. Hermeticism, a tradition inclusive of alchemy, denotes devotion to Hermes, the Greek form of Thoth. The egg, the foundation stone, the concealed and universal book – these alchemical and Masonic motifs all began beside the river, long before the age of cathedrals. And they traveled downstream, toward the Renaissance.

In 1460, Cosimo de' Medici (the great-grandfather of Catherine de Médicis, the rival of my ancestor Diane de Poitiers) sent a delegation of monks in search of books of archaic origin in the monasteries of Europe and the East. One of them returned from Constantinople with fourteen Greek manuscripts, the Corpus Hermeticum, a syncretic collection of esoterica composed around 200 CE which attributed its teachings to the mythic Hermes Trismegistus – Hermes Thrice Great – also known as Thoth. Marsilio Ficino, the chief scholar employed by the Medici family, completed the first translation of the Corpus Hermeticum in 1470. Along with the Jewish Cabala, which became available to scholars in Europe after the Jews' expulsion from Spain in 1492, Ficino's work was largely responsible for Renaissance mysticism.

92 *from the quarry*　The White Rock breakwater was constructed in 1953.

97 *reside here today*　The Semiahmoo (Half Moon) people of White Rock share common linguistic features with the Cowichan tribe on Vancouver Island (across the Strait of Georgia from White Rock), of whom the princess in the story was said to be a member.

97 *sixth century* BCE　Waltke, *Finding the Will of God*, pp. 62–64.

100 *refiner's fire*　Mal. 3:2.

101 *American Revolution*　Some of the remaining volumes – more than fifteen hundred – were inherited by Samuel Mather, Cotton's son, and then sold, by Samuel's daughter, to the printer Isaiah Thomas in 1814. These books are now part of the permanent collection of the American Antiquarian Society. Much of the original Mather library was gifted to Cotton Mather's nephew, Mather Byles, whose son brought many of the books with him when he emigrated to Canada. He did not bring them all: some were purchased, in fire sale fashion, in 1790 by Thomas Wallcut, and are now in the library of the Massachusetts Historical Society.

102 *on the walls*　Tales of mythological priest-magicians are central artifacts of the Kem literary tradition. It was with good reason that Clement of Alexandria, in the third century CE, called Egypt

"the mother of magicians." Among the many tales concerning Kem sages, the search for Thoth's sacred book (of which the Grail quest is but a more recent version) occupies a position equivalent to *Hamlet* in English literature. In Egyptology, the best-known versions of this myth cycle involve the competition between two magicians, Ptah-Nefer-ka and Setne. As Geraldine Pinch has demonstrated (*Magic in Ancient Egypt*, p. 50), Ptah-Nefer-ka is likely based on the historical figure of Hardjedef, who lived in the twenty-fifth century BCE. I have, accordingly, used the name Hardjedef in my adaptation of the tale.

102 *nested boxes* The mythological motif of nested boxes was a favorite of the Kem. Many burials employed sarcophagi stacked like Russian matryoshka dolls. In the tomb of Tutankhamun, three inner coffins lay nested within a stone sarcophagus, which in turn was encased within four gilded shrines. The symbolism of seven layers, in the case of the boxes of Thoth, or eight, with Tutankhamun, has long been of great interest to students of esoterica. For large-format photographs and detailed illustrations (folding out to thirty-six by fourteen inches) of Tutankhamun's tomb, see T.G.H. James's outstanding work, *Tutankhamun*.

102 *gates of paradise* The similarity between the ark of the covenant as described in the Bible and ceremonial arks used by the Kem, some of which are now in the Egyptian Museum in Cairo, is a source of comment and controversy among scholars. Such boxes, particularly when nested, were favorite motifs of the Kem (see previous note). Hardjedef's tale, which predates the Hebrew mythologies by more than a thousand years, is the archetypal example of this motif.

103 *and a barge* Budge, *Egyptian Magic*, p. 145.

PART II: THE JOURNEY OUTWARD

115 *was constructed* Berenice II was the wife of the Macedonian Ptolemy III, monarch of Egypt during the second century BCE. Together they initiated construction of the Edfu temple, upon the walls of which most of the Kem tales related in this book are inscribed. A myth tells how Berenice promised to sacrifice her hair to Aphrodite to ensure Ptolemy's safe return from his journey to avenge the murder of his sister. (Berenice loved Ptolemy a great

deal, or at least loved his politics. She had arranged the murder of Demetrius the Fair, Ptolemy's rival as her suitor.) In honor of Berenice's hair sacrifice, Aphrodite placed the tresses in the sky. They form the scatter of dim stars behind the constellation Leo, called today the Coma Berenices. (*Coma* is a term used in astronomy for a nebulous luminescent cloud. It means hair.) Berenice II survived her husband but was poisoned by her son.

116 *Holy City   Eben* is a word of Aramaic origin meaning stone; *shetiyah* means foundation. *Eben* probably derives from an earlier word, *banah*, to build or rebuild. The pronunciation, etymology, and symbolic value of *eben* are similar to those of *benben*, the Kem stone of origin. There is also the Hebrew word *ben*, meaning child (for the Kem, the *benben* stone was the child of the ancestors). In Hebrew, *shetiyah* also means drinking. The foundation stone, therefore, is the stone of sustenance, of the waters.

The quoted passage, from the folklorist Louis Ginzberg (*Legends of the Bible*, p. 5), comes near the end of a mythological description of the first day of creation. It continues: "In the sanctuary itself the Hekal [temple] is the centre, and the holy Ark occupies the centre of the Hekal, built on the foundation stone, which thus is at the centre of the earth. Thence issued the first ray of light, piercing to the Holy Land, and from there illuminating the whole earth."

122 *to the Kem   The Masonic tradition*, to which many founders of the American state belonged, is a branch of Hermetic philosophy, in turn derived from the Kem. The esoteric eye of Freemasonry, seated on the pyramid, is a Renaissance adaptation of the Kem *benben* stone.

Masonic influences on the early development of the United States are well established. See, for example, Knight and Lomas, *The Hiram Key*. Samuel Adams, Paul Revere, Benjamin Franklin, John Hancock, and George Washington, among many others, were all Masons. Washington swore his oath of office on a Masonic Bible.

123 *tangled history   The relationship* between the Hebrews and the Kem has long been a matter of debate (since the first century CE, in the works of the Jewish historian Flavius Josephus; and in the modern popular mind since Sigmund Freud's 1939 essay "Moses

and Monotheism"). The Jewish cultural identity – a distinct people, rich in arts and learning, pursued and exiled through many centuries of travail – depends on the distinction between the Hebrews and all other peoples. Yet there exists a substantial body of evidence in support of (and some evidence against, to be fair) a Kem origin for Hebrew culture. Most researchers have focused on the Amarna period of the Kem, during which the pharaoh Amenhotep IV changed his name to Akhenaten and attempted to revise the theology of Egypt under one god, the Aten (or Aton). During his reign, from 1353 to 1336 BCE, Akhenaten founded the world's first monotheistic religion. The most neutral study of this period, its characters, and its subsequent influence on history and culture is Dominic Montserrat's *Akhenaten: History, Fantasy and Ancient Egypt.*

At his city Akhet-aten (horizon of the Aten) in northern Egypt, Akhenaten abandoned the older model of megalithic temple construction, preferring instead to build with smaller stones. No image of the Aten was depicted inside the sanctuary, though external tableaux show the god as rays emanating from a disk resembling the sun.

Much has been made of Akhenaten's hymn of blessings to the Aten (Wilson, "The Great Hymn"):

> Every lion is come forth from his den;
> All creeping things, they sting.
> Darkness is a shroud, and the earth is in stillness,
> For he who made them rests in his horizon.
>
> At daybreak, when thou arisest on the horizon,
> When thou shinest as the Aton by day . . .
> Their arms are (raised) in praise at thy appearance.
> All the world, they do their work.
>
> All beasts are content with their pasturage;
> Trees and plants are flourishing.

The hymn is remarkably similar to psalm 104 (11–24): "[Springs] give drink to every beast of the field: the wild asses quench their thirst. By them shall the fowls of the heaven have their habitation, which sing among the branches. He watereth the hills from his chambers: the earth is satisfied with the fruit of thy works . . . Thou makest darkness, and it is night: wherein all the beasts of the forest do creep forth. The young lions roar after their prey and seek their meat from God. The sun ariseth, they gather themselves together, and lay them down in their dens. Man goeth forth unto his work and to his labour until the evening. O Lord, how manifold are thy works! In wisdom hast thou made them all: the earth is full of thy riches."

After Akhenaten's death (his body has never been identified), the monarchy was likely taken up by Smenkhkare (possibly his son), then by Tutankhamun (possibly another, younger son, or son-in-law, or half-brother *and* son). This boy king, whose name is known today only because his was the only pharaonic tomb to be discovered essentially intact, was forced by advisers to resume the old Kem theology. The religion of the Aten was suppressed; Akhenaten's city was abandoned. The blocks of his temple and residence were used in many other subsequent Kem building sites.

About eighty-five years (in the traditional chronology) after Akhenaten's death, the exodus of the Hebrews occurred. The mythopoeic chronicle of the Old Testament describes a people fleeing northern Egypt, devoted to one, non-iconic god, whose divine name, YHWH, was too sacred to pronounce. Instead, wherever the written name appeared in the scriptures, high priests vocalized the name as Adon, which translates in the English Bible as "the Lord." When the exiled Hebrews settled in Palestine, they utilized a sun disk, like the image of the Aten, as the royal seal of at least one of the kings of Judah, Hezekiah. See Deutsch, "Lasting Impressions."

There are many such correlations. The cartouche of the Aten was inscribed with the name Imram; the Bible refers to Moses as the son of Amram (Num. 26:59), the Hebrew equivalent. Across the Nile from Akhenaten's destroyed city, there is today an ancient village named Mal-lawi (Mallevi), meaning city of the Levites. The rod of Moses, crowned with the image of a serpent, was symbolically identical to the serpent scepter used to denote Kem royalty.

In his controversial book *Pharaohs and Kings: A Biblical Quest*, David Rohl makes a compelling case for the identification of major biblical characters (Joseph, Moses, Joshua, Saul, David, and Solomon) with figures of Kem pharaonic history. Rohl's research, which suggests a new chronology for the early biblical period, builds on the work of scholars such as Ahmed Osman, whose *Moses and Akhenaten: The Secret History of Egypt at the Time of the Exodus* re-evaluates many aspects of accepted archaeological theory.

The research conducted by Rohl, Osman, and others is thorough and precise. It has also been the subject of tremendous conflict. Heavyweight scholars have taken both sides of the argument. In one recent incident, Kenneth Kitchen, an Egyptologist of substantial stature, penned a long letter vociferously attacking Rohl's theories ("rubbish . . . sheer fantasy") and circulated it widely within the academic community. When the views of heretics within any tradition of knowledge become sufficiently irksome to traditionalists as to provoke strong censoring responses, it's a sure sign that the heretics have something important to contribute.

Religions typically discount the contributions of their earliest sacerdotal ancestors: Christianity downplays its substantial debt to Judaism; the holiest relic in Islam, the Kaaba of Mecca, was a religious icon millennia before the prophet Muhammad. In the Hebrew tradition, the situation is intriguing but unclear. A persecuted Kem religion disappears from northern Egypt, its leader vanishes, its records are almost completely destroyed. Immediately (in historical terms) thereafter, a religious exile occurs, undertaken by people fleeing the same geographic area. These refugees employ an iconography similar to the persecuted faith. They worship a deity whose spoken name is identical. Their leader, as if to disguise his heritage, answers to a truncated royal Egyptian name (Moses, which means "son of"). If such a situation were to arise today – in a remote corner of Borneo, for example, or within the urban tangle of American religious diversity – anthropologists would undoubtedly assume a fundamental connection between the two traditions. In fact, it would be difficult to argue otherwise.

Egyptian influences may extend beyond the Hebrew tradition. Recently at Qumran, in Jordan – possibly the Middle East's most thoroughly excavated archaeological site because of its association with the Dead Sea Scrolls and the mystical sect of the Essenes – the largest room of the ruins has been found to be a sun temple "situated at exactly the same angle as the Egyptian shrines dedicated to the sun cult." See Lönnqvist and Lönnqvist, *Archaeology of the Hidden Qumran*.

123 *Hebrews* The ancient Hebrew religion is not the same as the Judaism practiced today. The old faith was perhaps as distinct from contemporary rabbinic Judaism as that tradition is from Islam: different locus of worship, distinct holy relics and practices, same deity (in form if not in name). In the early Hebrew religion – before about 520 BCE, when the second temple was constructed – the office of the high priest did not exist. The Talmud had not yet been composed. We know nothing about archaic Hebrew practices prior to roughly 550 BCE, except what was adapted by the creators of the Bible. The core scriptures, Genesis through Kings, were invented – refashioned, revisioned, made from whole cloth, depending on your point of view – by Babylonian exiles preparing to return to Jerusalem. Its eventual form, if not its essence, was distinct from what had come before. Subsequent major evolution of the tradition, from the second through the fifth centuries of the Common Era, eventually resulted in the creation of what we now call Judaism. The antecedent religion and culture of the mythopoeic age is more accurately termed Hebrew, and should not be confused with its descendant, the Jewish religion – named for Yehuda, the fourth son of Jacob, founder of the tribe of Judah. To clarify this distinction in the narrative, I use the term Hebrews to describe the culture from the biblical creation to the end of the Babylonian exile, after which I use the contemporary term, Jews.

124 *from the garden* There exist many diverse versions of the Hebrew myths: oral, scriptural, apocryphal, Islamic, academic. In the modern era, the primary compilers of those myths have been Angelo Rappoport (1871–1950), Louis Ginzberg (1873–1953), and Raphael Patai (1911–1986). Ginzberg's versions are particularly extensive: his seven-volume opus *Legends of the*

Jews runs to thousands of pages. The index alone is more than six hundred pages. A less daunting volume, *Legends of the Bible*, covers the most popular tales in roughly 650 pages. Unless otherwise noted, I have adapted my versions of the Hebrew tales from Ginzberg.

124 *to be called*   Yates, *The Art of Memory*.

124 *the Kem's decline*   Contemporary Jews might find it strange that I use the terms "Messiah" and "kingdom of heaven" as foundational elements in the Hebrew tradition. After all, these aspects of the faith are not emphasized by Jews today, although belief in them persists. The Christian tradition is typically the one most associated with the coming of the Messiah and the return of divine order. These events, as the Book of Revelation prophesies, are believed by Christians to precede the Apocalypse. Islam preserves a similar set of visions and tales. But all the messianic mythical threads lead back to the Hebrews, after the Babylonian exile, hoping and praying for a redeemer to lead the people to final salvation.

124 *come into mind*   Isa. 65:17.

125 *unbounded possession*   Ginzberg, *Legends of the Jews*, vol. 1, p. 130.

129 *between 1635 and 1820*   The first of my ancestors to arrive in North America was Richard Mather, grandfather of Cotton Mather. Richard came with the Protestant migration in 1635. The last of the Old World ancestors to arrive were Scottish farmers, fleeing conflicts over the land. They came in 1820.

130 *same role*   The Stone of Scone, wrapped up with the political and mythic histories of Scotland, Ireland, and England, was used in coronation ceremonies in Ireland and Scotland from roughly 700 CE until 1292. The English monarch Edward I took possession of the stone in 1296, as war booty, and constructed the Coronation Throne in Westminster Abbey to house it. The stone was used in the coronation ceremonies of every English monarch from Edward II in 1308 to Elizabeth II in 1953 (with the exceptions of Edward V and Edward VIII, neither of whom was crowned). Eventually the pressure of Scottish nationalism resulted in the removal of the stone from the Coronation Throne on November 13, 1996, and its return to Edinburgh Castle, where it now lies.

The Stone of Scone is a rectangular block of yellow sandstone weighing 336 pounds. It measures twenty-six inches by sixteen inches by eleven inches and is decorated with a Latin cross. Geological studies of the stone indicate that it originates almost undoubtedly from Scotland or England, though an archaic myth claims it was the stone the Hebrew patriarch Jacob used for a pillow during his dream and later erected as Beth-El, "the house of God."

131 *fire of evening* In 1498, Albrecht Dürer completed a series of woodcuts, the most famous of which is titled after the four apocalyptic horsemen of the Book of Revelation (chapter 6). The figures – traditionally on white, red, black, and ashen horses, but in Dürer's version dark and skeletal – are imbued with alchemical imagery. One of the riders swings a set of scales, the symbol of final judgment since the earliest Kem. The others carry a sword, a bow, and a trident. Beneath the thundering hooves of the horses, a crowned man is devoured by a beast. Dürer's tableau embodies the artist's growing despair about the decadence and spiritual corruption of the church. In the first years of the sixteenth century, he turned increasingly to Hermetic philosophy. His copperplate engravings from 1514, *St. Jerome in His Study* and *Melencolia I*, are freighted with Hermetic and religious symbolism. These works, multilayered and interdisciplinary and brilliant in their obscurity, are the Renaissance equivalents of the essential Kem symbol: the stone of origin.

The visions of the Book of Revelation are typically viewed as mantic seizures: they reach forward through time, toward prophecy. But they also reach backward, to antecedent myths and symbols. To wit: the colors of the four horses – white, black, red, pale – are almost certainly derived from the Kem ritual called "driving the four calves," in which the animals symbolize a quaternity of completion. For the Kem, four was the symbol of totality and closure. In the ritual, each calf was chosen based on its color: white, black, red, pale ("speckled" or "ashen"). See Wilkinson's discussion of the calf-driving ritual in *Symbol and Magic*, p. 144.

In a similar context, the mythologist Joseph Campbell notes in *The Mythic Image* (p. 32) that "the recurrence of many of the best-loved themes of the older, pagan mythologies in the legends of the Christian Savior was a recognized feature intentionally stressed in the earliest Christian centuries. The meaning, for example, of the ass and ox in the Nativity scene would in the fourth century A.D. have been perfectly obvious to all, since these were the beasts symbolic in that century of the contending [Kem] brothers, Seth and Osiris."

133 *robust features*   A few months after I completed my stone work, I came across a photograph of a megalithic stone sculpture from Sulawesi in Indonesia, crafted by a culture of which about four hundred carvings are all that remain. No one knows when, precisely, they were made, or why. They predate recorded history. Some of the sculptures display human facial features; one of them is almost identical to the face I carved into my stone of origin.

135 *first people*   Chatters, *Ancient Encounters*.

136 *epochalyptic*   Although mythologies of the Apocalypse are typically associated with the Christian tradition, the Hebrews invented the idea. The literal meaning of *apocalypse* is "unveiling," but its religious connotation refers to a final, tumultuous period of human history after which history itself will cease. Time will come to an end. This conception of time's closure is particular to the emerging Hebrew culture in the first millennium BCE. I have coined the term "epochalyptic" to denote the epochal orientation of the Kem, the way in which they conceived of themselves as being immersed in rhythms of time, of epochs and ages and centuries that rolled upon one another in unending waves of emergence and return. For the Kem, time itself could not come to an end.

136 *they did not*   Although many modern depictions in books and films depict the enslaved Hebrews building the Giza pyramids, they were not involved in that endeavor. Teams of paid craftspeople, not slaves, built the pyramids. The archaeological record is definite about this, but less so regarding the question of whether some of those craftspeople belonged to the group that later evolved into the Jews. Originally, "Hebrew" was likely not an ethnic designation but an economic class named the Habiru (or Apiru), denoting one who sells a service. Scholars disagree about this term; possibly it connoted all Asian Semitic peoples, not

simply the workers referred to in pharaonic inscriptions. In either case, the Habiru were not subject to forced labor. However, inscriptions from around 1300 BCE – more than a thousand years after the pyramids of Khafre and his contemporaries were constructed – show prisoners from Canaan and Syria working on the temple of Karnak. This is the only period in the Kem's history when forced labor was used, and the ancestors of the Jewish people may have been the subjects of that enforcement.

136 *self-evident truth* In *Surpassing Wonder: The Invention of the Bible and the Talmuds* (p. 94), Donald Akenson provides an excellent summary of the way in which history and time were managed by the authors of the Bible: "Any new item is presented as having a meaning that can only be understood if it is placed alongside the earlier text. New ideas are given legitimacy by their being burnished with the patina of history: the newer an idea or practice is, the more it is claimed to be old."

136 *in the garden* In Jewish folklore, Samael was originally one of the seraphim, serpents of fire who guard the throne of God. *Seraphim* derives from the Hebrew *saraf nahash* (fiery serpent), which in turn derives from the Sumerian *siru*, serpent. Samael is traditionally identified with Satan, as well as the Kem god Set, adversary of Osiris and Horus.

139 *illumination* For the connection to India, see note for page 58.

139 *killed him* This method of murder, I have been told, is still employed by assassins in some Middle Eastern cultures, especially in blood feuds or conflicts involving women who refuse to enter into arranged marriages.

142 *nation to nation* Ginzberg, *Legends of the Jews*, vol. 1, p. 130.

143 *upon the waters* The similarity of names between the Hebraic twins and the Shebtiw twins, Aa and Wa, is surely not coincidental. The phoneme which initiates the name of both Hiwwa and Hiyya is represented, in Hebrew, by the letter hei (or the letter het), the symbol of divine revelation. But hei also signifies the simple act of breathing, of presence, as in the Hebrew word *heenayni*, "I am present." In Hebrew, the beginning letter of a word usually connotes the esoteric level of its meaning. In this sense, it could be argued that Hiwwa and Hiyya are names indicating "I, Wa, am present," and "I, Aa, am present."

144 *many versions*   Ginzberg, *Legends of the Jews*, vol. 1, p. 150.

146 *thirty high*   Approximately four hundred and fifty feet long, seventy-five feet wide, and forty-five feet high.

146 *by day*   Ginzberg, *Legends of the Bible*, p. 77.

J.R.R. Tolkien, whose *Silmarillion* is perhaps the finest work of modern mythography, relates a similar tale of the mariner Earendil in his ship Vingilot. Guided by the imperishable Silmaril stone, Earendil journeyed across the western sea in search of assistance in the war against the dark lord Melkor, "he who arises in might":

> Earendil . . . stood now most often at the prow of Vingilot, and the Silmaril was bound upon his brow; and ever its light grew greater as they drew into the West. And the wise have said that it was by reason of that holy jewel that they came in time to waters that no vessels save those of the Teleri had known; and they came to the Enchanted Isles and escaped their enchantment; and they came into the Shadowy Seas and passed their shadows, and they looked upon Tol Eressea the lonely Isle, but tarried not; and at the last they cast anchor in the Bay of Ledamar, and the Teleri saw the coming of that ship out of the East and they were amazed, gazing from afar upon the light of the Silmaril, and it was very great. Then Earendil, first of living Men, landed on the immortal shores. (pp. 247–48)

147 *Isaac and Ishmael*   Jews consider themselves to be descended directly from Abraham, as do Arabs. Jacob (Isaac's son and Abraham's grandson), the patriarch who changed his name to Israel after his wrestling match with the stranger, is considered the forebear of the twelve tribes of Israel. Ishmael, the son of Abraham by Hagar, is the mythopoeic forebear of the Arabs. In the modern world, the rift between the two groups is emphasized by a secondary ancestral distinction which has some Arabs descended from Esau, the elder twin of Jacob, whom Jacob tricked into surrendering his birthright for a bowl of soup.

148 *was a ruse*   Ginzberg, *Legends of the Jews*, vol. 5, p. 185.

149 *settle their differences*   In the Mesopotamian myth of Utnapishtim, from which the biblical account of the flood was derived, a dove and a swallow are first released. Both are unable to find land. It is the raven, sent after the others fail, who alone succeeds.

154 *shamir*   The mythological, radiant *shamir* appears in the myths of Judaism, but it may have an older origin. At the Temple of Horus, in Egypt, on the walls of which the last learned priests of the Kem wrote down as much of their legacy as they could recall, dwindling as it was with the slow demise of their culture, there is a reference to a protective deity. The god is embodied in the spear of the falcon lord, Horus the warrior, and was thought to have existed in the waters of Nun, before the creation of the world. The spear was a mythopoeic instrument, sentient and indomitable (though it was defeated, at least momentarily, in the first serpent battle). It was capable of cutting through anything. In Reymond's *Mythical Origin of the Egyptian Temple* (p. 97), the name of that spear deity is transliterated as Shm-hr.

156 *her children back*   Ginzberg, *Legends of the Bible*, p. 76.

156 *in such shapes*   Differing versions of the myth concerning the appearance of the bow describe it variously as an arrangement of clouds, a rainbow, or a military bow. The rainbow motif is resonant with modern sensibilities, particularly in *The Wizard of Oz*, which is a contemporary retelling of numerous myths. For the ancients, a military bow would have been the symbol of choice in establishing the covenant between Noah and the hosts of the Unnameable. As Richard Wilkinson has shown (*Symbol and Magic in Egyptian Art*, pp. 200–3), the bow held backward, or held aloft, was a gesture of submission and surrender in many cultures of the ancient Near East. For the Kem, among whom the turned-bow gesture may have originated, the bow possessed its own symbolic dialect: as arbiter, as indicator of status, as mediator between the human and the divine.

156 *of the ancients*   Kem priests were given the title Sem (Sem is the Greek name of Shem, and it is the origin of *Semite*, meaning "the descendants of Shem"). The Bible clearly indicates that Moses was a priest of the Kem: "And Moses was learned in all the wisdom of the Egyptians, and was mighty in words and in deeds" (Acts 7:22). In *From Fetish to God in Ancient Egypt* (p. 8, n3), E.A. Wallis Budge describes Moses' probable background: "All that the Bible tells us about Moses indicates that he had studied the various branches of Egyptian magic, and that he was a skilled performer of magical rituals and was deeply learned in the knowledge of the accompanying spells, incantations, and magical formulas of every description . . . The miracles he wrought in Egypt, and in the desert, suggest that he was not only a priest, but a magician of the highest order and perhaps even a Kheri Heb [high priest] of Memphis."

Although Hebrew folklore does not specifically indicate that Noah's son Shem was a priest of the Kem, a particular fable may hint at this designation. On the sea journey, Noah neglected to feed the lion; in its hunger, the lion struck Noah lame. Thereafter Noah's infirmity prohibited him from conducting priestly service. Shem undertook the offering when the ark found refuge. Noah's physical lameness, brought about by a failure of relationship with the lion, suggests a mythological association: Shem has earned the priesthood by meeting the lion's challenge, as the Kem priests fulfilled the challenge of the panther (they wore panther skin robes). Lion and panther (and jaguar, in South American shamanism) are essentially the same mythological animal, the predator whose fierceness and resolute clarity must be brought to the work of illumination.

Noah had two other sons, Ham and Japheth. Ham was the mythological patriarch of the Canaanites, of whom it is said in Genesis: "Cursed be Canaan! The lowest of slaves will he be to his brothers" (9:25, New International Version UK). The Canaanites, in turn, are the fabled ancestors of the modern Arabs. Shem, Noah's eldest son, was an ancestral patriarch of the Israelites. Already in the first chapters of the testaments, this enmity between brothers and peoples was well under way. But the Bible is not its only source: the Qur'an (17:4–7) returns the prophetic favor.

And We gave (Clear) Warning to the Children of Israel
in the Book, that twice would they do mischief on the

earth and be elated with mighty arrogance (and twice would they be punished)!

When the first of the warnings came to pass, We sent against you Our servants given to terrible warfare: They entered the very inmost parts of your homes; and it was a warning (completely) fulfilled.

Then did We grant you the Return as against them: We gave you increase in resources and sons, and made you the more numerous in man-power.

If ye did well, ye did well for yourselves; if ye did evil, (ye did it) against yourselves. So when the second of the warnings came to pass, (We permitted your enemies) to disfigure your faces, and to enter your Temple as they had entered it before, and to visit with destruction all that fell into their power.

Unless stated otherwise, Qur'an quotations are from the translation by Abdullah Yusuf Ali.

161 *Temple Mount* The location of Moses' encounters with Yahweh upon the mountain, during which he received a set of commandment tablets, broke them in anger at the pagan instincts of his people, and subsequently received a second set (how does one smash a gift of the divine and then sheepishly ask for another?), has traditionally been assigned to a mountain – no one knows exactly which one – in the Sinai Peninsula. It has also been suggested (by the Danish scholar Ditlef Nielsen as early as 1902, and more recently by Andrew Collins and Graham Phillips) that the divine mountain was al-Ma'daba, located in what is now southern Jordan, near Petra. In terms of myth, the location matters hardly at all; but in terms of the history of religion, the site of divine revelation is an essential element in the formation of Jewish identity. The exodus, as numerous scholars have shown, is still the prevailing myth of Jewish culture.

163 *Book of Illumination* Many scholars have noted the similarity between the Ten Commandments and several passages in the Kem "negative confessions" from chapter 125 of the Book of the Dead – which is itself an adaptation of the earlier Pyramid Texts, or the Book of Illumination.

163 *to carry them*   The nature, contents, and fate of the ark of the covenant constitute one of the most intriguing mysteries of the Bible. Ceremonial chests from the age of Tutankhamun, almost identical to the biblical description of the ark, can be seen in the Egyptian Museum in Cairo today (also see second and third notes for page 102). Originally the ark was placed upon the summit of foundation, the Shetiyah in Jerusalem; but it disappeared some time after construction of the first temple – possibly destroyed by invaders or apostates, perhaps hidden by high priests.

The ark lay at the center of Hebrew religion. Its loss would have been the cause of monumental sorrow. How does one deal with the disappearance of gifts from the hand of God? But curiously, the ark vanished from later scriptures, without comment. A shift in Hebraic consciousness, away from idols and toward the abstract numinous, probably accounts for some of the ark's obscurity. But its complete erasure from tradition is an enduring mystery (remember the first *Indiana Jones* movie?). Possibly the exiled Babylonian authors of the Old Testament, generations removed from the temple's destruction in 587 BCE, had no idea where the ark had gone. They were faced with the difficult challenge of rebuilding a religion without its central sacred symbol. But they had returned to the temple, at least, and this – a rebuilt stone structure with a foundation of bedrock at its heart – became the source of much subsequent Jewish mythology.

Aside from the foundation stone, nothing is left of the first temple (Solomon's temple) on Jerusalem's Temple Mount. The second temple, rebuilt after the Babylonian exile, fared little better: it was plundered and desecrated by Antiochus Epiphanes in 169 and 167 BCE, and later plundered again by the Roman Crassus, in 54 BCE. The Jewish revolt against the former desecration is celebrated today in the rituals of Hanukkah. The temple was renovated and enlarged by Herod the Great in stages beginning in 20 BCE; but it was destroyed again by the Romans in 70 CE. All that remains today is the Western Wall, or Wailing Wall. No definitive archaeological evidence links this wall to the original structure of the first or second temple.

The ark is reputed to be in Axum, Ethiopia. It is kept from public scrutiny by devoted priests and protected by a garrison of the Ethiopian army. Without access to the relic, it has been impossible for scholars to establish the veracity of this claim.

163 *all their journeys*   Exod. 40:38.

165 *Abraham*   In Hebrew, the past is denoted by the word *avar*. The Hebrew letters used for this word are ayin, vet, and resh. In the Book of Genesis, Abraham is called Ivri, and the Hebrews are the *ivrim*. These appellations, which are variants of *avar*, connote Abraham and his people passing into a new life, land, and set of beliefs. The defining aspect of this new life is its prohibition against human sacrifice.

165 *is strong*   The four italicized passages on pages 165–66 are adapted from Ginzberg's *Legends of the Jews*, vol. 1, p. 101.

169 *and pulled*   This connotation, interpreted either as "he takes by the heel" or "he supplants," derives from the legend of Jacob's birth, in which it is recounted that Jacob, who was born the second of twins, "took hold on Esau's heel" (Gen. 25:26). This event follows the prophecy (given to Rebekah, the mother of the twins) that has contributed to the enmity between Palestinian Arabs and Jews: "Two nations are in thy womb, and two manner of people shall be separated from thy bowels; and the one people shall be stronger than the other people; and the elder shall serve the younger" (Gen. 25:23).

Jacob is the patriarch of the Israelites, whereas Esau is the putative patriarch of the biblical tribe of the Edomites, an Arabic people who lived in what is now southwestern Jordan. According to tradition, the Edomites battled the Hebrews several times in antiquity; they were defeated by Saul and by David, and subsequently allied themselves with Nebuchadnezzar in the sack of Jerusalem. Later the Edomites were conquered again – by the Nabataeans – and many of them migrated to Judaea, a region that today is called the West Bank.

170 *toward the valley*   There are two traditional versions of this fable. The first, the biblical version (Gen. 32:24–28), is straightforward:

> And Jacob was left alone; and there wrestled a man with him until the breaking of the day.
> And when he saw that he prevailed not against him, he touched the hollow of his thigh; and the

hollow of Jacob's thigh was out of joint, as he wrestled with him.

And he said, Let me go, for the day breaketh. And he said, I will not let thee go, except thou bless me.

And he said unto him, What is thy name? And he said, Jacob.

And he said, Thy name shall be called no more Jacob, but Israel: for as a prince hast thou power with God and with men, and hast prevailed.

The folkloric connotation of the Jewish people as "God wrestlers" derives from this tale. *Israel* means "he who strives with God" or "God strives." The word possesses a suitably ambiguous meaning. Ginzberg tells a more complicated version (*Legends of the Jews*, vol. 1, p. 384) involving a wizard, sheep crossing a stream, and a business deal. In both versions, the site of the fable is at Mahanaim, "the place of encounter with the angels," which adjoins the ford of the Jabbok, a small stream. Neither version involves the primordial mountain, though the elements of the story also exist there: stream, angels, nighttime encounter. In mythological terms, the mountain must have been the site of the struggle: the angels ascended from its summit, God spoke from its holy seat, the prophetic vision of Jacob transpired beneath its stone altar. The ritual naming offered to Jacob as a result of his wrestling with the angel could not have taken place anywhere but upon the holy mountain (which is every mountain).

I have changed the timing of the wrestling match. In both the biblical and folkloric versions, Jacob encounters the angel – the archangel Michael, to be precise – later in his journey, after he leaves the mountaintop. Otherwise, I have preserved the narrative style (if not the structure, exactly) of the folkloric version told by Ginzberg.

175 *found the shamir* The tale of Solomon's search for the *shamir* is part of a complex myth cycle in the Hebrew tradition, but one that appears only indirectly in the Bible. Tradition relates that Solomon required the *shamir* as a means of circumventing the prohibition against the use of iron tools, as the Torah explicitly prohibits their use in creating an altar: "And there shalt thou

build an altar unto the Lord thy God, an altar of stones: thou shalt not lift up any iron tool upon them" (Deut. 27:5). The traditional reason for this prohibition is that iron is the metal used for making weapons; the temple, by contrast, is an object designed to evoke peace. This is an odd rationale. During the exodus, the weapon used to vanquish the enemies of the wandering Hebrews was the ark of the covenant, the embodiment of the Lord, most holy of sacred objects. The battle for Jericho is the most famous instance of the ark's use as a weapon, though it was used with great efficacy as the scourge of every enemy of the Hebrews. By the agency of a pillar of fire that emanated from it, or by means of a deadly, suffocating cloud surrounding it, or simply by its proximity to an enemy, the ark was a veritable avatar of destruction. The ark itself and its contents were the tangible symbols of the covenant between the Hebrews and the Unnameable. That covenant, as Akenson illustrates in *Surpassing Wonder* (p. 102), "is not primarily intended to bring peace, but victory." The Hebrews were not averse to sacred objects as weapons of war.

I take the view that the temple construction was intended to reflect a consciousness oriented toward the future, as though the temple itself was the earth rough-hewn and elemental, new and suffused with promise. The Bible provides an excellent description of the temple and its construction. It was, by all accounts, an elegant building. But the stone work was entirely distinct from that of the Kem. The craftsmanship was undertaken by Hiram of Tyre (see next note), who was brought in specifically for the task. I wonder if this distinctive work was intended to symbolize the Hebrews' break from the past, an abrogation of the past they shared with the Kem, the world's greatest stonemasons. The origins of the Hebrew culture, after all, are wrapped up with the Kem (see first note for page 123). The stonework of the temple was, perhaps, another instance of the Hebrew insistence on their own uniqueness. In the Hebraic cosmogony, their culture has no ancestor.

175 *up the mountain* Hiram of Tyre is a figure of tremendous importance in the Masonic tradition. The fact that a non-Hebraic craftsman was used as the chief architect and builder of the temple seems peculiar, though it's in keeping with the argument put forth in the

previous note: that the Hebrew people distanced themselves, perhaps intentionally, from the high craftsmanship of the Kem.

177 *stone and word*   These pillars, while not central to Hebrew folk-lore, have inspired a persistent mythology in Freemasonry. In the Masonic tradition, the pillars are called Jaquin and Boaz: "According to the 'old ritual' [of Freemasonry] these two great pillars had been hollow. Inside them had been stored the 'ancient records' and the 'valuable writings' pertaining to the past of the Jewish people. And amongst these records, the Freemasons claimed, had been 'the secret of the magical Shamir and the history of its properties'" (Hancock, *The Sign and the Seal*, p. 369).

180 *no longer therein*   Ginzberg, *Legends of the Jews*, vol. 4, p. 301.

183 *their approach*   The name of this king was actually Nebuchad-rezzar, though he is better known by his incorrect designation.

183 *succor and lament*   The folkloric record relates that some drank too much, too fast, and the shock of it killed them. The most dangerous act for someone near death from dehydration is, in fact, to drink a substantial amount of water. The resulting bodily reaction frequently results in death. The Bedouin tribes of the Arabian Peninsula, conditioned to the arid environment with all its attendant dangers, have long been experts at dehydration recovery. Their prescription involves drinking a small amount of water, washing the body, and slowly acclimatizing oneself with tiny sips over a long period.

The Hebrew captives had lost much already, and they rose up in a chorus of grief at the catastrophe of more death among themselves. Their anguish and exhaustion later inspired psalm 137 and, more than two thousand years later, the lines of a half-lame radical poet:

> We sat down and wept by the waters
> Of Babel, and thought of the day
> When our foe, in the hue of his slaughters,
> Made Salem's high places his prey;
> And ye, oh her desolate daughters!
> Were scattered all weeping away.
>
> (Byron, "By the Rivers of Babylon
> We Sat Down and Wept," stanza 1)

184 *southern desert* In Hebrew folklore (see Ginzberg, for example), the redeemed captives are identified as the sons of Moses (Eliezer and Gershom, names meaning "God is my helper" and "stranger in a strange land"). Historically, this identification is problematic. In the traditional chronology, Moses probably led the exodus around 1200 BCE (this is by no means a consensus view); the Hebrews were led captive to Babylon about 600 BCE. If the sons of Moses were among the captives, they would have to have been at least six hundred years old. Although this presents a chronological problem, it is not a conundrum for myth, in which characters frequently endure for centuries. In the Hebrew tradition, enviable spans are attributed to many sages and patriarchs: the famous Methuselah, grandfather of Noah and the son of Enoch, is said (in Genesis 5:27) to have lived for 969 years.

186 *into the fire* In alternative versions of this tale, it is Abraham instead of Daniel who is alone tossed into the fire. Or Daniel is absent from Babylon when his companions are punished. Or the angel Gabriel takes the place of Daniel.

186 *is different* Chicken pox is typically more serious in adults than children. The disease can be fatal in any age group, but most deaths (55 percent) are in the adult population. In North America, chicken pox is the leading cause of adult death by a viral illness that can be prevented by inoculation.

188 *become immortal* Adapted from Budge, *Legends of the Egyptian Gods*, p. 222.

190 *said Mishael* In Jewish mysticism, the four letters of the personal name of Yahweh – YHWH – are called the tetragrammaton. The combined letters are the source of a large body of esoteric material, but to my knowledge this symbolism has not previously been used in the context of the companions in the fire.

191 *threshing floor* Dan. 2:35. "Then was the iron, the clay, the brass, the silver, and the gold, broken to pieces together, and became like the chaff of the summer threshing floors."

PART III: PILGRIMAGE

198 *haunted by war* The original name of Jerusalem was Urusalim, a word of western Semitic origin meaning "foundation of God." In the Torah, the first five and most authoritative books of

Jewish scripture, Jerusalem is called Salem. This appellation derives from the concatenation of three Hebrew consonants: *sh*, *l*, and *m*. Like the language of the Kem, Hebrew does not write vowels; but when they are inserted in speech, the result is two possible words: *shalem*, meaning perfect and whole, or *shalom*, meaning peace. Salem is thus the spiritual center, the location of perfect wholeness and peace. As a geographic location, Salem (Jerusalem) is intended to be a symbolic intersection of the temporal and the eternal: the crossroads, the site of every mythic and divine encounter.

199 *gate of heaven*   Gershom Gorenberg provides a sobering and insightful view of the Temple Mount's role in current affairs in his book *The End of Days: Fundamentalism and the Struggle for the Temple Mount*.

200 *would reach it*   In the archaic era (i.e., before the Common Era), it was commonly believed that the primordial ocean encircled the lands of the known world. The journey of conquest undertaken by Alexander the Great was partially motivated by his desire to find the shores of the great ocean (he never did). See Stoneman, *Legends of Alexander the Great*.

201 *desert peoples*   In the Islamic tradition, Ishmael, not Isaac, is the sacrificial object in the story of Abraham upon the mountain. The conflicting accounts (between Islam and Judaism) arise in part from differing traditions regarding who is considered "firstborn." In the archaic Jewish and Christian traditions, a son or daughter born from a slave woman (as was Hagar) was not granted full familial membership. Jewish tradition still preserves (in spirit, if not in practice) the notion that Jewish identity is defined as having been born of a Jewish *mother*. Hagar's status as an Egyptian woman would necessarily have precluded – on two counts: she was a slave, and she wasn't Hebraic – any of her offspring with Abraham from being considered true Hebrews. The archaic traditions of Islam, on the other hand, granted familial and religious membership to a son or daughter born of a Muslim *father* (and a mother from any clan or class). If the mother was a slave, she redeemed her freedom upon giving birth. A folkloric twist in the Islamic tradition has Hagar as the wife, not the concubine, of Abraham – though she is not mentioned by name in the Qur'an.

By virtue of distinct classifications of heredity, both Isaac and Ishmael are the firstborn son: Isaac in the Jewish tradition, Ishmael in the Islamic. The biblical version of the sacrificial trial of Abraham and Isaac is detailed in Genesis 22. In the Qur'an, the trial of Abraham and Ishmael appears in 37:100-03. In some Islamic traditions, the sacrificial site was at Mecca, not upon the Temple Mount (in what was later to become Jerusalem).

201 *thorn bushes*   The Jewish version of this tale, which differs substantially from its Islamic counterpart, can be found in Genesis 21. The Islamic version appears briefly in the Qur'an (37:100-03) and in more detailed fashion in the works of the ninth-century CE Muslim chronicler al-Tabari (Abu Ja'far Muhammad ibn Jarir al-Tabari), particularly his *History of Prophets and Kings*. For a contemporary overview of early Islamic mythology, drawing on the work of al-Tabari and others, see Peters, *The Hajj*.

There exist many Islamic versions of the tale of Abraham's journey with Hagar and Ishmael. They differ in substantial ways: Ishmael's age, Hagar's character and status, the extent of Abraham's involvement. My version is a conflation of several traditional forms which appear in *The Hajj*.

204 *into the past*   See note for page 14.

205 *climbed them*   This is the source of the later ritual, enacted by pilgrims to Mecca, of climbing the two hills, al-Safa and al-Marwa, on the eastern side of the sanctuary: "Behold! Safa and Marwa are among the Symbols of God. So if those who visit the House in the Season or at other times, should compass them round, it is no sin in them. And if any one obeyeth his own impulse to good, – be sure that God is He Who recogniseth and knoweth" (Qur'an 2:158).

206 *hidden well*   This well, called Zamzam according to Islamic tradition, still flows today in the sanctuary at Mecca, where pilgrims drink from it.

208 *from their sleeping*   In Babylonian mythology, which in antiquity infused much of Arabic culture, the seven ancestral sages credited with the development of civilization are called the Sebettu. This designation is substantially identical to the Kem Shebtiw and undoubtedly derives from the same mythological ground. (For the sake of clarity, I have used the Kem spelling throughout.) Al-'Uzza, al-Lat, and Manat, the three divine sisters who appear in the so-called Satanic verses (53:19–22), are the mythological descendants of the sages. (In India, the seven sages are called the seven *rishis*. The motif of seven culture bearers is persistent; it appears in the myths of cultures worldwide, and has been used by numerous researchers as evidence for cross-cultural links in the archaic world.)

Islamic tradition asserts that the Kaaba enclosure was first built by Adam, then rebuilt by Abraham. The three sisters are thought to have entered the narrative later, after the descendants of Ishmael turned away from the religion of Abraham and worshiped idols. My narrative thus departs from tradition in two ways: by substituting the Shebtiw for Adam, and by providing a foundational role for the three sisters. My aim is to be consistent with the pre-Islamic mythologies of Saudi Arabia, in which Hebrew characters were probably not present until after about 500 BCE. The Hebrew tales, compiled after the Babylonian captivity, would have been delivered to the Arabian Peninsula by exiles and travelers. Before that time, the mythos of the Arabian peoples would likely have been rooted in the local and regional tales of the Sebettu, the goddesses, and the Babylonian pantheon (see third note for page 213 and note for page 218). With the advent of Islam, which in principle accepts Judaism as a legitimate tradition, the Hebrew tales of origin were adopted and adapted, rewritten backward, so that polytheism and paganism were supplanted as the original devotions of antiquity.

210 *from the Qur'an*   Peters, *The Hajj*, p. 9.

210 *same dimensions*   The holy of holies was twenty cubits (roughly thirty-five feet) in each dimension. See 1 Kings 6:20.

211 *Old Woman*   The traditional interpretation of the title Shayba is that it refers to the Queen of Sheba; but this designation is a mythological shorthand for the archaic female deities al-Lat, al-'Uzza, and Manat. The Old Woman is the mother goddess in her many guises.

211 *animosities proliferate*   Like the Bible, the Qur'an contains contradictory versions of how to understand and deal with the Other. Compare, for example, the following two passages.

> Be they Muslims, Jews, Christians, or Sabians,* those
> who believe in God and the Last Day and who do
> good have their reward with the Lord. They have
> nothing to fear, and they will not sorrow. (Qur'an
> 2:62, translation by Thomas Cleary)

(*The Sabians were a religious group from ancient Harran, now in southeastern Turkey. Harran is mentioned several times in the Bible but is of particular note as the place where Abraham's family settled after their departure from Ur in Genesis 11:31.)

> O ye who believe! take not the Jews and the Christians
> for your friends and protectors: They are but friends
> and protectors to each other. And he amongst you
> that turns to them (for friendship) is of them. Verily
> God guideth not a people unjust. (Qur'an 5:51)

The fifth sura includes one of the Qur'an's most aggressive suggestions for dealing with the Other (5:33): "The punishment of those who wage war against God and His Apostle, and strive with might and main for mischief through the land is: execution, or crucifixion, or the cutting off of hands and feet from opposite sides, or exile from the land: that is their disgrace in this world, and a heavy punishment is theirs in the Hereafter."

The unfortunate legacy of scripture – almost every scripture – is that the light it purports to shine also casts a great shadow.

212 *humps of camels*   I have borrowed this phrase from the ninth-century Christian doctor and translator of ancient manuscripts Ibn Ishaq (in Peters, *The Hajj*, p. 47).

213 *no one knows*   No archaeological evidence links the black stone of the Kaaba to the Kem, though an intriguing connection exists with regard to the name Kaaba. Taken individually, the sounds of the word correspond to three sacred Kem terms: *ka* (the double, or spirit self), *ab* (the heart), and *ba* (the soul). Perhaps linguistically, and perhaps mythologically, the Kaaba is the spirit-heart-soul. This interpretation reminds me of the Christian Trinity – Father, Son, and Holy Ghost – the three sisters of pre-Islamic mythology, and the divine triads that exist in countless religious traditions.

213 *Solomon's temple*   See, for example, psalm 118:22, "The stone which the builders refused is become the head stone of the corner," and Acts 4:11–12, "This is the stone, which was set at naught of you builders, which is become the head of the corner. Neither is there salvation in any other; for there is none other name under heaven given among men, whereby we must be saved."

213 *names of things*   My version of the tale of the three sisters is a conflation of several fragmentary myths of the pre-Islamic era. Since Muhammad's definitive act of casting out the idols in the Kaaba, in 630 CE, the pre-Islamic myths of the Arabian Peninsula have not been of general interest to Muslims (as the Kem foundation of Judaism is not of general interest to Jews). As a result, comparatively little is known about the authentic traditions of the Bedouin prior to about the sixth century CE.

   In *The Hajj* (p. 365), Peters notes: "The age of idolatry is long past for those who study idol worshipers, and so we can only very tentatively impose our conceptual patterns on the pre-Islamic Arabs performing sacrifice and other ritual acts before stones." The act of remembering the pre-Islamic tales is a mythological endeavor.

214 *by the wind*   The sounds made by "whispering" or "musical" sand derive from resonant qualities imparted by granular friction of the material. In addition to the "whispering" variety, squeaking, roaring, and booming sands exist. Booming sands can be found at Great Sand Dunes National Monument in Colorado (Bing Crosby's song "The Singing Sands of Alamosa" was inspired by them). See Nori, Sholtz, and Bretz, "Booming Sand."

   Also see second note for page 62.

214 *of the Kem*   Traditional sources (al-Azraqi, for example, and Ibn Ishaq, in his *Life of Muhammad*) identify the carpenter as Baqum, or Pachomios, a Coptic (or Greek) survivor of the shipwreck of an Egyptian vessel. The Copts were the last cultural vestige of the Kem. The Coptic Orthodox Church, a Christian sect descended from the early Copts who syncretized Kem culture into Christianity, exists in Egypt today.

215 *World Trade Center*   Minoru Yamasaki was a favorite architect of the Saudi royal family (he designed the Dhahran airport,

among other projects). Yamasaki described his vision of the World Trade Center as "a mecca, a great relief from the narrow streets and sidewalks of the surrounding Wall Street area." See Kerr, "The Mosque to Commerce."

218 *Arab peoples* There is some disagreement among scholars as to the extent of Hebraic influence on the pre-Islamic cultures of the Arabian Peninsula. It is known, at least, that in the centuries before Muhammad, the Bedouin already claimed descent from Abraham. But much of the Hebraic context of Islamic mythology was clearly modified by the Qur'an and by later Muslim chroniclers. The Qur'an, for example, asserts that Abraham "was not a Jew nor yet a Christian but he was true in Faith, and bowed his will to God's (Which is Islam), and he joined not gods with God" (3:67). This is a classic, almost invariable, response to mythological adoption. The Hebraic corollary is in their treatment of the Kem and Sumerian tales – the flood, the stone of origin – in which the cultural heritage of the myths is reassigned to the adoptive culture. Scripture is the archetypal mythology.

220 *Icelandic literature* Lewis, *The Arabs in History*, p. 95.

220 *hoped for* Peters, *The Hajj*, p. 26.

221 *no authority* Qur'an 53:23.

221 *angels in Islam* The Star Sura, the same scriptural segment that abrogates the intercessory status of the crones, grants limited intercessory powers to the (male) angels: "How many-so-ever be the angels in the heavens, their intercession will avail nothing except after God has given leave for whom He pleases and that he is acceptable to Him" (Qur'an 53:26).

221 *to a close* The Willendorf Venus, archaic indeed at about forty thousand years old, is one of a number of fantastically ancient goddess artifacts. The nature of their symbology is a matter of considerable debate among scholars. See, for example, "Venus Figurines: Sex Objects or Symbols?," chapter 14 in Rudgley, *The Lost Civilizations*.

221 *these crones* The evolution of religion in the West is basically the evolution of patriarchy. The male god made a slow ascension: prior to the Kem, masculine deities were typically of secondary status; with the Kem, they were endowed with powers sometimes lesser, and sometimes greater, than their female counterparts. Ra

and Osiris are considered the ruling deities of Kem theology; but Isis, whose epithets included "mistress of the sacred mountain," proved her power over both, in differing tales: by healing Ra after he was poisoned, and by raising Osiris from the dead. The Hebrews elevated the male deity while preserving a feminine aspect of divine manifestation: the Shechinah, the feminine soul of God (much lauded today in feminist schools of Judaism). In early Christianity, the male God reigned supreme; but his mother, Mary, was – and still is – venerated with considerable zeal. Islam dropped the feminine altogether: no female deities or angels or powers. (Qur'an 53:27 says, "Those who believe not in the Hereafter, name the angels with female names.") In the theological context of Islam, Allah is infinite, and therefore male as well as female. But in practice, the travails of Islamic women were begun when Muhammad cast out the female deities from the sanctuary; when al-Lat (the goddess) departed, and al-Lah (the god) remained.

221 *first to mind*   Casting out idols is a time-honored tradition in the religions of the Book. Whether it's Jesus overturning the tables of the money changers, or Muhammad in Mecca, or the Jews returning to Jerusalem after their captivity, idols and idolaters are the objects of consistent ire. One of the oldest mythological threads of this tradition is probably that of the Marsh Arabs, in Iraq, who preserve a tale in which Abraham – whom they call Bahram – cast out the idols of the Mandaean temple in Harran four thousand years ago.

222 *lost and won*   *Macbeth*, act 1, scene 1, lines 1–4. The crones of *Macbeth* derive from a mythological thread that begins thousands of years ago – no one knows exactly how many thousands – with the Venus figures and womb temples of the goddess tradition. See third and fourth notes for page 221, and Gimbutas and Campbell, *The Language of the Goddess*.

223 *the Unnameable*   Qur'an 4:1.64: "And there were messengers of whom We told you before, and messengers of whom we have not told you" (translation by Thomas Cleary).

229 *the Kaaba*   Nordegg's plan was inspired by Frederick Todd's design for the town of Mount Royal, adjoining Montreal. Todd, in turn, was inspired by the plan of Washington, D.C., with its

diagonal thoroughfares converging upon a central square. Pierre-Charles L'Enfant, a Mason, was the designer of Washington's original plan. Masonic – and therefore Kem – influences permeate its design. Nordegg's plan, with its curved avenues, is distinctively Masonic as well as Meccan.

237 *three sisters* One early concession made by Muhammad to win the allegiance of the Jewish populace of Medina (and to achieve status as a prophet within the Jewish tradition) involved the requirement that Muslims face Jerusalem while praying. This was changed in favor of Mecca, likely in early 624 CE, after conflict between Muslims and Jews increased on several fronts. The ancient and persistent animosity between the two groups, which is the source of the modern era's most dangerous instability, began, as all such conflicts do, as a village squabble.

237 *stretched out* In the Islamic tradition, hadith – which means story or news (*gospel* also means news) – are the remembered and mythological events surrounding the life of Muhammad. They are not parts of the Qur'an but oral traditions and teachings, eventually written down, that possess considerable authority. Al-Bukhari, an Islamic scholar who lived about two centuries after Muhammad, is generally regarded as the greatest hadith compiler. He gathered (it is said) six hundred thousand pieces of Islamic mythological history, then winnowed these down to about seven thousand "authentic traditions" which he published in ninety-seven books. Al-Bukhari, like the authors of the Christian gospels, was removed enough from the actual events he was describing that his tales are archetypal hybrids of fact and fable. They are ideal myths, entwining speculation with certainty. They reach back far enough to be true and false – the perfect mythic combination.

As in every tradition, the hadith are repositories of wisdom and folly. A particularly vicious hadith, a favorite of Osama bin Laden, asserts that in the final battle between Jews and Muslims, when the Jews will hide behind rocks and trees, the rocks and trees will call out, "Muslim, behind me is a Jew. Come and kill him" (Gorenberg, *End of Days*, p. vi). Another hadith describes the experience of divine revelation: sometimes as though a great bell were ringing, at other times in dreams like bright daylight, or in the form of a man, speaking simply from the fringe of the desert. There is considerable debate among contemporary Islamic scholars surrounding the question of what to preserve, and what to discard, of the hadith.

My version of Muhammad's "night journey" is derived from various hadith (Alawi al-Maliki al-Hasani, *Al-Anwar al-bahiyya*). Originally the tale involved two distinct aspects: the actual night journey (called *al-isra'*) and the Prophet's ascension to heaven (called *al-mi'raj*). But these were combined into a single fable early in Islamic history, and today they are taken as a single, continuous event.

237 *day of resurrection*   Israfil is the Arabic-Islamic version of the angel Raphael. Jibril and Mika'il are the equivalents of the angels Gabriel and Michael in the Christian and Jewish faiths, though each tradition deals with them distinctly. In the Jewish cosmology, Gabriel is the angel of judgment, whereas Michael is the angel of mercy. In the Christian system the roles are reversed.

238 *light of creation*   One hadith of many that describes these events says of Muhammad: "The roof of my house was opened and Jibril descended." Alawi al-Maliki al-Hasani, *Al-Anwar al-bahiyya*, part III.

239 *seal of prophethood*   A radiant point of energy between the shoulder blades is a feature of numerous shamanic and esoteric myths. It signifies the luminous body, the lens of awareness, the great secret of perception. The Toltec tradition of Mexico, in particular, emphasizes its importance.

239 *of a woman*   Buraq, the winged steed, is a mythological synthesis of sphinx, centaur, and Pegasus. There exist many diverse descriptions of the animal. Some chroniclers have given it a peacock tail, a white coat, long ears, and a stature approximating that of a small mule.

243 *through the hole*   The tying place of Buraq is more commonly described as having been somewhere on the Western Wall, though the hadith are by no means consistent on this point. Since as far back as the eleventh century, Islamic scholars have taken decidedly distinct points of view on the location of the hitching post. Proposed locations have included the foundation stone, the Mercy Gate, the Double Gate (also known as the Gate of Hulda

the Prophetess), and a niche – with a ring, inside the al-Buraq Mosque – near the southern end of the Western Wall.

Today the western edge of the al-Aqsa Mosque compound lies above the Western Wall (just south of the area used for Jewish prayers), on the Temple Mount (called the Noble Sanctuary by Muslims). The wall itself is called the al-Buraq Wall by Muslims. By way of this deliberate, overlapping architecture of devotion, Jewish and Islamic mythologies contest ownership of the area. This contest, which has persisted for more than a thousand years, involves advocates on both sides (including Christian advocates, supporting sometimes one side and sometimes the other) discounting and negating the religious and mythological claims of the other. For example, some Muslim groups assert that Jews have no claim to the Western Wall, and that their devotions in front of it are the footholds of a Zionist plot to wrest the entire area from Muslims, tear down the mosques and the Dome of the Rock, and establish a new Jewish temple. (Some Jews – and some Christians – believe that such an act would herald the arrival of the Messiah.) Sovereignty-minded Jews, for their part, frequently insist that Islamic claims for the sanctity of the wall and the Noble Sanctuary above – based on the many elements of Muhammad's night journey and on thirteen centuries of Islamic history – are simply modern political inventions aimed at foisting an Islamic presence onto a Jewish holy site, edging out the Jews, and eventually clearing Palestine of a Jewish presence. (Some Muslims believe that such actions would hasten the Day of Judgment.)

Many Muslims think of the entire Temple Mount as an extension of the al-Aqsa Mosque. Similarly, they consider the Western Wall – which is not on the Temple Mount but acts as one of its retaining structures – as the western foundation wall of the al-Aqsa Mosque. This architectural syncretism is faithful to the mythological reality: the Jewish tradition *is* the foundation of Islamic mythology.

With regard to documents concerning the Muslim-Jewish conflict over the Western Wall, it is surprisingly difficult to find accounts that are not freighted with religious hatred. Or, given the current situation in Israel/Palestine, perhaps it's not so surprising. For a reasonably neutral approach, see the United

Nations document entitled *United Kingdom Commission Report on the Western Wall (1930)*. This report was commissioned after clashes at the wall in 1929, and was reissued in 1968 after further conflicts during the Six-Day War. The report, which chronicles a tribunal on religious mythology, offers an insightful glimpse into the differing modes of consciousness that have contributed to ongoing strife in Israel/Palestine.

244 *of the waters* The Well of Souls, Bi'r al-Arwah, was venerated by Jews, Muslims, and later by Christian Crusaders who believed it was the site of the annunciation of John the Baptist (Ritmeyer, *Secrets of Jerusalem's Temple Mount*, p. 96). After Crusaders seized control of the site in 1099, the hole in the foundation stone was used as a chimney by Christian pilgrims who burned candles in the well below. The Crusaders also quarried fragments from the foundation stone itself, and sold these for their weight in gold.

The mythological designation of the site as a well of souls almost undoubtedly derives from the Kem tales of origin. Today the well is dry.

244 *long vanished* This contested location, which is roughly four feet by two, is described in some detail in Ritmeyer, *Secrets of Jerusalem's Temple Mount*.

244 *stone of origin* The hadith concerning Muhammad's night journey agree that the Prophet met and prayed with every sage of the world's unfolding. Mythologically, this must include the Kem prophets and deities, especially as Islam accepts (in principle, anyway) the existence of other valid traditions. See Qur'an 4:164: "And there were messengers of whom We told you before, and messengers of whom we have not told you" (translation by Thomas Cleary).

247 *religious kinship* From 685 to 691 CE, Caliph 'Abd al-Malik ibn Marwan initiated and organized the building of the Dome of the Rock, the Qubbat al-Sakhra. This site, in conjunction with the nearby al-Aqsa Mosque (completed by Marwan's son in 705 CE), is the defining element of al-Haram al-Sharif (the Noble Sanctuary), the mythological location referred to in the Qur'an as the "furthest mosque" to which Muhammad was taken on his night journey (though there was no actual mosque on the site during Muhammad's lifetime). Technically, the Dome of the Rock is a shrine and not a mosque. The surrounding thirty-five-acre complex, called the Temple Mount by Jews and Christians, is perhaps the world's holiest place.

247 *to the Guest* Vilnay, *Legends of Jerusalem*.

REFERENCES

Akenson, Donald. *Surpassing Wonder: The Invention of the Bible and the Talmuds*. Montreal: McGill-Queen's University Press, 1998.

Alawi al-Maliki al-Husani, Sayyid Muhammad. *Al-Anwar al-bahiyya min isra' wa mi'raj khayr al-bariyya* (The resplendent lights of the rapture and ascension of the Best of creation) [English translation online]. As-Sunnah Foundation of America. 1414/1993. <www.sunnah.org/ibadaat/fasting/index.htm>. [Cited January 17, 2003.]

Aldred, Cyril. *Egypt to the End of the Old Kingdom*. London: Thames and Hudson, 1965.

Ardagh, Philip. *The Hieroglyphs Handbook: Teach Yourself Ancient Egyptian*. London: Faber and Faber, 1999.

Armstrong, Karen. *A History of God: The 4000-Year Quest of Judaism, Christianity and Islam*. New York: Ballantine, 1993.

———. *The Battle for God: A History of Fundamentalism*. New York: Ballantine, 2000.

Avner, Uzi. "Sacred Stones in the Desert." *Biblical Archaeology Review* 27, no. 3 (May/June 2001): 31–41.

Baigent, Michael, and Richard Leigh. *The Elixir and the Stone: A History of Magic and Alchemy*. London: Penguin, 1998.

Bauval, Robert. "Investigation on the Origin of the Benben Stone: Was It an Iron Meteorite?" *Discussions in Egyptology* 14 (1989): 5–17.

Bauval, Robert, and Adrian Gilbert. *The Orion Mystery: Unlocking the Secrets of the Pyramids*. New York: Crown, 1995.

Benjamin, Walter. *Selected Writings*. Edited by Marcus Bullock and Michael Jennings. Cambridge, Mass.: Belknap Press, 1996.

Bierhorst, John. *The Mythology of North America*. New York: Quill, 1985.

Black, Jeremy, and Anthony Green. *Gods, Demons and Symbols of Ancient Mesopotamia*. London: British Museum Press, 1992.

Budge, E.A. Wallis. *Egyptian Magic*. 1901. Reprint, New York: Dover, 1971.

———. *Egyptian Religion*. 1899. Reprint, London: Arkana, 1972.

———. *The Egyptian Book of the Dead: The Papyrus of Ani in the British Museum*. 1895. Reprint, New York: Dover, 1975.

———. *From Fetish to God in Ancient Egypt*. 1934. Reprint, New York: Dover, 1989.

———. *Legends of the Egyptian Gods: Hieroglyphic Texts and Translations*. 1912. Reprint, New York: Dover, 1994.

Bunson, Margaret. *The Encyclopedia of Ancient Egypt*. New York: Gramercy, 1999.

Burland, Cottie, Irene Nicholson, and Harold Osborne. *Mythology of the Americas*. London: Hamlyn, 1970.

Campbell, Joseph. *Primitive Mythology: The Masks of God*. New York: Penguin, 1959.

———. *Oriental Mythology: The Masks of God*. New York: Penguin, 1962.

———. *Occidental Mythology: The Masks of God*. New York: Penguin, 1964.

———. *Creative Mythology: The Masks of God*. New York: Penguin, 1968.

———. *The Mythic Image*. Princeton: Princeton University Press, 1974.

Chang, Joseph. "Recent Common Ancestors of All Present-Day Individuals." *Advances in Applied Probability* 31, no. 4 (December 1999): 1002–26.

Chatters, James. *Ancient Encounters: Kennewick Man and the First Americans*. New York: Simon and Schuster, 2001.

Clagett, Marshall. *Ancient Egyptian Science: A Sourcebook*. Philadelphia: American Philosophical Society, 1989.

Clark, R.T. Rundle. *The Legend of the Phoenix*. Birmingham, U.K.: University of Birmingham Press, 1949.

———. *Myth and Symbol in Ancient Egypt*. London: Thames and Hudson, 1959.

Cleary, Thomas, trans. *The Essential Koran*. New York: Castle, 1998.

Danbey, Herbert. *The Mishnah*. Oxford: Oxford University Press, 1993.

Deutsch, Robert. "Lasting Impressions." *Biblical Archaeology Review* 28, no. 4 (July 2002): 42–51, 60–1.

Dunn, Chris. *The Giza Power Plant: Technologies of Ancient Egypt*. Santa Fe: Bear, 1998.

Eliade, Mircea. *The Sacred and the Profane: The Nature of Religion*. Translated by William R. Trask. New York: Harvest, 1987.

Ellis, Normandi. *Awakening Osiris: The Egyptian Book of the Dead*. Grand Rapids: Phanes, 1988.

———. *Dreams of Isis: A Woman's Spiritual Sojourn*. Wheaton, Ill.: Quest, 1995.

Faulkner, R.O. *The Ancient Egyptian Pyramid Texts*. Oxford: Oxford University Press, 1969.

———. *The Ancient Egyptian Coffin Texts*. London: Arris and Phillips, 1973.

Fowden, Garth. *The Egyptian Hermes: A Historical Approach to the Late Pagan Mind*. Cambridge: Cambridge University Press, 1987.

Fulcanelli [pseud.]. *The Mystery of the Cathedrals*. Las Vegas: Brotherhood of Life, 1984.

———. *The Dwellings of the Philosophers*. Boulder, Col.: Archive Press, 1999.

Gimbutas, Marija, and Joseph Campbell. *The Language of the Goddess*. New York: Thames and Hudson, 2001.

Ginzberg, Louis. *Legends of the Jews*. 7 volumes. Philadelphia: Jewish Publication Society, 1909–38.

———. *Legends of the Bible*. Philadelphia: Jewish Publication Society, 1992.

Gorenberg, Gershom. *The End of Days: Fundamentalism and the Struggle for the Temple Mount*. Oxford: Oxford University Press, 2002.

Hancock, Graham. *The Sign and the Seal: The Quest for the Lost Ark of the Covenant*. New York: Simon and Schuster, 1993.

———. *The Message of the Sphinx: A Quest for the Hidden Legacy of Mankind*. New York: Crown, 1997.

Haq, Syed Nomanul. *Names, Natures and Things: The Alchemist Jabir ibn Hayyan and His Kitab al-Ahjar (Book of Stones)*. London: Kluwer Academic Publishing, 1994.

Hoffman, Edward. *The Hebrew Alphabet: A Mystical Journey*. San Francisco: Chronicle, 1998.

Horne, Alexander. *King Solomon's Temple in the Masonic Tradition*. London: Aquarian Press, 1972.

Hornung, E. *The Ancient Egyptian Books of the Afterlife*. Translated by David Lorton. Ithaca: Cornell University Press, 1999.

James, T.G.H. *Tutankhamun*. New York: Friedman/Fairfax, 2000.

Kermode, Frank, and John Hollander, eds. *Oxford Anthology of English Literature*. 2 volumes. Oxford: Oxford University Press, 1973.

Kerr, Laurie. "The Mosque to Commerce: Bin Laden's Special Complaint with the World Trade Center." *Slate* [online], December 28, 2001. <slate.msn.com>. [Cited January 14, 2003.]

Killen, Geoffrey. *Egyptian Woodworking and Furniture*. Princes Risborough, U.K.: Shire, 1994.

King, L.W., ed. *Enuma Elish: The Seven Tablets of Creation, Or the Babylonian and Assyrian Legends Concerning the Creation of the World and of Mankind*. Vol. 1. 1902. Reprint, Escondido, Cal.: Book Tree, 1999.

Knight, Christopher, and Robert Lomas. *The Hiram Key: Pharaohs, Freemasonry and the Discovery of the Secret Scrolls of Jesus*. Boston: Element Books, 1997.

Koch, W. John. *Martin Nordegg: The Uncommon Immigrant*. Edmonton: Brightest Pebble, 1997.

Kugel, James. *Poetry and Prophecy: The Beginnings of a Literary Tradition*. Ithaca: Cornell University Press, 1990.

Kunz, George F. *The Curious Lore of Precious Stones*. 1913. Reprint, New York: Dover, 1971.

Lawton, Ian, and Chris Ogilvie-Herald. *Giza: The Truth: The People, Politics, and History Behind the World's Most Famous Archaeological Site*. London: Virgin, 1999.

Lev, Martin. *The Traveler's Key to Jerusalem*. New York: Knopf, 1989.

Lévi-Strauss, Claude. *The Way of the Masks*. Translated by Sylvia Modelski. Vancouver: University of British Columbia Press, 1998.

Lewis, Bernard. *The Arabs in History*. Oxford: Oxford University Press, 1993.

———. *What Went Wrong: Western Impact and Middle Eastern Response*. Oxford: Oxford University Press, 2002.

Lichtheim, Miriam, ed. *Ancient Egyptian Literature: A Book of Readings*. Vol. 1: *The Old and Middle Kingdoms*. Berkeley: University of California Press, 1973.

Lönnqvist, Minna, and Kenneth Lönnqvist. *Archaeology of the Hidden Qumran*. Helsinki: Yliopistopaino, 2002.

Lönnrot, Elias. *The Kalevala*. Translated by Keith Bosley. Oxford: Oxford University Press, 1989.

Master, Sharad. "A Possible Holocene Impact Structure in the Al'Amarah Marshes, near the Tigris-Euphrates Confluence." *Meteoritics & Planetary Science* 36, Supplement (September 2001): A124.

Matt, Daniel. *The Essential Kabbalah*. Edison: Castle, 1997.

Meeks, Dimitri, and Christine Favard-Meeks. *Daily Life of the Egyptian Gods*. Translated by G.M. Goshgarian. Ithaca: Cornell University Press, 1996.

Montserrat, Dominic. *Akhenaten: History, Fantasy and Ancient Egypt*. New York: Routledge, 2000.

Murray, Margaret. *Egyptian Sculpture*. New York: Scribner, 1930.

Nasr, Seyyed Hossein. *Ideals and Realities of Islam*. London: Unwin, 1979.

Naydler, Jeremy. *Temple of the Cosmos: The Ancient Egyptian Experience of the Sacred*. Rochester, N.Y.: Inner Traditions, 1996.

Nori, F., P. Sholtz, and M. Bretz. "Booming Sand." *Scientific American* 277, no. 3 (September 1997): 84.

Olson, Steve. "The Royal We." *Atlantic Monthly*, May 2002, pp. 62–64.

Osborne, Roger. *The Floating Egg: Episodes in the Making of Geology*. London: Pimlico, 1999.

Osman, Ahmed. *Moses and Akhenaten: The Secret History of Egypt at the Time of the Exodus*. New York: Inner Traditions, 2002.

Peters, Francis E. *The Hajj: The Muslim Pilgrimage to Mecca and the Holy Places*. Princeton: Princeton University Press, 1994.

Petrie, W.M. Flinders. *Egyptian Decorative Art.* 1895. Reprint, New York: Dover, 1999.

Piankoff, Alexandre. *The Wandering of the Soul.* New York: Bollingen, 1974.

Pinch, Geraldine. *Magic in Ancient Egypt.* Austin: University of Texas Press, 1994.

Reymond, Eve A.E. *The Mythical Origin of the Egyptian Temple.* New York: Barnes and Noble, 1969.

Ritmeyer, Leen, and Kathleen Ritmeyer. *Secrets of Jerusalem's Temple Mount.* New York: Biblical Archaeology Society, 1998.

Rohde, Douglas. "Somewhat Less-Recent Common Ancestors of All Present Day Individuals." In preparation. <http://tedlab.mit.edu/~dr/>. [Cited January 14, 2003.]

Rohl, David. *Pharaohs and Kings: A Biblical Quest.* New York: Crown, 1997.

Rothenberg, Beno. *The Egyptian Mining Temple at Timna.* London: Thames and Hudson, 1988.

Rudgley, Richard. *The Lost Civilizations of the Stone Age.* New York: Simon and Schuster, 1999.

Salaman, Clement, Dorine Van Oyen, William Wharton, and Jean-Pierre Mahé. *The Way of Hermes: New Translations of the Corpus Hermeticum and the Definitions of Hermes Trismegistus to Asclepius.* Rochester, N.Y.: Inner Traditions, 2000.

Schäfer, Heinrich. *Principles of Egyptian Art.* Translated by John Baines. Oxford: Clarendon, 1974.

Schumann, Walter. *Handbook of Rocks, Minerals and Gemstones.* Translated by R. Bradshaw and K.A.G. Mills. New York: Houghton Mifflin, 1993.

Schwaller de Lubicz, René A. *The Temple in Man: Sacred Architecture and the Perfect Man.* Rochester, N.Y.: Inner Traditions, 1977.

———. *The Egyptian Miracle: An Introduction to the Wisdom of the Temple.* Rochester, N.Y.: Inner Traditions, 1985.

———. *The Temple of Man: Apet of the South at Luxor.* Rochester, N.Y.: Inner Traditions, 1998.

Scott, Walter, ed. *Hermetica: The Ancient Greek and Latin Writings Which Contain Religious or Philosophic Teachings Ascribed to Hermes Trismegistus.* 1924. Reprint, Boston: Shambhala, 1993.

Sellers, Jane. *The Death of Gods in Ancient Egypt: An Essay on Egyptian Religion and the Frame of Time*. New York: Penguin, 1993.

Stoneman, Richard. *Legends of Alexander the Great*. London and Rutland, Vt.: J.M. Dent and Charles E. Tuttle, 1994.

Storm, Rachel. *The Encyclopedia of Eastern Mythology*. London: Prospero, 1999.

Thompson, William Irwin. *The Time Falling Bodies Take to Light: Mythology, Sexuality and the Origins of Culture*. New York: St. Martin's Press, 1981.

Tolkien, J.R.R. *The Silmarillion*. London: George Allen and Unwin, 1977.

Tring, J. *The Fire Tried Stone*. Cornwall, U.K.: Wordens of Cornwall, 1967.

United Kingdom Commission Report on the Western Wall (1930) [online]. Reissued in 1968 as UN document A/7057/Add. 1; S/8427/Add. 1. United Nations Information System on the Question of Palestine (UNISPAL). <http://domino.un.org/unispal.nsf/>. Search full text using title. [Cited January 14, 2003.]

Vilnay, Zev. *Legends of Jerusalem*. Philadelphia: Jewish Publication Society of America, 1973.

Von Franz, Marie-Louise, and Carl Gustav Jung. *The Grail Legend*. London: Hodder and Stoughton, 1972.

Waltke, Bruce. *Finding the Will of God: A Pagan Notion?* Grand Rapids: Eerdmans Publishing, 2002.

Watterson, Barbara. *Gods of Ancient Egypt*. London: Sutton, 1999.

West, John Anthony. *Serpent in the Sky*. Wheaton, Ill.: Quest, 1993.

Wilkinson, Richard. *Reading Egyptian Art: A Hieroglyphic Guide to Ancient Painting and Sculpture*. London: Thames and Hudson, 1992.

———. *Symbol and Magic in Egyptian Art*. London: Thames and Hudson, 1994.

Wilson, John A., trans. "The Great Hymn to the Aten." In Kate Stange, *The Akhet-Aten Home Page* [online]. Updated March 1, 2000. <http//kate.stange.com/egypt/hymn2.htm> [Cited March 16, 2003.]

Woldering, I. *The Art of Egypt*. New York: Greystone, 1963.

Yates, Frances. *Giordano Bruno and the Hermetic Tradition.*
Chicago: Chicago University Press, 1964.

———. *The Art of Memory.* Chicago: Chicago University Press,
1966.

———. *The Occult Philosophy in the Elizabethan Age.* New York:
Routledge, 1979.

Yusuf Ali, Abdullah, trans. *The Holy Quran* [online]. Islamic
Computing Centre, London. Originally published 1934–37.
<http://info.uah.edu/msa/quranYusufali.html>. [Cited January 14,
2003.]

Zimmer, Carl. "Ancient Continent Opens Window on the Early
Earth." *Science* 286 (December 1999): 2254–56.

INDEX